Lingering with the Works of Ted T. Aoki

This unique collection of essays from emerging and established curriculum theory scholars documents individuals' personal encounters and lingering interactions with Ted T. Aoki and his scholarship. The work illuminates the impact of Aoki's lifework both theoretically and experientially.

Featuring many of the field's top scholars, the text reveals Aoki's historical legacy and the contemporary significance of his work for educational research and practice. The influence of Aoki's ideas, pedagogy, and philosophy on lived curriculum is vibrantly examined. Themes include tensionality, multiplicity, and bridging of difference. Ultimately, the text celebrates an Aokian "way of being" whilst engaging a diversity of perspectives, knowledges, and philosophies in education to reflect on the contribution of his work and its continual enrichment of curriculum scholarship today.

This text will benefit researchers, academics, and educators with an interest in curriculum studies, educational research, teacher education, and the philosophy of education more broadly. Those specifically interested in international and comparative education, as well as interdisciplinary approaches—which include perspectives in arts, language and literacy, sciences, technology, and higher education curriculum—will also benefit from this book.

Nicole Y. S. Lee completed her PhD in Curriculum Studies with a specialization in Art Education in the Department of Curriculum and Pedagogy at The University of British Columbia, Canada.

Lesley E. Wong is a PhD candidate in the Department of Curriculum and Pedagogy, Faculty of Education at The University of British Columbia, Canada.

Joanne M. Ursino is completing her dissertation in Cross Faculty Inquiry in the Faculty of Education at The University of British Columbia, Canada.

Studies in Curriculum Theory Series
Series Editor: William F. Pinar, University of British Columbia, Canada

In this age of multimedia information overload, scholars and students may not be able to keep up with the proliferation of different topical, trendy book series in the field of curriculum theory. It will be a relief to know that one publisher offers a balanced, solid, forward-looking series devoted to significant and enduring scholarship, as opposed to a narrow range of topics or a single approach or point of view. This series is conceived as the series busy scholars and students can trust and depend on to deliver important scholarship in the various "discourses" that comprise the increasingly complex field of curriculum theory.

The range of the series is both broad (all of curriculum theory) and limited (only important, lasting scholarship) – including but not confined to historical, philosophical, critical, multicultural, feminist, comparative, international, aesthetic, and spiritual topics and approaches. Books in this series are intended for scholars and for students at the doctoral and, in some cases, master's levels.

Influences and Inspirations in Curriculum Studies Research and Teaching
Reflections on the Origins and Legacy of Contemporary Scholarship
Edited by Carmen Shields, Adam Garry Podolski, and John J. Guiney Yallop

Engaging Currere Toward Decolonization
Negotiating Black Womanhood through Autobiographical Analysis
Shauna Knox

Lingering with the Works of Ted T. Aoki
Historical and Contemporary Significance for Curriculum Research and Practice
Edited by Nicole Y. S. Lee, Lesley E. Wong, and Joanne M. Ursino

Restoring Soul, Passion, and Purpose in Teacher Education
Contesting the Instrumentalization of Curriculum and Pedagogy
Peter P. Grimmett

For more information about this series, please visit: https://www.routledge.com/Studies-in-Curriculum-Theory-Series/book-series/LEASCTS

Lingering with the Works of Ted T. Aoki
Historical and Contemporary Significance for Curriculum Research and Practice

Edited by Nicole Y. S. Lee, Lesley E. Wong, and Joanne M. Ursino

NEW YORK AND LONDON

First published 2022
by Routledge
605 Third Avenue, New York, NY 10158

and by Routledge
2 Park Square, Milton Park, Abingdon, Oxon, OX14 4RN

Routledge is an imprint of the Taylor & Francis Group, an informa business

© 2022 Taylor & Francis

The right of Nicole Y. S. Lee, Lesley E. Wong, and Joanne M. Ursino to be identified as the authors of the editorial material, and of the authors for their individual chapters, has been asserted in accordance with sections 77 and 78 of the Copyright, Designs and Patents Act 1988.

All rights reserved. No part of this book may be reprinted or reproduced or utilised in any form or by any electronic, mechanical, or other means, now known or hereafter invented, including photocopying and recording, or in any information storage or retrieval system, without permission in writing from the publishers.

Trademark notice: Product or corporate names may be trademarks or registered trademarks, and are used only for identification and explanation without intent to infringe.

Library of Congress Cataloging-in-Publication Data
Names: Lee, Nicole Y. S., editor. | Wong, Lesley E., editor. | Ursino, Joanne M., editor.
Title: Lingering with the works of Ted T. Aoki : historical and contemporary significance for curriculum research and practice / Nicole Y. S. Lee, Lesley E. Wong and Joanne M. Ursino.
Description: First Edition. | New York : Routledge, 2022. | Series: Studies in Curriculum Theory | Includes bibliographical references and index.
Identifiers: LCCN 2021031311 | ISBN 9780367479084 (Hardback) | ISBN 9781032154374 (Paperback) | ISBN 9781003037248 (eBook)
Subjects: LCSH: Curriculum planning–Research–Philosophy. | Education–Curricula–Research–Philosophy. | Curriculum change. | Aoki, Ted T.
Classification: LCC LB2806.15 .L56 2022 | DDC 375/.001–dc23
LC record available at https://lccn.loc.gov/2021031311

ISBN: 978-0-367-47908-4 (hbk)
ISBN: 978-1-032-15437-4 (pbk)
ISBN: 978-1-003-03724-8 (ebk)

DOI: 10.4324/9781003037248

Typeset in Galliard
by KnowledgeWorks Global Ltd.

To

Ted

Bill and Rita

And

Aokian scholars everywhere

Figure 0.1 Island with Snow Viewing Lantern (Mother Figure) | Photo: Joanne M. Ursino.

Contents

List of Figures — x
List of Contributors — xi
Foreword by William F. Pinar — xv
Acknowledgements — xxv

Introduction: Aokian Notes and Intergenerational Resonances — 1
NICOLE Y. S. LEE, LESLEY E. WONG, AND JOANNE M. URSINO

PART 1
Autobiography and Writing: Introduction — 17
BY NICOLE Y. S. LEE

1 Asking Who We Are in Place with Aoki's Poetics of Belonging — 21
AMANDA FRITZLAN

2 Whirling with Aoki at the Cross of Horizontal and Vertical Intentions: A Poet's Pondering with/in Language and Light — 33
ANAR RAJABALI

3 Finding the Human in the Middle of (In)visible Pandemics — 46
NICOLE Y. S. LEE

Interlude: Walking with Aoki — 58
RITA L. IRWIN

PART 2
Arts-Based Education Research and Stories: Introduction 61
BY JOANNE M. URSINO

4 An Aokian Sensibility at the Intersections of both Arts-Based Research and Relations 65
JOANNE M. URSINO

5 When Does an Haleliwia Become More Than an Haleliwia?: Abeying to a Poethics of Plants with Aoki 80
JOANNE PRICE

6 "That's My Way": Indwelling between the Two Worlds of Piano Teaching 94
JEE YEON RYU

Interlude: Letters from Ted 107
KAREN MEYER

PART 3
Curricular and Pedagogical Contexts: Introduction 111
BY LESLEY E. WONG

7 Walking across Contexts with Technology: An Aokian Methodology 115
LESLEY E. WONG

8 Visualizing and Reconceptualizing Transformative Sustainability Learning through an Aokian Lens 128
KSHAMTA HUNTER

9 Listen to What the Situation Is Asking: Aoki and Music Education 144
MARGARET O'SULLIVAN

Interlude: The Inspirited Curriculum 156
PETER P. GRIMMETT

PART 4
Curriculum Theorizing: Introduction 159
BY NICOLE Y. S. LEE

10 Thinking Creatively with Ted T. Aoki about Scholarship
   of Teaching and Learning 163
   BRUCE MOGHTADER

11 Lingering Notes: Sounds of Learning in Teacher Education 175
   YU-LING LEE

12 Contemplating the Relation between Theory and Practice
   through Three Aoki Inspirited Themes 186
   PATRICIA LIU BAERGEN AND KAREN MEYER

Index 199

Figures

P.1	Western Red Cedars and Cherry Blossom Tree in the Nitobe Memorial Garden | Photo: Nicole Y. S. Lee.	18
2.1	Untitled | Photo: Anar Rajabali.	43
Int.1	Nitobe Memorial Garden Walk | Photo Collage: Rita L. Irwin.	59
P.2	Nitobe Memorial Garden Bench and Tree | Photo: Joanne M. Ursino.	62
4.1	Photo Collage of Handmade Book Art | Photo Collage: Joanne M. Ursino.	67
4.2	Photo Collage of Notes in Handmade Book Art | Photo Collage: Joanne M. Ursino.	69
5.1	An Haleliwia Moment—Noticing Plants in the Language of Pedagogy | Photos: Joanne Price.	81
5.2	Haleliwia and Oak, Pine, Alder, Ash, and Willow Trees | Illustrations and Collage: Joanne Price.	92
Int.2	A Letter from Ted | Image: Karen Meyer	108
P.3	Nitobe Memorial Garden Path | Photo: Simon Wong.	112
8.1	Aoki's Bridge for Values Exploration offers a Transformative Sustainability Learning Model and a Competence Development Approach | Image: Natalie Hawryshkewich.	136
P.4	Nitobe Memorial Garden Sato-Zakura Tree | Photo: Simon Wong.	160
12.1	Nitobe Memorial Garden | Photo: Patricia Liu Baergen.	187
13.1	Nitobe Memorial Garden Lantern (Father Figure) | Photo: Simon Wong.	198

Contributors

Amanda Fritzlan completed her doctorate in curriculum studies at The University of British Columbia. Her research interests include the relationships with place that are a part of school-based education. As well, she studies and practices autobiography, autoethnography, and narrative inquiry as research methodologies. Teaching Indigenous art in elementary schools as a non-Indigenous teacher was the topic of Amanda's master's research. Her doctoral studies focus on mathematics teachers' experiences relating with community and place, particularly the ways in which they work with Indigenous knowledge and worldviews.

Peter P. Grimmett is Professor Emeritus at both SFU and UBC. A former Dean at SFU, he also served as the BC Deans appointment to the BC College of Teachers between 2007 and 2010. He has published 53 refereed journal articles, 11 books and 49 chapters in books, and in 2000 received an honorary doctorate from the University of Tampere, Finland. In 2014 he was awarded the Canadian Association for Teacher Education's Life-Time Research Achievement Award. His (2012) book, *Teacher Certification and the Professional Status of Teaching in North America: The New Battleground for Public Education*, locates recent developments in teacher certification and he is currently writing a book on the need to re-enchant curriculum and pedagogy in teacher education.

Kshamta Hunter is a PhD candidate in the Department of Curriculum and Pedagogy, Faculty of Education at The University of British Columbia (UBC). Kshamta's research explores the intersections of sustainability learning and leadership, using Transformative Learning and social innovation frameworks. She is interested in exploring and designing a comprehensive, responsive and relevant integrative curriculum and pedagogical approaches for the 21st century, through understanding the development of competencies for innovation toward sustainability. She holds a Masters in sustainability curriculum and pedagogy and is the Manager of Sustainability Engagement with the UBC Sustainability Initiative, where she is able to shape a lot of her research ideas into practice.

Rita L. Irwin is a distinguished university scholar and Professor of Art Education and Curriculum Studies, Faculty of Education, The University of British Columbia, Vancouver, Canada. She has held a number of university leadership positions as well as many leadership positions across the profession including being President of the Canadian Society for the Study of Education and the International Society for Education through Art. Her major research interests include practice-based research, participatory and community engaged research, international studies, arts-based research and a/r/tography set within questions related to sociocultural issues, teacher education, inquiry based learning, and contemporary art.

Nicole Y. S. Lee completed her PhD in Curriculum Studies, specializing in Art Education, in the Department of Curriculum and Pedagogy at The University of British Columbia, Vancouver, Canada. She holds a BFA in Visual Arts (studio), BEd, and MEd from York University, Toronto, Canada. Her a/r/tographic, curricular, and philosophical research develops a four-movement framework for cultivating a relationship with the unknown. Each turn layers concept, making, and breath, offering a curriculum for artful, purposeful, and meaningful living. Nicole's research is supported by the Social Sciences and Humanities Research Council of Canada.

Yu-Ling Lee is Assistant Professor in the School of Education at Trinity Western University. His areas of interest include design, technology, and philosophy of education. He is currently co-designing curricular technotheological learning spaces and co-making digital media as academic agency. You can find him on twitter @ yulingleephd.

Patricia Liu Baergen completed her PhD in Curriculum Studies at The University of British Columbia. Her research interests include curriculum studies, life history, theorizing pedagogy, and educational philosophy.

Karen Meyer holds emeritus standing after 26 years at The University of British Columbia. Teaching has been her life project, walking three paths. She has walked alongside teachers for two decades through job action, strikes, self-care issues, and inner-city school vulnerabilities. She supervised 11 Master's cohorts with practicing teachers. Karen's second path led her to Dadaab refugee camp in north-eastern Kenya. She worked with young teachers there who grew up in the camp and who face obstacles and uncertainties with inspiring resilience. Her third path offered support for graduate students, advocating for their passion, voice, and creative forms of writing.

Bruce Moghtader is Scholarship of Teaching and Learning (SoTL) Facilitator in the Centre for Teaching, Learning, and Technology at The University of British Columbia (UBC). His principal research interests include SoTL, education ethics, and knowledge economy.

Margaret O'Sullivan is a PhD candidate in Curriculum Studies in The University of British Columbia. The 2016 recipient of the National University of Ireland Denis Phelan Travelling Studentship Award for her doctoral studies, Margaret runs Music Generation Cork City, a music education partnership that provides music learning and creative opportunities for children and young people experiencing exclusion from participation in music-making. Her reflexive scholarly inquiry into the conceptualization of quality in community music education is inspired by her work in establishing this project, in combination with learning from practice in her 25 year career in cultural management and arts education.

Joanne Price recently completed a doctorate in Curriculum Studies and has since been living in mid Wales working as a study assistant and learning to speak Welsh anew. She is inspired by ways in which Ted T. Aoki's life as a pedagogue-who-walks-with relates to these experiences, and her daily walks in ffridd or wild upland areas. Here, she takes time to notice ways we might learn with and from plants and trees. Devoted to exploring original ways of responding to climate change, she writes stories in hopes of rejuvenating the planet and making room for different voices.

Anar Rajabali is an educator, poet and researcher. Her arts-based dissertation, *(Re)turning to the Poetic I/Eye: Towards a Literacy of Light* (2017), is a meditation on poetry, spirituality and the quest for knowledge and the recipient of ARTS Research Graduate Award at Canadian Society for the Study of Education. Her research engages poetry (textual and spoken), song, philosophy, autobiography, and curriculum theorizing. She is founder of Pearl Learning: English Language Education Centre and published works appear in: Creative Approaches to Research, Poetic Inquiry: Enchantment of Place, Art/Research International: A Transdisciplinary Journal and Journal of the Canadian Association for Curriculum Studies.

Jee Yeon Ryu completed her PhD in Curriculum and Pedagogy Studies at The University of British Columbia, specializing in music education. As a pianist, teacher, and researcher, she incorporates a variety of artistic genres into her pedagogical and scholarly practices, including erasure poetry, piano performance, video, and creative writing. Her works have been published in Music Education Research, International Journal of Education Through Art, Poetic Inquiry: Enchantment of Place, LEARNing Landscapes Journal, and Handbook of Arts-Based Research.

Joanne M. Ursino centres arts-based research and auto-poetic inquiry in a strong studio art practice. Joanne is completing her dissertation in Cross Faculty Inquiry in the Faculty of Education at The University of British Columbia. Her work and texts are intimate, intricate and engage feminist, anti-racist and queer discourses at the cutting edges of arts-based research, curriculum theory and language. Joanne has been making quilts for 30 years—alongside book arts/artist books and photography. Joanne's research is supported by the Social Sciences and Humanities Research Council of Canada.

Lesley E. Wong is a PhD candidate in the Department of Curriculum and Pedagogy, Faculty of Education at The University of British Columbia (UBC). Her areas of research include educational technology, educational design, online learning, and cyberbullying. Her doctoral work focuses on adolescent experiences and understanding of cyberbullying and is supported by the Social Sciences and Humanities Research Council of Canada.

Foreword by William F. Pinar

"This collection reflects a contemporary moment," the editors indicate. Accordingly, Nicole Y. S. Lee, Lesley E. Wong, and Joanne M. Ursino structure this collection of remarkable essays by "layering" the texts of Ted Aoki[1] "alongside his legacy then and now."[2] I'll try something similar, although I'll layer Aoki's texts less "alongside" and more at the end(notes), an attempt to perforate the present, at least insofar as it is portrayed in a text by Byung-Chul Han.[3] It is a temporal layering[4] that I'll also make spatial by highlighting Han in the main text. Aoki is audible in the endnotes. It is referencing that renders explicit the palimpsest the present moment can be. The erased past protrudes provided you interrupt your immersion in the present to read what the endnote numbers designate. There you experience Aoki enacting his "living pedagogy," one "midst curriculum-as-plan/curriculum-as-live(d),"[5] a spatial and[6] temporal concept that positions us not only suspended between Here and There but also between Then and Now.

Ted Aoki was an "untimely"[7] teacher, haunted[8] by history. He did not flee it—the internment, his daughter's death—but stayed suspended. Lingering he termed it, one of his key concepts and the title of this book that its essays enact. Lingering allows, as the editors point out, "one to go deeper into *that* paper, *that* idea, *that* tugging feeling that grips and haunts—the one that can only come from an individual because of their experiences, the one that was waiting to be articulated, and the one that matters."[9] Supplementing the spatial ("digging deeper") is the temporal ("their experiences"), as lingering allows the allegro of our lives to devolve into adagio, at least while we—alone and together—remain on that Aokian bridge[10] where he teaches us to dwell in-between what is, keeping the past[11] close-by to temporalize the present.[12] The editors know: "Lingering grants an opening for pause, breath, an experience of duration, and a *deepening of time* so that wisdom can grace one's presence."[13] In that lovely—and precise—series of images the spatial and temporal fuse.

An "acceleration of life," Han warns, "robs" us of the capacity for "contemplation," and it is "precisely" our incapacity to "linger in contemplation" which leads to a "general haste" and "dispersion."[14] Such grand (or meta-) narratives (the use of "we" without specification of place or time or culture) that Aoki helped deconstruct—destructive as they could be—can today provide meaning that went missing when we disappeared into our devices, dispersing both subjectivity and time so that any experience of "duration" is not possible.[15] The "compression" of events, information and images makes it impossible to *"linger,"* Han rues.[16]

Impossible? Perhaps not: "The end of narration, the end of history, does not need to bring about a temporal emptiness,"[17] Han advises, adding that in this pseudo-present[18]—in which historical time is absent—we can live "without theology and teleology," provided we live a *"vita contemplative."*[19] Han suspects that the current crisis could conclude "once the *vita activa*, in the midst of its crisis, again incorporates the *vita contemplativa.*"[20] The persisting problem of practice—not only what will I teach but how will I live? —could begin to be resolved once time and narrative restart, as the "right time," or the "right moment, only arises out of the temporal tension within a time that has a direction."[21] Remember where you've been and you'll see where you are; maybe you'll even glimpse where you're going: A perspective that, in Aoki's terms, allows as it reflects "dwelling aright"[22] in the situation.

Such "dwelling aright"—suspended on a bridge that is not a bridge, a "now" bookended by Then and Now and There and Here,[23] thereby hinting at what's ahead—takes time. Adjustment, attunement, and atonement take time. Everyone is implicated in what has transpired before us, as each of us carries the past inside us, a haunting effaced by our fascination with the screens at which we stare. The consequence is an interrelated series of crises: A "temporal crisis" (presentism) a cultural crisis (narcissism), an "identity crisis."[24] Submerged in the temporally-empty present, disabled from discerning difference by enclosure inside an ever-receding withering self (what Lasch perceptively characterized as a minimal self[25]), identity (as the interface between interiority and exteriority) disappears, replaced by online profiles (wherein self and identity are conflated) constantly curated on social media.[26]

Decades ago Aoki worried about the "reductionism" that occurs "when people closet themselves into solitudes of ethnic identities."[27] Referencing "the narcissistic 'I' of the 'me' generation," Aoki wonders if "in like way, does not understanding multiculturalism as solitudes of identities promote *ethno-narcissism* by regarding others strictly as "them," outside?"[28] Self-enclosed inside identity the singular self dissolves into a collective one, often static—even stereotypic, if now valorized positively.

Stasis—arrested (development) as depicted in Kafka's *The Trial*[29]—is not only identarian but temporal. Submergence in the pseudo-present erases singularity too, as time disappears into "empty duration," a "non-articulated, directionless time without any meaningful before or after, remembrance or expectation."[30] The next screen shot substitutes for something actually happening—embodied, often abrasive decidedly lived experience[31]—as it presents the "new," new ideas, new possibilities, a series of screen shots that then disappear.[32] "One begins ever anew," Han knows, "one zaps through 'life possibilities,' precisely because of an inability to bring any single possibility to a conclusion," adding that no longer is the "individual's life" structured like a "story," a "meaningful totality."[33] Collective life occurs in the Cloud, no civic square but a series of websites where we can shop, politics replaced by consumption, including of ourselves.

"Historical time *can* rush ahead," Han appreciates, "because it does not rest in itself, because its centre of gravity is not in the present."[34] Han errs when he declares that history does not permit any "genuine lingering," as that would only slow down "progressive progress."[35] Yes, history can encourage impatience, even frustration and rage, but it delays nothing. History is the narration of what's happening, and "out of nothing," Han admits, "narration makes a *world*."[36] But in our time "history gives way to *information*."[37] Information constitutes a "new paradigm," as an "altogether different temporality" is involved, what Han terms "atomized" or "point-time," between which "yawns an emptiness, an empty interval in which nothing happens, in which no *sensation* takes place."[38] Aoki might welcome a momentary absence of sensation—utter stillness—if that allowed one to linger.

For Han "point-time" precludes "contemplative lingering," as it lacks "narrative tension."[39] Aoki too found tension generative.[40] In the Age of Information the "senses" can be bombarded with—dispersed by—the onslaught of "new," sometimes "drastic perceptions."[41] In contrast, "lingering presupposes a gathering of the senses."[42] They disperse when we become submerged in images and information; the "internet" and "electronic mail" allow "geography, even the earth, disappear."[43] The person disappears as well,[44] as s/he exists only insofar as s/he makes sense, makes meaning, has a life: Once fused with the screen, "freed" from "meaning," "things begin to hover or whizz around without direction."[45] When meaning disappears, a "massification"[46] occurs as, Han cautions, "everything pushes into the present, leading to blockages."[47] Suddenly one is under arrest, going nowhere[48], as the "difference between Here and There ... disappears."[49] In desperation "one rushes from one event to another."[50] When rushing one is without footing or "hold," and "life today finds it hard to get a grip. Temporal dissipation throws it off balance. *It whizzes*."[51] Time feels "no longer fulfilling," as the fetishized "freedom" of the constantly and often compulsively "acting subject by itself does not produce any temporal gravitation."[52]

Lingering, one can slow down, even stop, suspended on that bridge which is not a bridge but is nonetheless a (non)place from which one can contemplate what is happening to and inside us. We can notice what time it is,[53] regain our "orientation,"[54] which is what whizzing withdraws from us.[55] Without being suspended on that bridge—when we are rushing, when our only thought is to get to the other side—we lose "any experience of duration,"[56] a loss Han attributes to "the fact that today we are unable to *linger*."[57] Han calls to us to let go of the "weightiness" of the "earth" and specifically of "work," and hover—a "hovering wandering with leisure" he puts it—and hovering we can detect the *"scent of hovering time."*[58] Such a scent, he suggests, can stop us in our tracks, as "hesitation"[59] is (non)movement[60] at the threshold"[61] of insight: A moment of immanence, when the in-between becomes not only

xviii *Foreword by William F. Pinar*

an empty space but a portal to the past, where the future can be found.[62] In time you too can be found, as a "stretch of time allows the self to come back to itself."[63] What Han terms "historical traction"[64]—what follows from "becoming historical,"[65]—"from the emphasis on the self," as it is the self who dictates "direction."[66] After reactivating the past—an idea that inspired Aoki too[67]—one then has "time," and time enables one to have a "*self*."[68] Without being-in-time—"without hold" is Han's phrasing—one is "adrift" and "without protection."[69] "Wisdom" requires "continuity" and "duration" in order to contest the "compulsion" to hanker after the "new."[70] Duration is what lingering initiates, what Aoki enacted when concluding several of his essays with "A Lingering Note," a subheading that is also a sound: "Allow me now to close with a lingering note, which hopefully, like the ring of a temple bell, echoes and re-echoes as it fades into silence."[71]

Enter this collection and you will hear that bell, still.

Notes

1. To learn about the life of Canada's pre-eminent curriculum theorist, see Liu Baergen, 2020.
2. From the editors' introduction, this volume.
3. 2017. The editors also quote this text.
4. Or juxtaposition: see Strong-Wilson, 2021, p. 21.
5. Aoki, 2003/2005, p. 426.
6. This conjunction Aoki emphasized to void either/or thinking, as the editors illustrate: "The following three examples—on the relationship between East and West, curriculum-as-plan and curriculum-as-lived, and leaders and followers—reveal some of the ways in which Aoki approaches the 'and'."
7. Aoki's teaching is untimely in the sense that "philosophy is essentially untimely because it is one of those few things that can never find an immediate echo in the present" (Heidegger, quoted in Rorty, 1991, p. 16). And "the return to things themselves or the return to the lived moment as a call or as a manifesto can by its very definition never be untimely" (Radhakrishnan, 2008, p. 12).
8. To hear that haunting, Aoki offers "short narratives—stories"—to "help us in breaking out of the seductive hold of an orientation to which we are beholden" (1992/2005, p. 191).
9. From the editors' introduction, this volume.
10. "The bridge is foundational to understanding his critique of bifurcation and binaries and what it means to dwell on the bridge," the editors explain. The metaphor is based on an actual bridge, as the editors also explain. In Aoki's (1979/2005, p. 345) words: "For 3 years, from 1975 to 1978, I served at UBC as a professor of curriculum studies. To seek momentary refuge from routinized activities ... I often wended my way to Nitobe's Garden." It was during his time at UBC that I met Ted. I remember still the table where we ate lunch at what was then the UBC Faculty Club: https://legacies.alumni.ubc.ca/the-ubc-faculty-club/
11. When World War II ended, what Aoki (1991/2005a, p. 248) remembers—he was in Edmonton taking summer-session courses at the University of Alberta—is a "night of raucous celebration on Jasper Avenue. The bombs that landed on Hiroshima and Nagasaki had done their jobs. I remembered, during the noise of celebration, the Hiroshima I had seen 11 years earlier while meeting friends of the family that lived there."

Foreword by William F. Pinar xix

12 "Leap to 1986. I was again in Hiroshima, this time as program chair for the Hiroshima Conference of the World Council for Curriculum and Instruction (WCCI). While there, I visited alone, within walking distance of the Hiroshima railway station, a Japanese garden I had visited as a youngster in 1934. I lingered, facing one memorialized tree, no longer a tree—a stark, twisted, black remnant of a tree, without foliage, with only a few twisted limbs. A memorial to what? Man's capacity for inhumanity?" (Aoki, 1991/2005a, p. 248).
13 From the editors' introduction, this volume. Italics added.
14 Han, 2017, p. 69. Acceleration substitutes activity for action, the latter term emphasizing intention and agency. "Such an approach," Aoki (1979/2005, p. 347) writes, "may reveal more fully within my lived human condition self-imposed or socially-imposed distortions that call for action—action that in the very acting will empower me to become a maker of my own history, a historical being engaged in his own personal and human becoming." The context is different but the point rings true here too, as Aoki is synthesizing (yes in the same sense that the fourth phase of the method of *currere* is synthesis) the active and contemplative life, personified in the person one is: "Here it is understood that to do something, one has to be somebody" (Aoki 1987/2005, p. 361). Again, the context is different but the point resounds the same.
15 Han, 2017, p. vi.
16 Han, 2017, p. 40. Later, Han (2017, p. 70) emphasizes that "contemplative lingering" requires "duration," as lingering is precluded by the speedy succession of "images" and "events." Without contemplative lingering we're without reflection, memory, or discernment, evident in the circulation of (mis)information over social media, evident in Aoki's era when magazines and newspapers printed (in our era "retweeted") whatever was said about public education: "Situated midst the texture of these media texts," Aoki (1993/2005b, p. 280) recalls, "I found myself both annoyed and delighted—delighted that education and miseducation are of public interest; annoyed by the way hypermedia tend to slither about a bit on the surface, suggesting a questionable premise that openness to people on talk shows assures surfacing of the truth." Today—with misinformation circulating throughout social media—"openness" almost ensures there will be no "surfacing of the truth."
17 Han, 2017, p. vii.
18 Presentism, Han (2017, p. 38) appreciates, removes both "in-between spaces: and "in-between times," thereby "*removing presence,*" leaving only two options: now—or nothing.
19 Han (2017, p. vii). We may do so without theology and teleology, he says, but not (I say) without history. That often but not always illusory linear path of progress is not absent in Aoki's work, as he takes note (for instance) of "bellwether signs in curriculum inquiry" (1978/2005, p. 90). Aoki knew that any academic field is a historical narration; he knew what chapter in curriculum theory he wanted written next and he intended to help write it. That he did.
20 Han, 2017, p. vii.
21 Han, 2017, p. 3. That direction can be backward, as both Han and Aoki invoke Aristotle when contemplating the problematic of praxis. Aoki reminded that: "For Aristotle, praxis was a holistic activity of the whole person—head, heart, and lifestyle, all as one" (1983/2005, p. 116). "In this sense," Aoki writes later, "good teachers are more than they do; they are the teaching" (1992/2005, p. 196). From the past he attempted to repair the present, in this instance recasting our conception of "teachers" and "teaching."
22 Aoki, 1986/2005, p. 163. Aoki is here discussing Miss O inhabiting the space of "tensionality" between planned and lived curriculum. The editors quote another Aoki passage to make this crucial point: "But in order to be able to see

what is right in a situation, one must have one's own rightness; that is, one must have a right orientation within oneself" (1987/1999/2005, p. 155).
23 Absolutizing the "Here removes the *There*," Han (2017, p. 38) knows, adding that the overpowering proximity of the "Here" erases the "aura" of "distance." What is true spatially is true temporally: Mindless immersion in the present erases the past and, in doing so, prohibits the future.
24 Han 2017, p. 43. While not addressing this point precisely, thirty years ago Aoki knew that alterity structured identity. "Increasingly," he notes, "we are called upon to reconsider the privileging of 'identity as presence' and to displace it with the notion of 'identity as effect.' What is being said here? We are being asked to consider identity not so much as some*thing* already present, but rather as a production, in the throes of being constituted as we live in place of difference" (1993/2005a, p. 205). Earlier—in his phenomenological phase—Aoki (1979/2005, p. 333) emphasized the singularity and subjectivity of identity formation: "So much of what we see and read about ethnicity are object studies about ethnic people, and by being factual, they tend to conceal the experiences of life-as-lived earthly. Hence, my interest here is to disclose even to some extent that which we tend to conceal, by attempting to bring into fuller view reflection upon what, for me, experiencing ethnicity has been like. I regard experiencing ethnicity as experiencing subjectively one's lived situation from one's own ethnic perspective. From my personal standpoint, and this is the only standpoint I experientially know, experiencing ethnicity has been and is experiencing being a Japanese Canadian in the time-space coordinates of my own historical situation in which I was born, and within which I have lived and am not living." While the post-structuralist and phenomenological traditions are often cast at odds with each other, on this issue we see their blurred boundaries: emphasizing identity "as effect" and as "lived experience" are hardly mutually exclusive. That is what is contaminated about identity: It is both what we make of ourselves and what others have made of us.
25 1984.
26 The conflation is evident when Moeller and D'Ambrosio (2021, p. 52) characterize one's social media profiles as "self-identity." No identity-as-interface now: You are (only) what others make of you.
27 1991/2005b, p. 381.
28 1991/2005b, p. 381. Emphasis added.
29 I emphasize this metaphoric meaning of the novel: Pinar, 1994, p. 38-40.
30 Han, 2017, p. 8.
31 "What seems to be concealed and hence unseen and unheard," Aoki knew, "is an understanding of thinking that might be understood as thoughtfulness—thoughtfulness as an embodied doing and being—*thought and soul embodied in the oneness of the lived moment*" (1992/2005), p. 196, italics added). All that dissolves when fused with the screen.
32 "Prolific identity, on and off the web, is to a large extent constituted by information, not simply by meaning," Moeller and D'Ambrosio (2021, p. 59, emphasis added) point out, adding: "It needs to be constantly updated... a *new* trip, a *new* activity, a *new* feeling are crucial to maintaining an active and presentable personal profile."
33 Han, 2017, p. 10.
34 2017, p. 16.
35 2017, p. 16.
36 2017, p. 12.
37 2017, p. 17. "Information immediately destructs itself," Moeller and D'Ambrosio (2021, p. 58) observe, "and needs to be replaced by new information. And so many website are now feeds."

38 Han, 2017, p. 17. In contrast to "knowledge", Han (2017, p. 40–41) asserts, "information" produces "no lasting" or "deep effects." Too simple and sharp a distinction, but I see his point. For me, it's the craftsmanship of (especially) humanities scholarship—conveying (however indirectly) the singularity of the person who crafted it—that encourages an "effect," not unlike the dyadic effect wherein one's own self-disclosure is said to stimulate others' self-disclosure.
39 Han, 2017, p. 18.
40 Aoki, 1996/2005, p. 318.
41 Han, 2017, p. 18.
42 Han, 2017, p. 87.
43 Han, 2017, p. 20.
44 No one disappears for Aoki; he keeps us in mind: "I can also picture you seated with the text of this writing before you as you are experiencing the reading of my paper. You are situated with yourself at the center, that central point of your being that allows you to say 'I'" (Aoki, 1986/2005, p. 143). For the non-Indigenous, contemplation—meditation (Kumar, 2013)—will do.
45 Han, 2017, p. 22.
46 Han, 2017, p. 23.
47 Han, 2017, p. 24.
48 "Everything is Here," Han (2017, p. 39) quips. Except "us" I'd add; we're in the Cloud.
49 Han, 2017, p. 28. When "Here and Now" is all there is, Han (2017, p. 37) knows, "in-between spaces" have no "meaning."
50 Han, 2017, p. 31.
51 Han, 2017, p. 31
52 Han, 2017, p. 79.
53 What time is it? Han (2017, p. 92) thinks it is a time when "work" is everything; non-work time is time to be "killed."
54 Han, 2017, p. 31. Focusing exclusively on a "goal," Han (2017, p. 37–38) appreciates, empties any "in-between space," relegating it to the status of "corridor," space without "value." Ridding ourselves of objectives—even "lingering"—does not, however, mean wandering aimlessly; there remains ahead of you the path that is yours alone.
55 "A major difference between the Aboriginal and Western worldviews," Aoki (2000/2005), p. 326, italics added) ventured, "is the *emphasis* of Western ideology on physical presence or objective reality, what some authors call 'outer space.' Contrast this to Aboriginal ideology, which is much more metaphysical and places a premium on the spirit, self, and being, or 'inner space.' A result is that there is likely to be more emphasis on the isolated individual in Western culture, whereas Aboriginal cultures support inclusiveness and connectedness through the life force in all living things." I italicized "emphasis" as it shows the shrewdness and subtlety of the man. The word salvages a generalization he knows in its absolute form is false: After all, phenomenology (to name just one tradition within "Western" culture, but the one that influenced him for decades) emphasized "lived"—in large part "inner"—experience.
56 Han, 2017, p. 33.
57 Han, 2017, p. 34.
58 Han, 2017, p. 34. I am reminded of Robert Musil who aspired, Peters (1978, p. 10) tells us, to be one of the "masters of the hovering life," for (quoting Musil) "their domain lies *between* religion and knowledge, *between* example and doctrine, *between amor intellectualis* and poetry, they are saints with and without religion, and sometimes too they are simply men who have gone out on an adventure and lost their way" (quoted in Peters, 1978, p. 10, emphasis added). For more on Musil see Pinar 2015, p. 201–213.

59 2017, p. 36. A "computer does not hesitate," Han (2017, p. 70) quips. True, but it can crash.
60 One can't park oneself on that bridge forever; lingering is no absolute value. Even Aoki limited lingering to a note, as in A Lingering Note. "Profound lingering would only produce boredom," Han cautions, as does "excessive activity" (2017, p. 84).
61 Han, 2017, p. 36
62 Han (2017, p. 39) puts it this way: "Transitions" imply "direction," and with it, "meaning."
63 Han, 2017, p. 46.
64 Han, 2017, p. 64. Han is discussing Heidegger here. Han notes that later in his life Heidegger shifts from historical to natural—seasonal—time (see 2017, p. 66, 83).
65 "Becoming historical," Toews (2008, p. 438) explains (discussing Kierkegaard and Marx), "involved a historical reconstruction of the current forms of self-identification—in this case, the reflective egoism of post-revolutionary bourgeois society—as a specific product of human practices in time. The goal was to experience the self that was simply given as a self that was historically particular and contingent. Implicit in this reconstructive activity was a conception of the self as not only product but also producer." Given the determinism of "contingency"—in our era, technologization and the erasure of history—I promote making explicit the sometimes pivotal power of individual agency in subjective and social reconstruction. Ted Aoki is a testament to that power.
66 Han, 2017, p. 64.
67 Aristotle's "sense of praxis," Aoki wrote, "I feel we need to restore" (1983/2005, p. 116). My concept of reactivation denotes additional—especially emotional—elements that "restore" does not imply, but the idea of bringing something from the past into the present—for the sake of repairing the present—is the same.
68 Han, 2017, p. 65.
69 Han, 2017, p. 72.
70 Han, 2017, p. 73. Han is still discussing Heidegger here but these are my thoughts too. Concerning compulsion, Han (2017, p. 97) reminds that for Aristotle, the *vita contemplativa* is "divine," free from "compulsion." Recall that Aoki too invoked Aristotle, "reveal[ing] for us a tradition that has become concealed, disappearing from the recesses of our memory," one that is "given to an ethical life" (1983/2005, p. 116). George Grant too went back (to Athens and Jerusalem) to find what could be reactivated in the present (e.g., "an ethical life"): see, for instance, Pinar, 2019, p. 39 n. 217.
71 1990/2005, p. 376.

References

Aoki, T. T. (1979/2005). Reflections of a Japanese Canadian teacher experiencing ethnicity. In W. F. Pinar & R. L. Irwin (Eds.), *Curriculum in a new key: The collected works of Ted T. Aoki* (pp. 333–348). Lawrence Erlbaum. https://doi.org/10.4324/9781410611390

Aoki, T. T. (1983/2005). Curriculum implementation as instrumental action and as situational praxis. In W. F. Pinar & R. L. Irwin (Eds.), *Curriculum in a new key: The collected works of Ted T. Aoki* (pp. 111–123). Lawrence Erlbaum. https://doi.org/10.4324/9781410611390

Aoki, T. T. (1986/2005). Interests, knowledge and evaluation: Alternative approaches to curriculum evaluation. In W. F. Pinar & R. L. Irwin (Eds.), *Curriculum in a new key: The collected works of Ted T. Aoki* (pp. 137–150). Lawrence Erlbaum. https://doi.org/10.4324/9781410611390

Aoki, T. T. (1986/1991/2005). Teaching as in-dwelling between two curriculum worlds. In W. F. Pinar & R. L. Irwin (Eds.), *Curriculum in a new key: The collected works of Ted. T. Aoki* (pp. 159–165). Lawrence Erlbaum. https://doi.org/10.4324/9781410611390

Aoki, T. T. (1987/1999/2005). Toward understanding computer application. In W. F. Pinar & R. L. Irwin (Eds.), *Curriculum in a new key: The collected works of Ted T. Aoki* (pp. 151–158). Lawrence Erlbaum. https://doi.org/10.4324/9781410611390

Aoki, T. T. (1987/2005). Inspiriting the curriculum. In W. F. Pinar & R. L. Irwin (Eds.), *Curriculum in a new key: The collected works of Ted T. Aoki* (pp. 357–365). Lawrence Erlbaum. https://doi.org/10.4324/9781410611390

Aoki, T. T. (1990/2005). Sonare and videre: A story, three echoes and a lingering note. In W. F. Pinar & R. L. Irwin (Eds.), *Curriculum in a new key: The collected works of Ted T. Aoki* (pp. 367–376). Lawrence Erlbaum. https://doi.org/10.4324/9781410611390

Aoki, T. T. (1991/2005a). Five curriculum memos and a note for the next half-century. In W. F. Pinar & R. L. Irwin (Eds.), *Curriculum in a new key: The collected works of Ted T. Aoki* (pp. 247–261). Lawrence Erlbaum. https://doi.org/10.4324/9781410611390

Aoki, T. T. (1991/2005b). Taiko drums and sushi, perogies and sauerkraut: Mirroring a half-life in multicultural curriculum. In W. F. Pinar & R. L. Irwin (Eds.), *Curriculum in a new key: The collected works of Ted T. Aoki* (pp. 377–387). Lawrence Erlbaum. https://doi.org/10.4324/9781410611390

Aoki, T. T. (1992/2005). Layered voices of teaching: The uncannily correct and the elusively true. In W. F. Pinar & R. L. Irwin (Eds.), *Curriculum in a new key: The collected works of Ted T. Aoki* (pp. 187–197). Lawrence Erlbaum. https://doi.org/10.4324/9781410611390

Aoki, T. T. (1993/2005a). Legitimating lived curriculum: Toward a curricular landscape of multiplicity. In W. F. Pinar & R. L. Irwin (Eds.), *Curriculum in a new key: The collected works of Ted T. Aoki* (pp. 199–215). Lawrence Erlbaum. https://doi.org/10.4324/9781410611390

Aoki, T. T. (1993/2005b). The child-centered curriculum: Where is the social in pedocentricism? In W. F. Pinar & R. L. Irwin (Eds.), *Curriculum in a new key: The collected works of Ted T. Aoki* (pp. 279–289). Lawrence Erlbaum. https://doi.org/10.4324/9781410611390

Aoki, T. T. (1996/2005). Narrative and narration in curricular spaces. In W. F. Pinar & R. L. Irwin (Eds.), *Curriculum in a new key: The collected works of Ted T. Aoki* (pp. 403–411). Lawrence Erlbaum. https://doi.org/10.4324/9781410611390

Aoki, T. T. (2000/2005). Language, culture, and curriculum.... In W. F. Pinar & R. L. Irwin (Eds.), *Curriculum in a new key: The collected works of Ted T. Aoki* (pp. 321–329). Lawrence Erlbaum. https://doi.org/10.4324/9781410611390

Aoki, T. T. (2003/2005). Locating living pedagogy in teacher "research": Five metonymic moments. In W. F. Pinar & R. L. Irwin (Eds.). *Curriculum in a new key: The collected works of Ted T. Aoki* (pp. 425–432). Lawrence Erlbaum. https://doi.org/10.4324/9781410611390

Han, B. C. (2017). *The scent of time: A philosophical essay on the art of lingering* (D. Steuer, Trans.). Polity.
Kumar, A. (2013). *Curriculum as meditative inquiry*. Palgrave Macmillan.
Lasch, C. (1984). *The minimal self: Psychic survival in troubled times*. Norton.
Liu Baergen, P. (2020). *Tracing Ted Tetsuo Aoki's intellectual formation: Historical, societal and phenomenological influences*. Routledge. https://doi.org/10.4324/9781003029557
Moeller, H. G., & D'Ambrosio, P. J. (2021). *You and your profile: Identity after authenticity*. Columbia University Press.
Peters, F. G. (1978). *Robert Musil: Master of the hovering life*. Columbia University Press.
Pinar, W. F. (1994). *Autobiography, politics and sexuality: Essays in curriculum theory 1972–1992*. Peter Lang.
Pinar, W. F. (2015). *Educational experience as lived*. Routledge.
Pinar, W. F. (2019). *Moving images of eternity: George Grant's critique of time, teaching, and technology*. University of Ottawa Press.
Radhakrishnan, R. (2008). *History, the human, and the world between*. Duke University Press.
Rorty, R. (1991). *Essays on Heidegger and others. Philosophical papers. Volume 2*. Cambridge University Press.
Strong-Wilson, T. (2021). *Teachers' ethical self-encounters with counter-stories in the classroom: From implicated to concerned subjects*. Routledge.
Toews, J. (2008). *Becoming historical: Cultural reformation and public memory in early nineteenth-century Berlin*. Cambridge University Press.

Acknowledgements

This work would not have been possible without William Pinar and Rita Irwin, the co-editors of *Curriculum in a New Key: The Collected Works of Ted T. Aoki*. We are indebted to Bill for his teachings in EDCP 508 (951): Special Course in Curriculum and Pedagogy: Ted T. Aoki over the years, where many of the contributors of this volume studied the works of Aoki. Bill gave us the opportunity to publish this book in his Studies in Curriculum Theory Series with Routledge, and we remain grateful for all of his support. The idea for this book emerged from the 2019 Canadian Society for the Study of Education (CSSE) symposium "Lingering with the Works of Dr. Ted T. Aoki" that featured scholarship from Elise Chu, Amanda Fritzlan, Huynh Mai Phuong (Jenita), Nicole Lee, Lesley Liu, Bruce Moghtader, and Joanne Ursino. With heartfelt gratitude to this group, we thank them for their support in the early development of this publication. We would like to acknowledge Peter Grimmett for his personal sharing at the CSSE symposium, which inspired our intergenerational approach to Aokian scholarship. Special thanks to Angela Baldus for her work on the book index. We appreciate Karen Meyer, whose interdisciplinary approaches to academic writing inspired our editorial work. Finally, we express our gratitude to Rita for her way of embracing Aokian theory as living practice, which sparked our passion for an Aokian way of being-in-the-world.

Nicole, Lesley, and Joanne

Introduction
Aokian Notes and Intergenerational Resonances

Nicole Y. S. Lee, Lesley E. Wong, and Joanne M. Ursino

Many of the contributors of this text first encountered the celebrated and vitalizing Canadian curriculum scholar Ted Tetsuo Aoki through the graduate course on his work in the Department of Curriculum and Pedagogy, Faculty of Education, The University of British Columbia (UBC) offered by William F. Pinar. Some encountered Aoki through Carl Leggo's seminars. As part of these intellectual, scholarly, and affective communities, the authors studied Aoki's writings in *Curriculum in a new key: The collected works of Ted T. Aoki* (Pinar & Irwin, 2005) and came to know Aoki's ideas and his legacy theoretically and experientially. Even before encountering the text, however, they met Aoki through conversations with teachers and mentors who embody and carry the spirit of his ideas, pedagogy, and philosophy. Aoki's influence has a wide reach in curriculum studies and is vibrant among curriculum theorists. There are countless thinkers who have embraced his call to "dwell together humanly" (Aoki, 1991/2005a, p. 439). This includes those who have studied and taught alongside him as well as students who continue to study, read, and write in relation to his numerous texts. Aoki's life-giving corpus enables multiplicities to flourish, and those who have come to love his ideas and ways of being-in-the-world "rejoic[e] in the abundance and intricacy of the world, entering into its living questions, living debates, living inheritances" (Jardine, 2006, p. 8). His work remains generative and enriches scholarship today.

This collection reflects a contemporary moment: a return that considers the significance of Aoki's teachings and a layering of the depth and breadth of intergenerational voices alongside his legacy then and now. During the preparation of this manuscript, the co-editors have often ruminated upon the tracing of academic and theoretical genealogies. Borrowing the words of Canadian curriculum scholar David Jardine (2006), who understands knowledge ecologically, "the work of this curricular topic, or topography or place not only has gone on before us, but it will go on after us, too" (p. 8). Echoing Jardine's (2006) words, the undertakings in this book are part of "an intergenerational project, not just a pathological one handed to an isolated individual" (p. 8) that "require[s] our attention and our work and our care for their well-being, for their 'furtherance' (Gadamer, 1989, p. xxiv)" (p. 11). As

DOI: 10.4324/9781003037248-1

expressed by Sarah Ahmed (2010), a British-Australian feminist writer and independent scholar, "what passes through history is not only the work done by generations but the 'sedimentation' of that work as the condition of arrival for future generations" (p. 241), and this book can be understood as a sedimentation that will contribution to other sedimentations. With these meditations, we bring together the intergenerational voices of emerging scholars Amanda Fritzlan, Kshamta Hunter, Nicole Y. S. Lee, Bruce Moghtader, Joanne M. Ursino, and Lesley E. Wong; and early career scholars Patricia L. Baergen, Yu-Ling Lee, Joanne Price, Anar Rajabali, and Jee Yeon Ryu. Interwoven between the chapters are interludes by three senior curriculum scholars who have had personal connections with Aoki: Peter Grimmett, Rita L. Irwin, and Karen Meyer. All of the contributing authors have been influenced by Aoki and his way of being-in-the-world, as well as the place from which his scholarship thrived.

The University of British Columbia and the Nitobe Memorial Garden

UBC Point Grey campus, situated on the traditional, ancestral, and unceded territory of the Musqueam people, is geographically located on the headland overlooking the Strait of Georgia and marking the southern entrance to Burrard Inlet. This strategic lookout point towards the Salish Sea, the land and home of the Musqueam people for millennia, was taken by the "British government as a Colonial Admiralty reserve" in c. 1860 and used as a military base in World War II (1930–1945) to defend the British Columbia coastline against Japanese naval attacks (The University of British Columbia, 2021). Positioned an ocean away from Asia, this place of socio-political, historical, and cultural complexity is the site from/through which Aoki discusses the imaginaries of "East and West" (Aoki, 1996/2005a) and experiences of ethnicity as a Japanese Canadian teacher (Aoki, 1979/2005). On the Western tip of the headland stands The Nitobe Memorial Garden, a traditional Japanese garden and teahouse that celebrate the memory of Dr. Inazō Nitobe (1862–1933), whose goal was "to become a bridge across the Pacific". Within the garden is a bridge that prompted Aoki's wonderings on the in-between and the *and*. Aoki writes about the Nitobe Memorial Garden both as a place of compelling invitation and one that inspires his metaphors.

It does not take long for one to notice gaps in the representation of equity seeking groups and of institutional affiliations in this collection of writing. The co-editors questioned the assumption that invited individuals can serve as representatives who can speak for the whole. At the same time, it was equally problematic that particular voices are not presented in these pages. In curating this volume, the co-editors grappled with the tensionality of presences and absences, moved deliberately away from tokenistic representation, and let the process guide what unfolds. Although this does not absolve the gaps, the body of work does reflect the condensations and accumulations of a moment in time, grounded in a particular place and a specific web of relations. Following Aoki's (1987/2005a) shift to the ontological, this text focuses on the "isness" rather than the "whatness" of individuals (p. 355)—how one lives into their own curricular paths rather than how particular curricular paths can be generalized for all. Like Aoki (1987/2005b), the authors "participate in a questioning of the questions we typically ask when we, in and through our very living, tell our stories—stories that inevitably tell who we are and, as well, our understanding of how our world is" (p. 349). Each author considers how they dwell in tensionality in the in-between, the liminal, and the middle of multiplicities in their lived experiences. With the intention to amplify each individual voice alongside Aoki's writing, the co-editors approached the editing process as an ongoing conversation and developed a dialogic relationship with contributors. With each volley of drafts, we seemed to be asking each other and ourselves, "What would Ted say?"

Multiplicity of Voices

This book is a collection of responses to *Curriculum in a New Key* that amplifies the significance, influence, and relevance of Aoki's work in diverse areas: autobiography, writing, and connections to land; language and poetic inquiry; leadership and ontologies of becoming; ecological communities and cultural knowledge systems; method and arts-based research; autoethnographic storytelling in music education; the role of technology across contexts; environmental sustainability; community music education; Scholarship of Teaching and Learning; teacher education; and curriculum theorizing and contemplative practices.

The chapters and interludes between parts reflect a multitude of disciplines, fields of study, angles, cultural backgrounds, knowledges, life experiences, writing styles, and philosophies within education. Though contributors may be inspired by and cite similar passages, individual understandings of the text in relation to one's positionality; situational, spatial, and temporal contexts; and civic particularity show pedagogically the divergent ways in which a text can be entered, interpreted, built upon, carried, embodied, and lived. The differences in styles and techniques of writing, including prose, poetry, and drama, showcase the distinctiveness of authorial voice.

The chapters invite and hold space for complicated conversations (Pinar, 2012) among people from different walks of life. In an early gathering of scholars at a 2019 Canadian Society for the Study of Education (CSSE) symposium that prompted the publication of this text, William Pinar who chaired the panel remarked: "we all have our own instrument to play". Indeed, Aoki (1991/2004e) summons us "to release… from the hold of this metaphysical totality that reduce… 'belonging together' to the eminence of togetherness in belonging *together*… By thinking differently" (p. 396). With the gentle guidance of mentor teachers inspired by Aokian ways of being-in-the-world, students have always been encouraged not to become more like someone else, but to grow and lean into themselves. Each chapter articulates a unique approach to an Aokian way of being-in-the-world, which provokes possibilities of practices for the self, classrooms, and higher education settings.

An Aokian Way of Being-in-the-World

An Aokian way of being-in-the-world, not articulated as a methodology as "the *-ology* of any methodology defines it as logocentric" (Aoki, 2003/2005, p. 447), is concerned with living out commitments to sustaining attention: to being with others and being in multiplicity and tensionality, discerning one's self in relation, attuning to the pedagogic good, maintaining critical awareness while nurturing kindness, and understanding experience. It entails being in the midst of lived entanglements, engaging the "curricular landscape that allows multiplicity to grow in the middle" (Aoki, 1993/2005b, p. 214), and working with/through the messiness. The authors of this volume discuss these commitments through own practices of: abeying, advocating, analyzing, attending, caring, collaborating, cycling, documenting, dwelling, editing, evaluating, facilitating, healing, inquiring, inspiring, languaging, leading, listening, making, mediating, mentoring, piano playing, philosophizing, reading, researching, seeing, storytelling, sustaining, theorizing, thinking, walking, whirling, wondering, and writing. Here, practice is conceptualized as every day, habitual, and ritualistic actions and activities carried out over time. As South Korean-born Swiss-German philosopher Byung-Chul Han (2017) notes, "a *vita contemplativa* [contemplative life] without acting is blind, a *vita activa* [active life] without contemplation is empty" (p. 112). Such practices present a foundation for contemplation, and in turn, contemplation shapes one's activities and actions.

An Aokian lingering is a contemplative gesture, and in many ways, Aokian scholarship is slow scholarship, because "contemplative lingering gives time. It widens the being that is more than being-active. When life regains its capacity for contemplation, it gains in time and space, in duration and vastness" (Han, 2017, p. 113). Lingering grants an opening for pause, breath, an experience of duration, and a deepening of time so that wisdom can grace one's presence. Mountz et al. (2015), as part of a network of feminist geographers, recognize that:

> Everyone has a paper tucked away somewhere that she has been working on for years. Given the chance to marinate, ideas ripen, often resulting in some of our most thoughtful, provocative, and important work. Good scholarship requires time: time to think, write, read, research, analyze, edit, and collaborate. High quality instruction and service also require time: time to engage, innovate, experiment, organize, evaluate, and inspire.
>
> (p. 1237)

Contemplative lingering allows one to go deeper into *that* paper, *that* idea, *that* tugging feeling that grips and haunts—the one that can only come from an individual because of their experiences, the one that was waiting to be articulated, and the one that matters. Canadian curriculum scholar Cynthia Chambers (2004) observes that "deciding what matters, finding the path with heart, requires sustained attention" (p. 7). The temporal aspects of these commitments allow for attunement, meaningful connections, and the capacity to dwell authentically.

Key Resonances

Although this part offers a brief review of Aokian ideas that resonate throughout the book, it is not intended to be a summary, substitute, or updated edition of Aoki's writing. The editors present these key resonances with the anticipation that they might ground a reading of the coming chapters and encourage readers to experience Aoki's work for themselves.

Opening the key resonances is a return to the bridge. Inspired by the Nitobe Memorial Garden at UBC, Aoki often conjures the image of a bridge to invite a contemplative, lingering pause—"a moment of authentic dwelling" (Aoki, 1991/2005a, p. 438)—in the in-between space and multiplicities of two or more elements that are being "bridged or brought together to conjoin in an 'and'" (Aoki, 1996/2005a, p. 315). Aoki (1996/2005a) describes how

> on this bridge, we are in no hurry to cross over; in fact, such bridges lure us to linger. This, in my view, is a Heideggerean bridge, a site or clearing in which earth, sky, mortals, and divine, in their longing to be together, belong together.
>
> (p. 316)

For Aoki (1991/2005a), "any true bridge is more than a merely physical bridge" (p. 438) as "they are dwelling places for people... to understand what it means to dwell together humanly" (pp. 438–439). The bridge is foundational to understanding his critique of bifurcation and binaries and what it means to dwell on the bridge.

Critiquing the valorization of bifurcation and either/or binaries, Aoki (1993/2005a) lists a series of dichotomous constructs wherein he troubles their structure "as hierarchy with privilege bestowed to the first named" (p. 294). He notes that "this either/or framework has become dominant, so prevalent that we have tended to adopt it as a reality, forgetting that it has been constituted historically and culturally" (Aoki, 1993/2005a, p. 294). He highlights how a question that skews "closed to a simplistic binary either/or—either good or bad; either black or white; either positive or negative; either achievement centered or child-centered" (Aoki, 1993/2005c, p. 280), refuses a deeper conversation that opens up possibilities. Instead, he chooses to embrace tensionality and complexity. The following three examples—on the relationship between East and West, curriculum-as-plan and curriculum-as-lived, and leaders and followers—reveal some of the ways in which Aoki approaches the "and".

1 "East and West" is a prevalently constructed binary, yet these distinct entities can be bridged and connected with an "and" (Aoki, 1996/2005a, p. 315). The "and" is understood as a site which is "both this and that" and "neither this nor that" and is intended as a dwelling space in-between two separate entities. This space is a dwelling between two distinct and separate entities and generates possibility and newness (Aoki, 1996/2005a). His explorations of hybridity, third space, and ethnicity stem from his exploration of "East and West". The conjoining and capability of the word "and" between the individual entities of "East" and "West" generates a new and doubled identity of hybridity (Aoki, 1996/2005a, p. 319). This hybridity contains traces of both identities and ethnicities in an empowering form of newness. The ambivalence of encompassing "both this and that", both "East and West", and "modernism and non-modernism" marks the opening of a third space where newness is generative (Aoki, 1996/2005a, p. 319).

2 Aoki (1991/2005b) acknowledges "the presence of at least two curricula, the curriculum-as-plan and the curriculum-as-lived" (p. 250). He explains that "we all know of the curriculum-as-plan often manifested in the syllabus, the course outline, or the course text, typically reflecting objective understandings. On the other hand, the curriculum-as-lived is one that students experienced situationally" (Aoki, 1991/2005b, p. 250). It is a curriculum that "invites", that "stirs teachers and students to animated living", it is "charged with life", here Aoki (1987/2005a) lingers with the possibilities of how "we live curriculum" (p. 362). Aoki (1986/1991/2005) does not ask that we forsake one for the other, rather that the we engage with the tension between the two—the zone of between (p. 163), and that curriculum planning (p. 165) recognize the aliveness in the relation between student and teacher and dwell in this resonant, situated space. An attunement to the aliveness of the situation inspirits curriculum, which attends to the "lived situation of people in classrooms and communities" (Aoki, 1987/2005a, p. 362).

3 For Aoki (1987/2005b), leadership speaks to the relationship between leader and follower because "they make sense only when… the two are held together" (p. 350). Leadership is not "the management sort of authority" (Aoki, 1987/2005b, p. 351) nor "expertness in doing tasks of curriculum development" (Aoki, 1986/1991/2005, p. 165), but rather "a deeply conscious sensitivity… that acknowledges in some deep sense the uniqueness of every teaching situation" (Aoki, 1986/1991/2005, p. 165). Aoki (1987/2005b) understands that "'to educate' itself means, in the original sense, to lead out (*ex-ducere*)" (p. 350) and that "to lead is to lead others out, from where they now are to possibilities not yet" (p. 350).

He (1987/2005b) asserts that "a leader must be a true follower—in leading, he must follow... that which is true to that which is good in the situation within which he dwells" (p. 351)—the pedagogic good.

As master scholar, theoretician, and pedagogue, Aoki is deeply committed to the pedagogic good and his insights on this are profound:

> In a human situation, which is often a situation of action, it asks of us to see what is right. But in order to be able to see what is right in a situation, one must have one's own rightness; that is, one must have a right orientation within oneself. Not to be able to see what is right is not error or deception; it is blindness.
> (Aoki, 1987/1999/2005, p. 155)

With a concern for discerning what is good and right within oneself as well as within a situation, Aoki (1991/2005c) traces four models of evaluation orientations—paradigms that are used to guide this search in an educational context. He details what the ends-means, praxical, emic, and critical-hermeneutic orientations entail—so that "the form of evaluation [can] be appropriate to the phenomenon to be evaluated and that the evaluation approach [can] be responsive to the interests to be served by the evaluation" (p. 168). Importantly, Aoki (1991/2005c) reveals the perhaps implicit ideas, on ways of being-in-the-world and knowing the world, embedded in each evaluation orientation. Each carries serious implications when being used to judge what is good and right in pedagogical situations.

Such a commitment to what is good and right in a situation depends on an individual's capacity for discernment. With a constant consideration for the human, the humanity in situations, and the experiential world of humans, Aoki cautions against "deny[ing] the humanness that lies at the core of what education is" (1992/2005, p. 188) and the "reduction of teachers and students from beings-as-humans to being-as-things" (1984/2005, p. 129). Aoki (1983/2005) distinguishes concepts of "instrumentalism" and "praxis" in the context of curriculum implementation (p. 122). The first perspective, "implementation as instrumental action" (Aoki, 1983/2005, p. 112), invokes a producer-consumer paradigm, where individuals are regarded as things and are "oriented towards interest in control, efficiency and certainty" (p. 122). The second perspective, "implementation as situation praxis" views a school as "a community of human beings" (Aoki, 1983/2005, p. 122) where mutual respect and understanding can foster personal empowerment. For Aoki (1984/2005), "what we must have is a view or action that humanizes (p. 122), because "viewing the teacher instrumentally effectively strips him/her of the humanness of his/her being, reducing him/her to a being-as-thing, a technical being devoid of his/her own subjectivity" (p. 115). Tangibly, this entails a "mindfulness [that] allows the listening to what it is that a situation is asking" (Aoki, 1987/1999/2005, p. 155)—one that recognizes such an attunement as "a hermeneutic act, remembering that being in the situation is a human being in his becoming" (Aoki, 1987/1999/2005, p. 155).

Aoki (1986/1991/2005) notes how "indwelling in the zone [of in-] between… is not so much a matter of overcoming the tensionality but more a matter of dwelling aright within it" (p. 163). "Living in tensionality" is a "mode of being… of living simultaneously with limitations and with openness, but also that this openness harbours within it risks and possibilities as we quest for a change from the is to the not yet" (Aoki, 1986/1991/2005, p. 164). For Aoki (1987/2005b), "it is not so much the elimination of the differences, but, more so, the attunement of the quality of the tensionality of differences that makes a difference" (p. 354). The language of attunement runs throughout Aoki's writings, which evokes an image of listening. Evident in Aoki's (1990/2005) metaphor of the violin string, attunement is deeply linked to tensionality, where "to be alive is to be appropriately tensioned and that to be tensionless, like a limp violin string, is to be dead" (p. 360). "Seek[ing] appropriately attuned tension, such that the sound of the tensioned string resounds well" (Aoki, 1991/2005d, p. 382) in the context of living means an "attunement to the aliveness of the situation" (Aoki, 1986/1991/2005, p. 162) so that one might come to live well. Aoki (1990/2005) extends an invitation to "linger a while and listen to a few conversation pieces, short sayings about listening, the ear, and the world of sound" (p. 372), so "that we come to be more fully sonorous beings than we are" (p. 373). This call to linger, to follow the stray note is a sensory shift to open ourselves "to a deeper realm beyond the reach of the eye, a realm where we might begin to hear the beat of the earth's rhythm" (Aoki, 1990/2005, p. 375).

This key resonances part began with a metaphor, which "grounds the subject" and closes now with its partner, metonymy, which "lets it take flight" (Aoki, 2003/2005, p. 446). While metaphor anchors in depth, metonymy "generates a 'horizontal' or lateral space of discourse, one that does not fix a 'subject location' (Aoki, 2003/2005, p. 446). It is in the line of words on the page and their relation each to the other. Within this line of words—metonymically—understanding and meaning unfolds (Aoki, 1996/2005b, p. 417). In and of itself it offers an ordinary logic and yet "metonymy's implications are radical, general and deeply disturbing to our subjective ground" (Aoki, 2003/2005, p. 446). Rather than it being "the narration of any life. It is living itself" (Aoki, 2003/2005, p. 447). This turn, towards living itself and the unfolding of understandings and meanings, fittingly carries us into an overview of the chapters.

Overview of the Text

The main body of the text is divided into four parts with three chapters in each. Before each part is a brief introduction that deepens the threads between the chapters in the set.

The first part, Autobiography and Writing, features individual living inquiries into the landscapes of interiority and identity. Authors explore the question: who am I (becoming) in relation? The second part, Arts-Based Educational Research and Stories, brings together a collection of compelling narratives that use arts-based and autoethnographic approaches to play with form. Writers offer narratives that decenter traditional academic writing and invite the reader to attune themselves to the complexities of stories unfolding. They ask: what is my relationship with others in the human, non-human, and more-than-human worlds? The third part, Curricular and Pedagogical Contexts, gathers papers that speak to specificities of systemic, organizational, and disciplinary structures. Contributors study their experiences of working within schools, community establishments, and higher education and ask: how can Aokian scholarship illuminate the everyday tensions within the systems we work? The fourth part, Curriculum Theorizing, assembles philosophers of teaching, learning, theory, and practice from teacher education, Scholarship of Teaching and Learning, and higher education milieus. Authors inquire: how might one traverse binaries and linger on the bridge between teaching and learning, theory and practice?

Part 1 on autobiography and writing begins with Chapter 1: *Asking Who We Are in Place with Aoki's Poetics of Belonging*. Amanda Fritzlan opens the book with a reflection on Aoki's role in guiding her own autobiographical writing since she first encountered his work about ten years ago. Dwelling with the complexities of belonging in place, Fritzlan examines who she is in place—entering into the histories of her family and their families and how she came to consider Vancouver, British Columbia, Canada, place her home. She comes to appreciate the invitation to poetic and autobiographical curricular inquiry that calls this place home, and also begins to recognize it as a responsibility.

Chapter 2, *Whirling with Aoki at the Cross of Horizontal and Vertical Intentions: A Poet's Pondering with/in Language and Light* by Anar Rajabali, invites the reader to a space amidst the horizontal and vertical:/, a third space and in-between place—an inspired site of living pedagogy from which her poetry comes. Through the lens of an Ismaili Muslim, Rajabali aspires to seek balance between her material and spiritual life. In relation to her poetic inquiry and Sufi practice of whirling, the author reflects on Aokian lessons from dwelling in live(d) experiences channels the past, the present, and the future as it be/coming, an interplay of flickering light.

Concluding the part, Nicole Y. S. Lee meditates upon lingering questions around the complexities of her 2020 teaching experience during multiple (in)visible pandemics: COVID-19, neoliberalism, racism, and xenophobia in Chapter 3, *Finding the Human in the Middle of (In)visible Pandemics*. Writing in relation to the traumatic from the perspective of a Chinese Canadian female pedagogue, Lee urges the importance of finding the human in Aokian ways. Through reading Aoki's life-affirming words, the author undergoes both a hardening and a softening as she re-engages personal meaning of being an educator and of leading with humility and Aokian humiliation. Lee summons courage and vulnerability in dwelling aright in webs of relations.

Connecting "Part 1: Autobiography and Writing" and "Part 2: Arts-Based Education Research and Stories" is an interlude by Rita L. Irwin, titled *Walking with Aoki*. Irwin revisits her own scholarship as she walks with her doctoral students through the Nitobe Memorial Garden at the University of British Columbia. The walk prompts her to think about Aoki's profound contribution in the genealogy of ideas and in the shaping of scholars' way of being-in-the-world. Irwin reflects upon how a/r/tography emerged in lingering between making, learning, and inquiring, and in sharing this vibrant space with her students. Irwin's interlude lures us to consider the following questions: How does a genealogy of ideas and scholarship of which one is part shape one's way of being-in-the-world? How do walking methodologies enable lingering? How do physical spaces enable and enrich theoretical understandings of being-in-the-world?

Part 2 on "Arts-Based Education Research and Stories" commences with Chapter 4: *An Aokian Sensibility at the Intersections of both Arts-Based Research and Relations*. Joanne M. Ursino offers ten fragments that intertwine autobiography alongside her coursework on the scholarship of Aoki. Ursino writes of the proximities, relations, and citations that take place over time in the academy. She concludes this chapter with a three-fold layering that dwells on a recent art education conference, her arts-based research, and the offering of a found poem in a temporal reading of *Curriculum in a New Key: The Collected Works of Ted T. Aoki* (Pinar & Irwin, 2005).

In Chapter 5: *When Does an Haleliwia Become More Than an Haleliwia?: Abeying to a Poethics of Plants with Aoki* by Joanne Price, the potential of thinking alongside Aoki's texts brings creative, devotional, and regenerative renderings to their understanding of educational practices. When Price first encountered a remote woodland herb known as Haleliwia in mid Wales, they felt called to pause and attend to its way. Price wanders with Aokian resonances among the silences, resistances, and hopes that inhabit a place of personal transition—both a return and the marking of a new moment. Here, they walk to reclaim a sense of self—sharing a quiet curiosity opening to visions, rhythms, and faraway voices as punctuations to the text. It is an expression of gratitude to Aoki in relation to more than human worlds for teaching a way of learning to live in both careful and exhilarating ways.

Part 2 ends with Chapter 6: *"That's My Way": Indwelling between the Two Worlds of Piano Teaching* by Jee Yeon Ryu, where the author shares three autoethnographic stories and reflective narratives about the importance and value of children's individual ways of exploring music and piano playing. Inspired by the teachings of Aoki, children's unique ways of learning to play the piano are presented as "small stories" (Nutbrown, 2011) and "tales" (van Maanen, 2011). Reminiscent of short, impressionistic vignettes, the stories illustrate the meaningful and memorable teaching and learning moments of Ryu's everydayness as a piano teacher. Ryu both questions and reflects on *what* we teach and *how* we teach (Aoki, 1986/1991/2005, p. 161). She suggests an indwelling between exploring music and piano playing that moves towards a more "inspiriting" (Aoki, 1987/2005a, p. 357) piano pedagogy and curriculum for young children.

An interlude by Karen Meyer, titled *Letters from Ted*, joins "Part 2: Arts-Based Education Research and Stories" and "Part 3: Curricular and Pedagogical Contexts." Meyer conceptualizes Aoki's letters, a collection of over 60 hand-written texts, as epistolary pedagogy. The letters tell a story, from beginning to end, of the author's five-year tenure as director of a politically contentious academic unit focused on curriculum (1998–2003). Aoki walked beside Meyer as a mentor and teacher through these correspondences, offering critical thoughts, pointing to possible obstacles dressed in rhetoric, and pushing her to reinterpret and relocate "curriculum" as a critical site of living practice. Meyer's interlude provokes us to think about the following questions: How might mentorship unfold through correspondences? How can curriculum be reinterpreted and relocated as a critical site of living practice? How might obstacles, wrapped in language, prompt moments of choice?

Part 3 on Curricular and Pedagogical Contexts starts with Chapter 7: *Walking across Contexts with Technology: An Aokian Methodology*. Lesley E. Wong examines context and meaning making by situating herself within the Nitobe Memorial Garden. Through personal, professional, and educational contexts, Wong examines three of Aoki's themes—the limits of binaries, instrumentalism and praxis, and bridges of lingering and multiplicity—to speak to the role of technology in the classroom and lives of students. Wong examines hybrid experiences and the lived experience of third spaces to discuss pedagogical practices of technology inclusion within the curriculum. The Nitobe Memorial Garden enables Wong to reflect on her own lived experiences, the words of past research participants, and thus reflect on her own teaching practices. Wong draws parallels and explores her own understanding of technology to open spaces of multiplicity in both the classroom and speaks to its lingering effects during the COVID-19 pandemic.

In Chapter 8: *Visualizing and Reconceptualizing Transformative Sustainability Learning through an Aokian Lens* by Kshamta Hunter relates the relevancy of Aoki's writing as a researcher and educator for Education Sustainable Development (ESD). Hunter extends Aoki's work on curriculum-as-lived, curriculum-as-plan, and praxis to contemporary understandings and challenges of sustainability teaching and learning. While situating her own research through an Aokian lens, Hunter revisits her own sustainability curriculum, specifically the leadership program for post-secondary students. She invokes Aoki's bridge metaphor to propose a transformative learning model for sustainability education.

This part ends with Chapter 9: *Listen to What the Situation is Asking: Aoki and Music Education* by Margaret O'Sullivan. O'Sullivan engages with Aoki's conceptualizations of community to consider how community music education is cast as radical outsider in the practice and study of music education.

O'Sullivan discusses how community music education dwells in situations of curriculum-as-lived in comparison to moments in relation to structures that reify European classical music traditions. Using currere, O'Sullivan relates moments from her career, in education settings outside of the institutional mainframe of schooling and the conservatoire, to better understand the influential role of dominant theory-practice paradigms in her career as an instigator of arts and music education programs.

Bridging "Part 3: Curricular and Pedagogical Contexts" and "Part 4: Curriculum Theorizing" is an interlude by Peter Grimmett, titled *The Inspirited Curriculum*. Writing with the urgency of resisting the politics of instrumentalism, Grimmett expands on the possibilities of turning commonplace teaching into a practice that invokes joyous study and learning. Inspired by Aoki's impassioned heart for curriculum and pedagogy, he promotes studying with and for students, conceptualizing inspirited curriculum as an ongoing engagement with the material world, infused with life and spirituality. Grimmett's interlude calls us to linger with the following questions: How might one resist the politics of instrumentalization in education? What might teachers study with and for students and find delight in educational work together? How might a curriculum come to be inspirited?

Chapter 10: *Thinking Creatively with Ted T. Aoki about Scholarship of Teaching and Learning* by Bruce Moghtader leads the last part on Curriculum Theorizing. The author turns towards the Scholarship of Teaching and Learning (SoTL). Noticing how Aoki's dwelling in the space between theory and practice contributes to deliberations on the valuing and evaluating of teaching, as he creatively nurtured the pedagogical space for thinking and doing, Moghtader argues that Aoki's attention to the relationship between theory and practice strengthens the disciplinary and interdisciplinary considerations pertaining to SoTL. Through investigating a range of evaluation paradigms, the author seeks to better understand the conceptual and theoretical approaches to teaching and the intricacies of educational research.

In Chapter 11: *Lingering Notes: Sounds of Learning in Teacher Education*, Yu-Ling Lee traces the emphasis placed globally in teacher education to reform, with policies that can excessively promote professional practice while concomitantly de-intellectualizing teacher education (Clarke & Phelan, 2017). Lee weaves his experience as a student and teacher, thinking and theorizing new curricular lines of movement with a reflection on pedagogical being and curriculum-as-lived (Aoki, 1986/1991/2005). He draws on Aoki's call to be "more fully sonorous beings" (Aoki, 1990/2005, p. 373) to linger on the stories and complexities of teachers, students, and their pedagogical beingness.

This part and the volume culminates with Chapter 12: *Contemplating the Relation between Theory and Practice through Three Aoki Inspired Themes* by Patricia Liu Baergen and Karen Meyer. The writers engage three Aoki (Pinar & Irwin, 2005) inspired themes to contemplate the complicated relation between theory and practice: disrupting binary thinking, curriculum-as-lived, and the unplanned curriculum. They offer their situated voice, suggesting that Aoki positioned himself concurrently in both scholarly practice and pedagogical practice, subscribing to a non-linear relationship between theory and practice, as, for Aoki, every moment of practice is saturated in/with theory.

The chapters and interludes juxtapose theory and practice in contemporary curriculum studies, research, and academic writing, which are threaded together by Aokian theoretical frameworks and experiences with Ted T. Aoki in individual living situations. The contributing authors consider insights gained not only from *Curriculum in a New Key*, but through embracing a certain Aokian "way of being". Each piece reflects an attunement—in tensionality, in relation, and in a desire to live well—to the pedagogic good of the situation in which they find themselves. May this work move readers as our teachers and mentors have moved and are continuing to move us.

References

Ahmed, S. (2010). Orientations matter. In D. Coole & S. Frost (Eds.), *New materialisms: Ontology, agency, and politics* (pp. 234–257). Duke University Press. https://doi.org/10.1215/9780822392996-011

Aoki, T. T. (1979/2005). Reflections of a Japanese Canadian teacher experiencing ethnicity. In W. F. Pinar & R. L. Irwin (Eds.), *Curriculum in a new key: The collected works of Ted T. Aoki* (pp. 333–348). Lawrence Erlbaum. https://doi.org/10.4324/9781410611390

Aoki, T. T. (1983/2005). Curriculum implementation as instrumental action and as situational praxis. In W. F. Pinar & R. L. Irwin (Eds.), *Curriculum in a new key: The collected works of Ted T. Aoki* (pp. 111–123). Lawrence Erlbaum. https://doi.org/10.4324/9781410611390

Aoki, T. T. (1984/2005). Competence in teaching as instrumental and practical action: A critical analysis. In W. F. Pinar & R. L. Irwin (Eds.), *Curriculum in a new key: The collected works of Ted T. Aoki* (pp. 125–135). Lawrence Erlbaum. https://doi.org/10.4324/9781410611390

Aoki, T. T. (1986/1991/2005). Teaching as in-dwelling between two curriculum worlds. In W. F. Pinar & R. L. Irwin (Eds.), *Curriculum in a new key: The collected works of Ted T. Aoki* (pp. 159–165). Lawrence Erlbaum. https://doi.org/10.4324/9781410611390

Aoki, T. T. (1987/1999/2005). Toward understanding "computer application". In W. F. Pinar & R. L. Irwin (Eds.), *Curriculum in a new key: The collected works of Ted T. Aoki* (pp. 151–158). Lawrence Erlbaum. https://doi.org/10.4324/9781410611390

Aoki, T. T. (1987/2005a). Inspiriting the curriculum. In W. F. Pinar & R. L. Irwin (Eds.), *Curriculum in a new key: The collected works of Ted T. Aoki* (pp. 357–365). Lawrence Erlbaum. https://doi.org/10.4324/9781410611390

Aoki, T. T. (1987/2005b). Revisiting the notions of leadership and identity. In W. F. Pinar & R. L. Irwin (Eds.), *Curriculum in a new key: The collected works of Ted T. Aoki* (pp. 349–355). Lawrence Erlbaum. https://doi.org/10.4324/978141061139

Aoki, T. T. (1990/2005). Sonare and videre: A story, three echoes and a lingering note. In W. F. Pinar & R. L. Irwin (Eds.), *Curriculum in a new key: The collected works of Ted T. Aoki* (pp. 367–376). Lawrence Erlbaum. https://doi.org/10.4324/9781410611390

Aoki, T. T. (1991/2005a). Bridges that rim the Pacific. In W. F. Pinar & R. L. Irwin (Eds.), *Curriculum in a new key: The collected works of Ted T. Aoki* (pp. 437–439). Lawrence Erlbaum. https://doi.org/10.4324/9781410611390

Aoki, T. T. (1991/2005b). Five curriculum memos and a note for the next half-century. In W. F. Pinar & R. L. Irwin (Eds.), *Curriculum in a new key: The collected works of Ted T. Aoki* (pp. 247–256). Lawrence Erlbaum. https://doi.org/10.4324/9781410611390

Aoki, T. T. (1991/2005c). Layered understandings of orientations in social studies program evaluation. In W. F. Pinar & R. L. Irwin (Eds.), *Curriculum in a new key: The collected works of Ted T. Aoki* (pp. 167–186). Lawrence Erlbaum. https://doi.org/10.4324/9781410611390

Aoki, T. T. (1991/2005d). Taiko drums and sushi, perogies and sauerkraut: Mirroring a half-life in multicultural curriculum. In W. F. Pinar & R. L. Irwin (Eds.), *Curriculum in a new key: The collected works of Ted T. Aoki* (pp. 377–387). Lawrence Erlbaum. https://doi.org/10.4324/9781410611390

Aoki, T. T. (1991/2005e). The sound of pedagogy in the silence of the morning calm. In W. F. Pinar & R. L. Irwin (Eds.), *Curriculum in a new key: The collected works of Ted T. Aoki* (pp. 389–401). Lawrence Erlbaum. https://doi.org/10.4324/9781410611390

Aoki, T. T. (1992/2005). Layered voices of teaching: The uncannily correct and the elusively true. In W. F. Pinar & R. L. Irwin (Eds.), *Curriculum in a new key: The collected works of Ted T. Aoki* (pp. 187–197). Lawrence Erlbaum. https://doi.org/10.4324/.9781410611390

Aoki, T. T. (1993/2005a). Humiliating the Cartesian ego. In W. F. Pinar & R. L. Irwin (Eds.), *Curriculum in a new key: The collected works of Ted T. Aoki* (pp. 291–301). Lawrence Erlbaum. https://doi.org/10.4324/9781410611390

Aoki, T. T. (1993/2005b). Legitimating lived curriculum: Toward a curricular landscape of multiplicity. In W. F. Pinar & R. L. Irwin (Eds.), *Curriculum in a new key: The collected works of Ted T. Aoki* (pp. 199–215). Lawrence Erlbaum. https://doi.org/10.4324/9781410611390

Aoki, T. T. (1993/2005c). The child-centered curriculum: Where is the social in pedocentricism? In W. F. Pinar & R. L. Irwin (Eds.), *Curriculum in a new key: The collected works of Ted T. Aoki* (pp. 279–289). Lawrence Erlbaum. https://doi.org/10.4324/9781410611390

Aoki, T. T. (1996/2005a). Imaginaries of "East and West": Slippery curricular signifiers in education. In W. F. Pinar & R. L. Irwin (Eds.), *Curriculum in a new key: The collected works of Ted T. Aoki* (pp. 313–319). Lawrence Erlbaum. https://doi.org/10.4324/9781410611390

Aoki, T. T. (1996/2005b). Spinning inspirited images in the midst of planned and live(d) curricula. In W. F. Pinar, & R. L. Irwin (Eds.), *Curriculum in a new key: The collected works of Ted T. Aoki* (pp. 413–423). Lawrence Erlbaum.

Aoki, T. T. (2003/2005). Interview. In W. F. Pinar & R. L. Irwin (Eds.), *Curriculum in a new key: The collected works of Ted T. Aoki* (pp. 441–447). Lawrence Erlbaum. https://doi.org/10.4324/9781410611390

Chambers, C. (2004). Research that matters: Finding a path with heart. *Journal of the Canadian Association for Curriculum Studies, 2*(1), 1–19.

Clarke, M., & Phelan, A. (2017). *Teacher education and the political: The power of negative thinking*. Routledge.

Gadamer, H. G. (1989). *Truth and method*. Continuum Press.

Han, B. C. (2017). *The scent of time: A philosophical essay on the art of lingering* (D. Steuer, Trans.). Polity.

Jardine, D. W. (2006). Introduction. In D. W. Jardine, S. Friesen, & P. Clifford (Eds.), *Curriculum in abundance* (pp. 1–11). Lawrence Erlbaum

Mountz, A., Bonds, A., Mansfield, B., Loyd, J., Hyndman, J., Walton-Roberts, M. ... Curran, W. (2015). For slow scholarship: A feminist politics of resistance through collective action in the neoliberal university. *ACME: An International E-Journal for Critical Geographies, 14*(4), 1235–1259.

Nutbrown, C. (2011). A box of childhood: Small stories at the roots of a career. *International Journal of Early Years, 19*(3–4), 1–16. https://doi.org/10.1080/09669760.2011.629491.

Pinar, W. F. (2012). *The character of curriculum studies: Bildung, currere, and the recurring question of the subject.* Palgrave Macmillan.

Pinar, W. F., & Irwin, R. L. (2005). *Curriculum in a new key: The collected works of Ted T. Aoki.* Lawrence Erlbaum. https://doi.org/10.4324/9781410611390

The University of British Columbia. (2021, May 11). *A brief history of UBC.* Retrieved May 15, 2021, from https://archives.library.ubc.ca/general-history/a-brief-history-of-ubc/

van Maanen, J. (2011). *Tales of the field: On writing ethnography* (2nd ed.). The University of Chicago Press. https://doi.org/10.7208/chicago/9780226849638.001.0001

Part 1
Autobiography and Writing
Introduction

Nicole Y. S. Lee

This part on autobiography and writing features a collection of chapters by Amanda Fritzlan, Anar Rajabali, and Nicole Y. S. Lee in which scholarship flows from an interest in the self: its civic particularity; its embeddedness in space-time, history, place, language, and situation; and its personhood and human-beingness. Though the authors come from diverse walks of life, each traces Aoki's profound and meaningful influence as they walk with him in their own becoming. Leaning into Aoki's (1991/2005) call to "dwell humanly" (p. 437), Fritzlan, Rajabali, and Lee share their complex experiences in and of Canada, questioning the constructions of otherness and their implications to personal understandings of belonging. The authors acknowledge painful personal and collective histories, seek to learn from them, and find a way through them with reflective writing practices. The narrative thread in the autobiographical writings reveal a contemplative attentiveness toward one's interiority, in relation to the social, political, cultural, and spiritual worlds in which the authors participate. In telling their stories of becoming, the authors consider their situatedness in the multiplicity and in-between space of *and*s. They explore the tensionality of such an existence of in-dwelling and how they attune to the elements that are being bridged. The autobiographical writings in this part have germinated in the quiet spaces of each author's interiority, yet the texts reflect an intensity of strength, ardour, and force of conviction in their way forward (see Figure P.1).

Aoki, a British Columbia-born Japanese Canadian who has lived through World War II, is no stranger to otherness and the in-between space of both and neither. In Grade 1, he (1979/2005) recounts how there were two classes, one "regular" for the Occidentals and one for Orientals (Japanese and Chinese Canadians) (p. 335). From visiting Japan in his youth, Aoki (1979/2005) "felt that as a Japanese Canadian, [he] was both Japanese and

DOI: 10.4324/9781003037248-2

Figure P.1 Western Red Cedars and Cherry Blossom Tree in the Nitobe Memorial Garden | Photo: Nicole Y. S. Lee.

non-Japanese. [He] felt [he] was both insider and outsider, 'in' yet not fully in, 'out' yet not fully out" (p. 335). At The University of British Columbia, Aoki (1979/2005) experienced "a sense of not belonging" when he learned that "the faculties of law, applied science, and medicine on the campus, and the School of Education, then downtown, disallowed the entrance of Japanese Canadian students" (p. 336). As a cadet in the Canadian Officers Training Corps before Pearl Harbour (1942), in 1941, a dialogue between the Commanding Officer and Aoki reveals how his Canadianness was not enough for him to stay. Along with other Japanese Canadians, he was "subjected to the federal government's policy to evacuate... from the west coast of British Columbia to southern Alberta (Irwin, 2005, xxii). Aoki's wife, June, experienced the evacuation in April 1942 (Aoki, 1992/2005, p. 193).

These narratives can be challenging to confront as pieces of Canadian history. Yet, Aoki's grace and generosity exude in his recognition that the condition of being in a tension situation is "a condition that makes possible deeper understanding of human acts that can transform both self and world, not in an instrumental way, but in a human way" (Aoki, 1979/2005, p. 336). The authors in this part follow Aoki's (1979/2005) summon to probe into what it means to be who they are, to "touch the essence of what it means to be human—the essence of what it means to become more human" (p. 336). In the exploration of who she is in place, Fritzlan follows her family history of moving, in protest of the Vietnam War (1955–1975), from the United States to Canada and conceptualizes tensions around belonging when family members have different viewpoints. In tracing her relationship to language worlds, Rajabali discusses her family's move from East Africa to Canada to flee the dictatorship of Idi Amin in the 1970s, her experiences of growing up as Ismaili Muslim in Vancouver, Canada, the gradual loss of her mother tongue, and her practices of connecting with her heritage. With a desire to understand the notion of presence and the perception of humanity in the Other, Lee studies her teaching experience in the COVID-19 crisis as a Chinese Canadian female pedagogue. These three chapters offer ontological, phenomenological, and hermeneutical potentials for thinking about the self and other.

Either pulled from the text or inspired by the chapters, the following questions suggest directions for considering the themes that the authors of this part tackle.

Chapter 1: Asking Who We Are in Place with Aoki's Poetics of Belonging—Amanda Fritzlan

1 How does one's civic particularities and connections to place shape one's autobiography?
2 What are the curricular possibilities that emerge from land and their significance in relation with Indigenous knowledges?
3 How does the metaphor of a bridge summon an ethics of relationality?

Chapter 2: Whirling with Aoki at the Cross of Horizontal and Vertical Intentions: A Poet's Pondering with/in Language and Light—Anar Rajabali

1 What does it mean to dwell poetically within the spiritual?
2 What potentials flourish in the in-between spaces, middle spaces, spaces amidst, spaces of slashes, and third spaces in which one is inhabiting?
3 How do the arts enable access to what is unsaid but still felt?

Chapter 3: Finding the Human in the Middle of (In)visible Pandemics—Nicole Y. S. Lee

1 What happens in the in-between space and the "and" of self and other?
2 How does one recognize the presence of and see the humanity in the other?
3 How does Aoki's writing on vulnerability and trauma offer strength and possibilities to walk courageously?

References

Aoki, T. T. (1979/2005). Reflections of a Japanese Canadian teacher experiencing ethnicity. In W. F. Pinar & R. L. Irwin (Eds.), *Curriculum in a new key: The collected works of Ted. T. Aoki* (pp. 333–348). Lawrence Erlbaum.

Aoki, T. T. (1991/2005). Bridges that rim the Pacific. In W. F. Pinar & R. L. Irwin (Eds.), *Curriculum in a new key: The collected works of Ted. T. Aoki* (pp. 437–439). Lawrence Erlbaum.

Aoki, T. T. (1992/2005). Layered voices of teaching: The uncannily correct and the elusively true. In W. F. Pinar & R. L. Irwin (Eds.), *Curriculum in a new key: The collected works of Ted. T. Aoki* (pp. 187–197). Lawrence Erlbaum.

Irwin, R. L. (2005). Preface. In W. F. Pinar & R. L. Irwin (Eds.), *Curriculum in a new key: The collected works of Ted. T. Aoki* (pp. xix–xxii). Lawrence Erlbaum.

1 Asking Who We Are in Place with Aoki's Poetics of Belonging

Amanda Fritzlan

> *My sister writes, "Out walking with the boys today I saw the very beginnings of the spring woodland wildflowers. Trout lily leaves are up, some Dutchman's breeches just starting to form blooms, and one bloodroot bud and still-curled leaf" (personal correspondence, April 17th, 2020). This email affects me for days. I miss those flowers, first to appear when the snow finally melts. Even the thought of them fills me with a longing, a memory of being there on that land in rural Eastern Ontario where I grew up, a desire to return.*

Introduction

Aoki has been a guide for my autobiographical writing that considers place since I first encountered his work about ten years ago. His writing was included in the coursework for my Master's in Education degree at The University of British Columbia (UBC). I am drawn to and I draw from his poetic engagement with the tensions of belonging and not belonging in this place, the West Coast of Canada. Aoki shares personal narratives of the discrimination he has faced as a Japanese Canadian. He includes experiences from his childhood on Vancouver Island and from his forced displacement from the West Coast to Alberta during the Second World War. Throughout his writing, Aoki attempts to articulate the ambiguous space of being both an insider and an outsider in the place he was born and calls home.

I grew up in Eastern Ontario and now live on the West Coast of Canada, in Vancouver. This is the traditional territory of the Squamish, Musqueam, and Tsleil-Waututh Nations. As an elementary school classroom teacher, I take my students outside and we learn together the names of trees. I am beginning to learn the histories of this place and consider my complicity in the colonization of this land and the ongoing colonial practices in education. In doing so, I also am beginning to question how I belong here, ask who I am in this place.

Writing about who I am in place involves entering into the histories of my family and their families and how I came to call this place home. I look to Aoki's practice of considering his own civic particularity. He writes of the significance of his identity as a Canadian-born Japanese Canadian. The concept

DOI: 10.4324/9781003037248-3

of Canadian citizenship is troubled by Aoki's stories of experiencing discrimination. As well, the dilemma of being both an insider and an outsider echoes in his telling of a visit he made to Japan for the first time (Aoki, 1979/2005). Engaging with Aoki's work, I am provoked to consider how my own civic particularity may hold tensions of belonging in place.

Inquiring into the ways in which communities of people with historical and cultural difference may live well together is a common theme in Aoki's curriculum theorizing. He points to the situated nature of education, describing a "curriculum-as-lived" experienced by particular students and teachers. Teaching, he argues, is a "mode of being" not an installation of a "curriculum-as-planned" (Aoki, 1986/1991/2005, p. 160). This approach to education requires an acknowledgement of the cultural and historical diversity that dwell together in a place. For Aoki, place can be as large as the Pacific Rim and as small as a classroom. He asks: "How can a curriculum be built so invitingly that teachers and students extend a welcoming hand?" (Aoki, 1987/2005, p. 362). I come back to this question as I write of my experiences as a teacher and now as a doctoral candidate in curriculum studies.

Chambers and Ng-A-Fook are two other Canadian curriculum theorists who write about who they are in relation to place. Their work provides additional theoretical framing of my inquiry. Chambers (2012) steps back into her childhood relations, explores her early family life, and experiences of a university career as she theorizes a curriculum for place. Retelling his family's stories of arrival in Canada, Ng-A-Fook (2013) questions his own assumptions of their integration as immigrants and particularly his school experiences. He writes, "I did not question the ways in which such educational assimilation works as a process of narrative zombification for forgetting our inheritance of a colonial past" (pp. 7–8).

Writing about relationship with land in Canada requires an acknowledgement of histories of colonization. Asking who I am in place is an attempt to ethically engage with the land and communities where I live and work. Dion (2007) identifies a "perfect stranger" position that claims to know nothing about other, in this case, Indigenous people in Canada (p. 330). She works with educators to build consciousness of their own relationships to Indigenous culture, identity, and history. This is an awakening to not knowing and to the hard work of self-knowledge.

I include in my writing stories of a bridge. It is a literal bridge that I travel across daily on my way from home to the school where I teach. This particular bridge becomes a metaphor as I articulate with words its structure and function. Aoki offers the metaphor of a bridge to address ethics of relationality in place. He states, "any true bridge is more than a merely physical bridge… Indeed, it is a dwelling place for humans who, in their longing to be together, belong together" (Aoki, 1991/2005a, p. 438). The bridge is a generative space that is not entirely a place. It is a poetic pathway to an act of staying with the difficulties of difference. "Poetry can inspirit our curriculum studies[,]" writes Leggo (2018), "by opening up innovative ways for paying attention to language, which, in turn, opens up new ways of knowing and becoming, and new ways of researching the experiences of daily, quotidian, human experiences" (p. 18).

Aoki's bridge supports his experience of the ways in which he is able to "hear the rhythmic measure of the earth, our place of dwelling, where its earthy humus provides nurturance to new meanings of humiliation that are springing forth" while "lingering in this space of lived tensionality of difference" (Aoki, 1993/2005, p. 300). As I write, lingering on the bridge, what do I hear?

Theorizing a Curriculum of Place through Personal Narratives

Writing of personal experiences, Aoki transforms the unique and personal into a theory of living curriculum for many. Aoki recalls that as a Grade 1 student in Cumberland British Columbia, "for some reason" he was not in the class that consisted entirely of "Japanese and Chinese Canadians" but in the "regular class" (Aoki, 1979/2005, p. 335). At the end of the school year, he remembers that he was placed in a Grade 2 class for the following year, while all his Japanese and Chinese classmates were placed in a Grade 1-A class. Aoki describes this event as his "first 'learning' experience of social division by ethnicity" and points to the presence of a "hidden curriculum" (Aoki, 1979/2005, p. 336).

Dwelling with the complexities of belonging in place, Aoki analyses the experiences in his own life. About a visit to Japan in his youth he shares, "In Japan I felt that as a Japanese Canadian, I was both Japanese and non-Japanese. I felt I was both insider and outsider, 'in' yet not fully in, 'out' yet not fully out" (Aoki, 1979/2005, p. 335). Another example of a sense of not belonging for Aoki takes place on the campus of the UBC during a time when Japanese students were not allowed entrance to "the faculties of law, applied science, and medicine on the campus, and the School of Education, then downtown" (Aoki, 1979/2005, p. 336). In this instance clearly, the curriculum is not hidden.

Aoki asks: "But where does a Japanese Canadian like me belong?" (Aoki, 1979/2005, p. 336). His experiences reflect being a Nisei, second generation Japanese Canadian, and an evacuee from the West Coast in the time surrounding World War II, subject to racist policy and actions. With the 1941 invocation of the Emergency War Measures Act, Aoki (1979/2005) explains, he was forced to leave his home on the West Coast and become a manual labourer in Alberta (Aoki 1991/2005b). Aoki (1979/2005) recounts that a shortage of teachers in Alberta during the war led to the 1944 Alberta Government School Emergency Act, and an opportunity for him to enter the Normal School for teachers in Calgary. However, he also recalls that this admission came with the reality of a bylaw that forbade Japanese Canadians living in the city of Calgary (Aoki, 1979/2005).

Aoki describes in himself a searching nature, a need to find meaning, "discomforted by the very comfort that seemed to surround me" (Aoki, 1979/2005, p. 343). In practical terms, this led him to leave his position after the war as an Assistant Principal in Lethbridge and become a Junior Professor at the University of Alberta. He describes a desire to "probe more deeply into what it means to be Japanese Canadian in Canada" and how, through his probing, he felt like he was "beginning to touch the essence of what it means to be human—to become more human" (Aoki, 1979/2005, p. 336). He elaborates on this kind of probing as an opportunity that "comes more readily to one who lives at the margin—to one who lives in a tension situation ... a condition that makes possible deep understanding of human acts that can transform both self and world, not in an instrumental way, but in a human way" (Aoki, 1979/2005, p. 336).

Chambers (2003) comments that, "Aoki calls for the location of new places to speak" and that he "begins the project with himself" (p. 49). Aoki's autobiographical writing becomes a language for seeing difference while belonging together. He addresses the challenges for "the enunciatory spaces of difference in the Pacific Community" (Aoki, 1995/2005, p. 308). For him, these spaces are "marked by different kinds of cultural histories, all involved somehow in articulating in multiple ways, positively and negatively, progressively and regressively, often conflictually, sometimes even incommensurably" (Aoki, 1995/2005, p. 308). In 1995, he writes critically about the vision of "multicultural Canada" as a "metaphorical language of diversity" (Aoki, 1995/2005, p. 306). He asserts that "within such imaginary rests a notion of community as a totality such that in its heterogeneity exists some kind of homogeneity" (Aoki, 1995/2005, p. 306).

Similarly, Chambers writes extensively about place and what makes a distinctly Canadian curriculum theory. Following in Aoki's footsteps she starts with her own journey, including her Scottish and Irish ancestry (Chambers, 2012), and her connections to First Nations identity through marriage and having children (Chambers, 1994). Reflecting on the changing geographies of her home throughout her life she writes, "born into a nomadic family in the midst of a diasporic society, I have mourned the lack of home and hated my need to belong and my confusion about where I did" (Chambers, 2006, p. 30). She makes a connection between her desire to find a place that is home and her work in studies of education. Chambers (2006) describes herself as:

> A curriculum theorist who found the particular messy and difficult and sought the refuge in the abstract ... one whose difficult pilgrimage to find home was relentless and unforgiving; one whose desire to belong was outstripped only by her fear that she never would.
>
> (p. 30)

Like Aoki, Chambers dwells in the complexity of diversity and difference in Canadian life and education; she also calls on a need, an urgency, to connect curriculum to place. She sees no choice in multiple voices calling the same place home (Chambers, 2008, p. 125) and looks to ways of being in place, including acknowledgement of painful histories, as a vital commonality. "It is not the grudge but the grief that matters, and what we are going to do about it. It is where we are that matters" (Chambers, 2008, p. 125).

Butler et al. (2015) acknowledge and build on the work of Chambers, writing about decolonization and curriculum that extends beyond theory into relationship with people and the land:

> As researchers and educators, this work calls us beyond theoretical engagement, toward building and sustaining relationships with Indigenous communities. It also calls us, following Chambers, toward genuine engagement with the landscape that underlies and sustains our colonial institutions—with its complex past and with its uncertain future.
> (Butler et al., 2015, p. 57)

While reaching to an international conception of curriculum studies, Ng-A-Fook (2013), like Aoki, begins where he is, examining how he came to be where he is, walking amongst conflicts of defining home and belonging. His grandfather, Ng Fook, moved to Guyana as an indentured Chinese labourer and then to the United States where he was able to raise money to send his son to school in Scotland. From there, Ng-A-Fook's father and Irish-Scottish mother immigrated to a town in Northern Ontario where he was raised. He looks critically on the process of assimilation as an immigrant and asks, "How might we then begin to advocate for a curriculum of decolonization that asks teachers and students to remember colonialism's narratives of forgetting?" (Ng-A-Fook, 2013, p. 8).

Engaging with writing and theorizing about education and land in Canada requires a respect for Indigenous peoples' relationships with land. Marker (2018) explains, "Indigenous knowledge systems are predicated on a common sense that experience and reality cannot be abstracted from the phenomena of the power of place" (p. 3). As a non-Indigenous, fifth-generation European settler, I feel the ground under me shift as I learn of and from stories that live in place. My sense of having an intimate relationship with a particular place is challenged. I wonder how well I know this place, and again, who I am in this place.

Methodology: Autobiographical Writing in Place

It is through a process of writing autobiographically, of writing the world as experienced, and of telling stories that, as researchers, we may synthesize our experiences to reveal the complexities between ourselves and our worlds. Pinar (2016) communicates, "We are not the stories we tell as much as we are the modes of relation to others our stories imply, modes of relation implied by what we delete as much as by what we include" (p. 191–192).

For autobiography in education research, we create fictions through interpreting experience as we tell stories of our lives, our families, our histories of education, etc.

Autobiography is valuable in educational research as a method of inquiry into the social and political expressions of the self. These expressions are largely determined by origins and may be assumed and so unknown to the researcher themselves (Pinar, 2016). Aoki (1995/2005) considers the underlying assumptions for his autobiographical writing in education. He reflects, "upon my own narrative imaginary within which I've been inventing my stories of personal experiences of my schooling days, and, as well, upon my own life experiences as a Canadian with the label of an Asian minority" (Aoki, 1995/2005, p. 312). My personal assumptions and unchallenged narratives that emerge through autobiographical writing about relationship to this place inform my future relationship to my work as an educator and researcher.

A "curriculum-as-lived" (Aoki, 1986/1991/2005) becomes intertwined with the stories that emanate from classrooms, hallways, gardens, and all of the places that teaching and learning occur. A member of my doctoral supervisory committee reminds me that my stories are not just my own. The stories I tell are in relationship to others who live in this place, to those I write about, to those who read my stories. Research that matters, Chambers (2004) explains, must matter not only to the researcher but also to others (p. 7). I use autobiography to engage with my experiences of teaching and learning in this place with an ethic of responsibility. And, I ask myself whose stories I am also telling as I recount my experiences.

Leggo (2018) reflects on his experiences supervising graduate students at UBC with Aoki, "A big gift of Ted's influence is that he called others to hear their voices—unique, idiosyncratic, embodied—voices that had often been silenced by fear of what was possible or impossible in graduate research" (p. 22). The narratives that follow I have written and rewritten over several years of my graduate studies at UBC. My story of a bridge began in a course with Carl Leggo. Narrative exploration of my civic particularity started to take form in a course focused on the work of Aoki with William Pinar. As I write this chapter, I appreciate the invitation to poetic and autobiographical curricular inquiry that calls this place home. I also begin to recognize it as a responsibility.

Asking Who We Are in Place

Civic Particularities and Connection to Place: Belonging, Not-Belonging, and the Spaces in Between

I am writing this part of the paper in the place that I spent my childhood and teenage years, Brooke Valley, with the white pine trees, cicadas, and humidity. My sister and my mother are nearby. I have returned to visit, and to renew connections. A few days ago, I took part in the 50th reunion of the resettlement of this intentional rural community built on values of peaceful living and shared land. As an adult, I consider how this place and the people here shape who I am today. Chambers (2006) writes of visiting a place: "A tour implies obligations ... Visiting, though, is a form of renewal, a way of renewing and recreating people, places and beings, and their relationships to one another" (p. 35). During my stay, I recreate my relationships here, bringing with me experiences from my life while I was away.

My parents left the United States to come to Canada before I was born in protest to the Vietnam War. I have dual citizenship. Part of me is resentful of the disconnect from my parents' lives in the United States. It was a relational rupture; grandparents, uncles, aunts, and cousins othered, not just by a border, but by ideology as well. My parents left. I went back to visit as an outsider, as one who could see mainly faults.

My great-great-grandfather, Jan Anders Olofsson, was buried in Bellingham, Washington, in 1914. He came to the United States from Untersaker, Sweden, in the late 1860s and settled with his wife, Marguerite, in Funk, Nebraska. They had nine children, five of whom survived, before Marguerite died in childbirth. After their mother's death, my great-grandfather and his siblings left their home to be raised in the households of neighbours. They held onto their Anglicized last name, Olson. I know almost nothing of the lives of the people in this story, but imagine intense loneliness and sorrow, a feeling of being far from home. I don't know who lived on the land where my ancestors settled before they arrived. I realize my own colonial assumption in hearing this story from family that the land was empty and uninhabited, terra nullius.

I rethink the story of my parents and their friends resettling in Eastern Ontario on large parcels of inexpensive land. This is the traditional territory of the Anishinabewaki, Huron-Wendat, and Omàmiwininiwak Nations (Native Land Digital, 2018).

Telling and Listening to Stories That Live with Place

A colleague of Tsleil-Waututh ancestry handed me the story of "Chief Watsauk and the Salmon." She suggested that I take it to work with a group of four- and five-year-olds. At the time, I was in the role of Aboriginal literacy teacher. What I saw in my hands was a bag of felt pieces and a short, typewritten script. Most of the students had heard this story before from their own storytellers. They helped me along but soon lost interest in teaching me and in the felt pieces.

Archibald's (2008) storywork principles include responsibility and respect, as well as interrelatedness, holism, reciprocity, reverence, and synergy. Storywork involves protocols for telling stories, respecting who the story belongs to, and where or by whom the story can be told. Traditionally, Indigenous storywork teaches lessons to young people but not in schools; it is brought into schools because that's where the young people are (Archibald, 2008, p. 79). The story of "Chief Watsauk and the Salmon" teaches a respectful relationship between humans and salmon.

Several years later, I encountered the story of "Chief Watsauk and the Salmon" again. This time it was as a Grade 7 classroom teacher. A Métis teacher visited our classroom and told the story. She taught us to listen with our eyes, our ears, and our hearts. The students each made a visual story cycle for "Chief Watsauk and the Salmon" and practised telling the story to one another several times. A few weeks later, they shared the story with their Kindergarten student buddies.

"Chief Watsauk and the Salmon" lives with this place beyond my encounters with it and the walls of a school. The lessons this story offers are mediated by those who share, tell, and listen.

Bridges and Gaps

I created a series of narratives called "Bicycle Writing" in a course with the late Carl Leggo in the spring of 2012 as part of my Master's in Education. He read out loud to our small cohort from his own writing of home in Corner Brook, Newfoundland. He shared with us his stories grounded in the details of everyday life, while giving attention to quality of voice and rhythm in telling. The lessons of the time spent in that course still come to me as I reflect, eight years later. The act of telling and of listening was something different than the writing. The writing itself was an act for myself; there was no perfect poetry, no template. I found my writing in the form of stories surrounding my bicycle commute from home to work as a classroom teacher. I wrote of my grief for a recently passed family member, my frustration of school policies, and the deeply embedded obstacles of social and historical differences in the community that I worked with each day. Now, in 2020, in my doctoral work, I return to my "Bicycle Writing." I reread and rewrite the story of a bridge that I ride across and of the gaps it contains.

I approach the North Shore of Vancouver, British Columbia, via the Iron Workers Memorial Bridge. In 1925, the original version of this structure, now used as an adjacent railway crossing, became the first bridge to span the Burrard Inlet. Stl'atl'imx scholar Peter Cole explains, "fences and bridges are control and containment measures!" (Cole & O'Riley, 2008, p. 58). The Iron Worker Memorial Bridge is part of Highway 1 that stretches between the Atlantic and Pacific coasts of Canada. Highway 1 connects, it assimilates, it nationalizes, and it binds. On all accounts, this bridge symbolizes Western mechanization and measured efficient rapid transportation. The irony of the twice daily congestion that sits on that bridge, jammed in gridlock traffic—people sitting in silent aggravated isolation compartmentalized by steel and rubber—confounds me and motivates me to ride my bike to work.

The early morning view by bike from the top of the bridge is spectacular, pink clouds over mountains with snow, fog, or rain onto blue green water below. Water and sky are part of land. Recently, this view has been partially obscured by tall spikes built to stop suicide jumpers. I step off my bike and rest my face between the cold steel railings for the full view.

Before this bridge, boats were used to cross the inlet. Today, there are many different boats in the inlet including tugboats, cruise ships, motorboats, sailboats, Tsleil-Waututh canoes carved from large cedar trees, huge container cargo ships, and oil-carrying tank ships. There is currently one oil tank ship per week that is filled on the south shore of the inlet, east of the Iron Workers Memorial Bridge. The tanker ship makes its way out of the inlet, around the south end of Vancouver Island, and into the open ocean. A federally backed pipeline expansion plan for carrying diluted bitumen from Alberta would result in approximately seven oil tank ships per week, layering the bridge through Coast Salish unceded territories to Pacific Rim markets.

Aoki writes of bridges that rim the Pacific:

> "What is a bridge?" Merely to describe and characterize physical bridges and their metaphorical extensions in transportation and communications, however, even when one includes in the account the wonders of science and technology that make them possible and their implications for commerce, trade, and culture, falls short of capturing the essential properties of the physical structure of bridges, transportation, and communications. It falls still farther short of grasping the human meaning of the bridges for humankind.
> (Aoki, 1991/2005a, p. 438)

The metaphor of the bridge, of standing on the bridge, is for an action of being in the space of attention and imperfection, finding an ethic of acknowledging the impossible gaps of cultural historical difference (Rogoff, 2002), while of attempting to humanly hold all the complications of dwelling together well, in this place.

Discussion and Conclusions

A curriculum in relationship with land involves engagement in one's own personal, cultural, historical understanding. Uncovering my own history of relationship to Canada as an alternate to the United States through an autobiographical process becomes a part of how I approach my studies. Butler et al. (2015) warn that defining who we are in relationship with land and governance through education, in particular, is limited by the infrastructures and methodologies we construct and practise as educators.

> We must rethink the symbolic bases of meaning that define what it means to be a "citizen" in our society, and what alternate cultural and educational trajectories might enable a student to enter into these conversations.
> (Butler et al., 2015, p. 50)

Aoki, Chambers, Marker, Ng-A-Fook, and other curriculum theorists and practitioners return again and again to the question of who we are in place, writing across personal histories of immigration, displacement, Indigenous identity, histories in place, decolonization, technology, and globalization in relation to education. What it is to be Canadian is central to these conversations. However, Marker (2015) reminds us that the US-Canadian border is imposed over land that is continuous as traditional Indigenous territories.

Chambers (1999) identifies four challenges for curriculum theorists: (1) "write from this place"; (2) "a language of our own"; (3) "interpretive tools of our own"; and (4) "topography for Canadian curriculum theory" (p. 147). These challenges speak to the need for personal, local writing connected to land as the genesis of curricular conversations. Regarding the role of place, Chambers asserts: "we need to write in a detailed way the topos—the particular places and regions where we live and work—and how these places are inscribed in our theorizing, as either presence or absence, whether we want them there or not" (Chambers, 1999, p. 147). It is in the understanding of place and who we are in relationship that we can begin the journey across difference and unreconciled histories of land.

Writing of relationship with land in education raises the questions: "Who are we in place?" and, "What is appropriate in place?" The interrelationship of these two questions creates a curricular possibility that emerges from land. The term "place" indicates a particular relationship with particular land that makes meaning through culturally grounded practices and values as well as personal histories and experiences. In seeking, searching for meaning, Aoki also writes of the space in between difference and lingering in this space. Autobiographical work as a practice for engaging with curriculum studies requires attention to this tension.

Considering what is appropriate in place means learning of the social and cultural histories and practices of a place. In Canada, Indian Residential Schools practised forced cultural assimilation of Indigenous students from the 1870s to 1996 with devastating effects of cultural genocide and ongoing intergenerational trauma (Truth and Reconciliation Commission of Canada, 2015). Decolonization and reconciliation in education require living relationships in and with place. They call on "a transactional form of imagination that asks us to see ourselves implicated in the lives of others not normally considered relatives" (Donald, 2012, p. 93).

Within Aoki's poetics of both belonging and of not belonging is an ethic of relationality in education that connects the places we live with a responsibility to understand how we see ourselves and how we see others. Autobiographical writing provides a venue for this reflective approach to curriculum theorizing. Aoki (1979/2005) employs a metaphor of flowers, the Japanese sakura or cherry blossom, and the Canadian rose to illustrate seeing in more than one way. While living in Alberta he writes:

I intend to come home to B.C., and when I come home, I will want to view the sakura and the rose, so beautiful and bountiful are they in British Columbia. But in seeing them, I will be seeing myself—for I know that what I see and how I see is because of who I am. I am what I see.

(Aoki, 1979/2005, p. 348)

References

Aoki, T. T. (1979/2005). Reflections of a Japanese Canadian teacher experiencing ethnicity. In W. F. Pinar & R. L. Irwin (Eds.), *Curriculum in a new key: The collected works of Ted. T. Aoki* (pp. 333–348). Lawrence Erlbaum.

Aoki, T. T. (1986/1991/2005). Teaching as indwelling between two curriculum worlds. In W. F. Pinar & R. L. Irwin (Eds.), *Curriculum in a new key: The collected works of Ted. T. Aoki* (pp. 159–165). Lawrence Erlbaum.

Aoki, T. T. (1987/2005). Inspiriting the curriculum. In W. F. Pinar & R. L. Irwin (Eds.), *Curriculum in a new key: The collected works of Ted T. Aoki* (pp. 357–365). Lawrence Erlbaum.

Aoki, T. T. (1991/2005a). Bridges that rim the Pacific. In W. F. Pinar & R. L. Irwin (Eds.), *Curriculum in a new key: The collected works of Ted. T. Aoki* (pp. 437–439). Lawrence Erlbaum.

Aoki, T. T. (1991/2005b). Five curriculum memos and a note for the next half-century. In W. F. Pinar & R. L. Irwin (Eds.), *Curriculum in a new key: The collected works of Ted. T. Aoki* (pp. 247–261). Lawrence Erlbaum.

Aoki, T. T. (1993/2005). Humiliating the Cartesian ego. In W. F. Pinar & R. L. Irwin (Eds.), *Curriculum in a new key: The collected works of Ted T. Aoki* (pp. 291–301). Lawrence Erlbaum.

Aoki, T. T. (1995/2005). In the midst of doubled imaginaries: The Pacific community as diversity and as difference. In W. F. Pinar & R. L. Irwin (Eds.), *Curriculum in a new key: The collected works of Ted. T. Aoki* (pp. 303–312). Lawrence Erlbaum.

Archibald, J. (2008). *Indigenous storywork: Educating the heart, mind, body, and spirit.* UBC Press.

Butler, J., Ng-A-Fook, N., Vaudrin-Charette, J., & McFadden, F. (2015). Living between truth and reconciliation: Responsibilities, colonial institutions, and settler scholars. *Transnational Curriculum Inquiry, 12*(2), 44–64. https://ojs.library.ubc.ca/index.php/tci/article/view/187629

Chambers, C. (1994). Looking for home: Work in progress. *Frontiers: A Journal of Women Studies, 15*(2), 23–50. http://doi.org/10.2307/3346760

Chambers, C. (1999). A topography for Canadian curriculum theory. *Canadian Journal of Education, 24*(2), 137–150. http://doi.org/10.2307/1585924

Chambers, C. (2003). As Canadian as possible under the circumstances: A view to contemporary curriculum discourses in Canada. In W. F. Pinar (Ed.), *International handbook of curriculum research* (pp. 221–252). Lawrence Erlbaum.

Chambers, C. (2004). Research that matters: Finding a path with heart. *Journal of the Canadian Association for Curriculum Studies, 2*(1), 1–19.

Chambers, C. (2006). The land is the best teacher I ever had: Places as pedagogy for precarious times. *Journal of Curriculum Theorizing, 22*(3), 27–37.

Chambers, C. (2008). Where are we? Finding common ground in a curriculum of place. *Journal of the Canadian Association for Curriculum Studies, 6*(2), 113–128.

Chambers, C. (2012). "We are all treaty people": The contemporary countenance of Canadian curriculum studies. In N. Ng-A-Fook & J. Rottman (Eds.), *Reconsidering Canadian curriculum studies: Provoking historical, present, and future perspectives* (pp. 23–38). Palgrave Macmillan.

Cole, P., & O'Riley, P. (2008). Coyote & Raven discuss mathematics, complexity theory and Aboriginality. *Complicity: An International Journal of Complexity and Education, 5*(1), 49–62. http://doi.org/10.29173/cmplct8781

Dion, S. (2007). Disrupting molded images: Identities, responsibilities and relationships – Teachers and Indigenous subject material. *Teaching Education, 18*(4), 329–342.

Donald, D. (2012). Forts, colonial frontier logics, and Aboriginal-Canadian relations: Imagining decolonizing educational philosophies in Canadian contexts. In A. A. Abdi (Ed.), *Decolonizing philosophies of education* (pp. 91–111). Sense.

Leggo, C. (2018). Loving language: Poetry, curriculum, and Ted T. Aoki. *Alberta Journal of Educational Research, 64*(1), 14–34.

Marker, M. (2015). Borders and the borderless Coast Salish: Decolonising historiographies of Indigenous schooling. *History of Education: Journal of the History of Education Society, 44*(4), 480–502.

Marker, M. (2018). There is no *place of nature*; there is only the *nature of place*: Animate landscapes as methodology for inquiry in the Coast Salish territory. *International Journal of Qualitative Studies in Education, 31*(6), 453–464.

Native Land Digital. (2018). https://native-land.ca

Ng-A-Fook, N. (2013). Reconsidering our attendance to curriculum development as ... events, subjectivities, and a cosmopolitan praxis. *Journal of the American Association for the Advancement of Curriculum Studies, 9*(1), 1–16.

Pinar, W. F. (2016). Autobiography and an architecture of self. In J. M. Paraskeva & S. R. Steinberg (Eds.), *Curriculum: Decanonizing the field* (pp. 177–194). Peter Lang.

Rogoff, I. (2002). Hit and run: Museums and cultural difference. *Art Journal, 61*(3), 63–73.

Truth and Reconciliation Commission of Canada (2015). Honoring the truth, reconciling for the future. http://nctr.ca/assets/reports/Final%20Reports/Executive_Summary_English_Web.pdf

2 Whirling with Aoki at the Cross of Horizontal and Vertical Intentions
A Poet's Pondering with/in Language and Light

Anar Rajabali

Through striking new curricular language, Ted Aoki (2003/2005) contends the living site of pedagogy as a space amidst the horizontal and vertical: /, a third space that is generative and holds possibility and promise. With Aokian vigour, I contemplate this in-between place—an inspired site from which my poetry comes. As an Ismaili Muslim, I aspire to seek balance between my material and spiritual life. I find meaning at the meeting point of horizontal and vertical existence. Here, my own metaphoric writing becomes a rhizomean reality where newness springs forth bridging personal and pedagogical understandings. As I conceptualize the process of my poetic inquiry to the Sufi practice of *whirling*, attending to both ground and sky, I lyrically dance at this vibrant and vulnerable pinnacle where body, word, and spirit commingle (Rajabali, 2017). With this poetic posture, I reflect on the Aokian echoes and lessons that are gained. Dwelling in live(d) experiences channels the past, the present, and the future as it is be/coming, an interplay of flickering light.

I met Aoki through the sounds of his words, in his vowels, consonants, and conjunctions as he writes, "to dwell poetically is to be in the dwelling place of mortals where one may hear the inspirited beat of the earth's measure. So, inspired, the sounding forth, may echoes of geo-metron sound and resound" (Aoki, 1990/2005, p. 375). I have lingered in his syllables like a shadow casting light and listened to the reciprocal reverberations of Aoki's language landscape in words that are lyrical and calling like a sparrow's song. I mingle with him somewhere in the middle, in the "ands," and experience a rhizomean reality "replete with a multiplicity" (Aoki, 1996/2005, p. 419). Here, meanings are in constant re/creation, spinning inspirited images, and resounding echoes. I know him in the slash: /, amid horizontal and vertical intentions, being and becoming, living and lived, East and West, and poignantly of living and Spirit. To read Aoki is to feel alive, to have one's senses peaked where theorizing is a "complex pedagogical performance of that rich remembrance" (Pinar, 2005, p. 26). Ruminating with Aoki is to participate

DOI: 10.4324/9781003037248-4

in an intimate dialogue, that is, to explore the ontological ground of what it means to be a human being in wor(l)ds in social, political, cultural, and spiritual ways. To invest in this theorizing is to journey to know oneself. It is to break the ground of who we are, to un/root language, to find what is hidden and concealed, to discover essence and what is real.

I follow Aoki's intellectual footprint and walk with him on this bridge of inquiry, a dwelling space where teacher and student meet in a third space of spiritual spheres. I embark on a rhizomean path of mediation and meditation, Aoki's and my own, and experience a synergistic unfolding in the folds of imagination, intuition, intention, and improvisation. I evoke the poet Hafez who writes of the intimacy of language and that the words we speak become "the house we live in" (Ladinsky, 1999, p. 281).

I understand that language exists in the said and the unsaid, in the silences and pauses in-between, in the commas like a crescent moon. As a poet, I linger in both white space and in words where Aoki describes his wife, June's, calligraphy of possessing both presence/absence.

Through striking curricular language, Aoki (2003/2005) contends the *living* site of pedagogy as a space midst the horizontal and vertical, a third space that is generative and holds promise and possibility, and marks the double rich meanings of experience: "it is now a space textually accented with a mark: /, a graphically tectonic space, a space marked by differences neither strictly vertical nor strictly horizontal, a space that may allow generative possibilities" (Aoki, 1996/2005, p. 420).

In the reciprocal cycles of Aoki's presence and absence, what rises in-between? Fels (2013) eloquently writes of the slash and how it plays in her life, provoking "a desire for reciprocal engagement that breathes love into being, we become presence/absence of each other" (p. 43). For me, there are openings for transcendence, a third space that gives rise to vertical experiences, of what I experience in poetry and poetic writing as an "intimate immensity" (Bachelard, 1958/1964, p. 2010). In turn, to feel something that is unnamed but present. *And poetry is called forth by love.* Aoki asks us to be open to this possibility and I am lovingly lingering in my teaching, writing, and poetry, re/searching this space where humans as creatives and creators indwell (Aoki, 1996/2005).

I have stated that I aspire to live at the cross of the vertical and horizontal as an Ismaili Muslim living in the world seeking balance between material and spiritual ways of being. I find happiness here in all my endeavours and poetry becomes my live(d) site of pedagogy, of my contemplative pedagogy in action. It is where I live well with wholeness. Aoki (2003/2005) writes of this space as a "site of metonymy–metaphoric writing, metonymic writing" (p. 429). I know the generative power of metaphor—rich imagery laden language ripe with revelation and newly found understandings, of newness coming into being like waves of the ocean, rippling lines of love, and devotion. With Aokian vigour, I attend to this poem which rises from the depths of my body, in horizontal and vertical ways of writing, a living representation of my phenomenological perceptions giving me intimate vision.

In My Belly

It starts in the belly,
a belly of stone, unsettling to this labourer
a poet is a lifter of things
snow peaked mountainous like moving
melting into rivers and washing over dirt and pebbles meandering through crevices and cracks—
It runs through my blood capillaries
carrying consonants and vowels pulsing through the veins
scarlet thick and rushing to my wild swelling syncopated heart
now speaking only in syllables
and musical tongues
lungs full of language
exhaling words like breath on a mirror
or wing-like wispy mist on the green seas
To be seen and then scatter into the edges.
What was once my shadow is now in front of me,
the sun no longer between us.
I step into it as the poem
penetrates my flesh,
closer than my flesh,
hanging onto bare bones
as the moon now rises
in my belly.

Whirling in Aoki's Slash/: The Posture of the Poet

> We come out of nothingness, scattering stars like dust. The stars form a circle and in the centre we dance.
> —Jalaluddin Rumi

In this excerpt from Jalaluddin Rumi's poem to his teacher, Shams Tabrizi, he lyrically dances depicting both presence and absence. We come from "nothingness" but not emptiness—a Supreme soul as in a volcano breaking into particles fragmenting into luminous nuggets of stars hurled in the open waiting seamless sky. We are parts of a whole, the sum of parts. In this interpretation, we carry some ultimate Truth in us and to dance—forming circling intuitive patterns—is to feel the rhythm of our bodies reflecting the music of the universe that lives in/for us. Here, there is re/birth, re/creation, and community but also individuality. Each star carries its own light and Ted Aoki (1996/2005) eloquently writes of conventional linear language of curriculum and instruction where learning is reduced to evaluation against a standardized norm: "In in an overconcern for sameness, fails to heed the feel of the earth that touches the dancing feet differently for each student" (p. 418).

To bridge Aoki and Rumi is to acknowledge that both were "defenders of interiority," in love with the cosmos and that perhaps the "most rational knowledge is first mystical" (Irigaray, 2002, p. 3). Here, language is human as dwelling poetic and requires a (re)turning to, where meanings are revealed in perpetuity of eternal possibilities and interpretations. To circle like Rumi's stars, with every turn shedding more light and patterns of feeling and thought, is to dwell with/in Aokian ideas and to be in remembrance of spirit and nature. I am lured to linger in Aoki's words as a language of light as Carl Leggo (1999), a passionate student of Ted Aoki, writes of his own research as "an invitation to listen to light, to savour it on the tongue, to rub it in the hands, to roll naked in the light, to smell the light, and to know that light is a language revealing and concealing" (p. 124). Here is re/search as inspirited revelation, in the slashes, and slants of light.

I see inspirited poetry happening as that creation in the space between living and writing and writing and living (and whirling).

I have stated whirling is my inquiry and I conceptualize my process as the Sufi dance—*Sama*—where I write and live at the intersection of my material and spiritual worlds where intellect and Faith are intertwined. I enact a contemplative praxis towards a poetic pedagogy in what Lincoln and Denzin (2005) call a sacred pedagogical practice. I communicate the lived experience of the mystical with/in the context of Ismaili and Sufi traditions where I have shed light on the Aokian question *What does it mean to dwell poetically within the spiritual?* (Rajabali, 2017) as an artist/researcher/teacher. So, in poetry, I share my path of healing and meaning where I pledge to contemplative practices in the classroom to honour diversity and plurality.

As in Aoki, I am writing my experience of phenomena as seen through the I/eye that is living it, towards unveiling and revealing the essence or the heart of what is holding my attention and intention. In turn, I hope others come away with a strong felt sense and understanding of what *this* has felt like. In whirling as inquiry, I am highly peaked, attentive, and engaged in all moments. Spirituality, therein, is not only a way of being in the world but is a way of interpreting the world; a stance to spirit reflects one's deep yearning for meaning. This becomes a dialogical encountering that is giving, generative, and gracious. The whirling dervish—the Sufi *Sama*—with one hand to the heavens and the other to the earth, represents the materialization and spiritualization (Bochner & Ellis, 2002) of this re/search endeavour as well as my spiritually secular existence as an Ismaili Muslim in the striving for balance in (re)search *as* life. That is, the negotiation between the sacred and the profane aspects of human becoming. In this space of aesthetic expansion is where whirling as a pedagogy acknowledges the act of meaning making as passing through from level to level in bringing out the very essence of the inquiry. In turn, this is re/search that is revelatory. In this space is a continuum—a turning back and a moving forward.

To be in a place of reflective attentiveness (Steinbock, 2007) is being both inward and outward, giving and taking, and knowing light/ness and dark/ness. This *Sama* gives rise to faith in human possibility. To whirl between my artist/researcher/teacher identities is to be in a place of both touching the familiar and unfamiliar in sensual and textual ways (Irwin & Springgay, 2008). I move into heightened and summit places of both pain and beauty in re/writing and re/turning that exists at the intersections of knowing and being.

Here is the posture of the poet, I find in Aoki's slash. I imagine the right arm directed to the sky, the left arm turned towards earth, feet firm and grounded, head, and tilted/. Both arms open to receive, bridging human love with divine love. Here is a place midst the horizontal and the vertical, of what is and *what is not yet*. I dwell in rhizomean revelations with/in Aoki's conjunctions: and ... and ... and ... and. There is a tuning in and a turning in. Conceptualizing poetic posture as whirling is to be in a posture of humility, that is, to sense "... a deeper realm beyond the reach of the eye, a realm where we might begin to hear the beat of the earth's rhythm" (Aoki, 1990/2005, p. 375).

In whirling as inquiry, meanings are horizontally and vertically generated where the vertical space is not fixed but expansive into transcendent possibility: An infinite line as in Rumi's universe that I opened this section. Frost (1939/2007) writes of the figure a poem makes, "It should be of the pleasure of a poem itself to tell how it can. The figure is in the same as for love. No one can really hold that the ecstasy should be static and stand still in one place" (p. 1156).

I Write Poetry

> The Sufi's spin in remembrance
> of God yearning
> to fill the heart with Love
> one hand toward the heavens
> the other
> down
> ward
> to the Earth.
> I have seen them spinning
> sublime swirling cloaked cloud
> butterflies
> a whirling womb of wanting
> till only Heart
> remains
> now Luminous.
> I cannot spin
> I am clumsy
> without balance
> or grounding.
> So, I write poetry

to stir the heart of
what lies within
I write poetry
to open silent wings
I write poetry
to *Spin*.

M/other Tongue

> Each of us is born into a concrete language of our mother tongue. This mother language with which we are home is the language belonging to a community—a language of sharing, a language of familiarity... a language with a profound respect of the other as self.
> —Ted T. Aoki, from *The Dialectic of Mother Language and Second Language*

In theorizing second language acquisition and education, Aoki understands bilingualism as a hermeneutic dialectic rooted in the lived and educational spaces with/in the mother tongue and acquired languages (Irwin, 2010). In resisting dualisms and polarities, and by asking us to dwell in the places in-between, therefore, becomes an ethical plea to resist cultural assimilation. By embracing pluralism not only as an ideal, but an inherent value to human development and learning, language then ties intricately, intimately, and symbiotically to one's cultural, spiritual, and emotional well-being. To erase language is to lead to the gradual erosion of self. To embrace language, Aoki (1987/1991/2005) writes, is to foster respect of the "other as self." To understand Aoki's "middle," is to slip into the language of both *this and that* and to slip in, out, and through one's mother tongue and one's new forming language. Entering the world of the second language "is a circular journey in which there is always a returning homeward, a re-turn" (Aoki, 1987/1991/2005, p. 242) where understanding and learning happens at the root of what one knows and connects with most profoundly and primarily. Most poignantly, to know that there is a life behind language: body, heart, and mind. Language learning is not just a means to an end but a means with deeper layered meanings where Aoki states he is *viscerally* connected to his mother tongue.

I poetically reach into my own autobiographical memory and lived experience as Aoki encourages teachers to do. I lost my mother tongue when I was young. My parents came to Canada in the 1970s suddenly leaving East Africa. It was a perilous time under the dictatorship of Idi Amin who was persecuting certain ethnic groups and there was the threat of violence. And they had to flee. Coming to Vancouver, my father found a house in an area where we were a distinct minority and growing up, I became the only child of colour on my street and in my school. I was teased, mercilessly, and my parents were victims of many racist encounters. These I remember. I was spoken to and conversed only in English at home. Here, at this time and place, somehow diversity seemed a burden not a blessing. I found comfort and lingering hope in my own faith, teachings, and customs as our community started to build a life and home in Canada.

Growing up, I still lived with/in two language worlds, one viscerally connected to me in the very gut, flesh, and bones of my being with memories that I do not fully remember but feel. Inspired by Aoki's play on meanings, I now place his rhetorical metonymic device—the slash (/) between M/other to signify how my mother tongue became my other tongue re/presenting my disconnect with my own language. Further, leaving my language world as symbolic of being seen and treated as "other."

I whirl with a poem—to horizontal and vertical places—as my language un/known brings nostalgia, comfort, and connection. To have gained the language of poetry, brings me to the Aokian in-between spaces of past/present and East/West and absence/presence. This is a language born from the soul where the tongue speaks the words that the whole body just feels, touches, and remembers.

M/other Tongue

>I could not speak my mother tongue
>a baby of exile
>I left Dar es Salaam when I was one
>from the red aching dirt to the green vast
>promising pastures
>I made Canada my home
>English please:
>>*Assimilate. Integrate. Reciprocate.*
>
>I spoke it.
>I became it.
>I owned it.
>My own language languishing
>into the hazy setting Tanzanian sun
>dropping
>into the depths
>of the unknown.
>In the summers, my grandparents would visit.
>Nanabapa, a proud man in a constant brown suit and fedora
>I, often, ponder at his photograph
>perched on my parents' antique wooden piano
>gathering specks of settling dust
>where he remains
>furnishing his medals of honour
>the stories of which I do not know
>lost inside
>my mother tongue.

I recall the mornings
he would eat a slow purposeful breakfast—
warm milk with cornflakes and chai,
Uganda toast, yellow, that would disappear into the hot tea
to be fetched out with a spoon
slurping
the only language we fully shared beyond the broken offerings
of English and Gujarati
our distance apparent as those couples
who eat meals in a ritualistic silence
in gestures that speak of the immediate desires
of a few drops of milk,
a cube of sugar,
a brown speckled ripening banana,
Oh, how are lives met in the in-between
of time, space, and culture
and how I long to speak to you now, Nanabapa,
I would say:
> Kemcho tame, Nanabapa, badhu barabar che?
> Tame juvan hatha eni wattu karo?
> How are you grandfather, all is well?
> Please tell me the stories of your youth?
But what I have are these memories
heavy, at times, dissolving like Uganda toast
in chai—
Wet. Sloppy. Ready to be lifted
and consumed like these words
I write
that bring you out, up and back to
Me.

F/Light

In this chapter, I am dwelling in live(d) experiences, language, and light. Light has been a lingering theme threading through my own re/search with poetry as claiming, naming, and framing my scholarship. I have stated that I am becoming literate in light (Rajabali, 2017). Leggo (2006) writes of poetry as both an epistemology and an ontology, a way to know the world and a way to become in the world through words. In this personal and phenomenological research space that is unfolding, peaking and leading to revelatory knowing—through the Aokian lens—I am re/attuning and re/turning to myself. In this sense, my pedagogical presence has been informed by my poetry which speaks from autobiographical memories. Aoki (1992/2005) writes, "what seems urgent for us at this time is understanding what teaching truly is, to undertake to reattune ourselves such that we can begin to see and hear our doings as teachers harboured within the pedagogical presence of our beings, that is, of who we *are* as teachers" (p. 197). In poetry and writing *I tune in and I turn in*, a sensual and sensory reminder of experiences lived and living, symbiotically informing my whole being as teaching and teacher, of one who strives to live lyrically.

As an a/r/tographer, my identities are fluxing, fluid, and flowing between being artist/researcher/teacher, all informing in rhythmic ways my living and scholarship. Each slash conceptualized as *slants* of light. I have re/named my methodology of a/r/tography as a/r/tobiographical writing which narrates, documents and reflects on the personal stories informed by my identities (Rajabali, 2017). The stress on "biography" details various aspects of a life and the explication of specific intimate experiences that illuminate the inquiry at hand. Aoki writes of teaching as speaking from autobiographical memory which provides this foundational layering to the profession (Pinar, 2005). For me, this is layering light, where method becomes movement, meaning, and motivation.

In the slants of light that flickers and shadows is to dwell in the midst of human unfolding leading to transcendence and verticality. This verticality experienced as an epiphany giving rise to emotion in heightened or profound understandings and knowledge. I ask: How do I know and listen for verticality in my teaching, for opening of silent wings…What rises in the in-between of what is unsaid but still *felt*? What lingers, luminates and lifts? Aoki asks me to listen and his writing is full of light, which is far reaching, a light that can be heard with language that resounds bodily like a young flower peaking in the dirt, *I lean in to hear her rising up.*

In this poem, I enter the world of sound, of *sonare*, Aoki's hearkening into listening. My memory also enters the world of sound and I am "lingering in the sonorous shadow" (Aoki, 1990/2005, p. 371). With *spinning inspirited images*, I whirl into the past with words that are remembered and imprinted upon me, each throwing and shedding light with this poetic flickering that brings me and my father into F/light. Rumi teaches when light flames the heart, home will always be found (Chittick, 2003).

Brushing of Wings

> I heard it first in the kitchen
> whilst buttering brown toast—
> a flash of feathery blue wings,
> disbelieving, then in the corner of my vision,
> a flapping rush right through
> the open patio door
> surprising invitation, a wild welcoming
> to walls, momentary conviction
> entering the living room to
> a piano, a couch, a lamp,
> photographs, books
> meeting bird and beak

a mirror—
I am screaming down the corridor
with my small sister in tow
our arms flailing to the sounds of wildness
not looking behind to slam
the bedroom door and lock it too, impenetrable
safety now crouching
hearing the voice
of my father hushing and
the brushing of wings against the piano keys—
A fluttering dance of fear and faith.
I envision his rough rugged hands,
somehow tender here,
guiding beating bloodied body
toward one of the open windows
releasing into the soft sun
in a few minutes, it was over.
We hear silence
and come to see him
staring out the window soaked
in the midday light half silhouetted, wingless.
I think of that bird, a Steller's jay, suspended
in the in-between of flight feeling
the rushing of wind against her vivid wings
catching that bold breath of momentary freedom—
before finding the open beaks
of her young, this call to duty
that keeps her fiercely moving.

Absence/Presence Profound

In this chapter, I have walked with the teacher I have never met. I have dwelled lyrically in Aoki's words as I have been unfolding with/in this scholarship, always surprised at where I arrive, this phenomenological place of possibility. There has been rhythm, here, and I am leaning into listening to the deeper realm beyond the I/eye. I have whirled in the Aokian echoes and resonances of his words at the cross of the vertical and horizontal, conceptually a generative space for me as poet, researcher, and teacher—as human becoming.

In this work, there is absence/presence profound of a teacher who is still teaching, who is still teacher, who teaches me to be *still* and then to move purposefully and softly. In turn, this is a mindful and ethical engaging where "… thought and soul [are] embodied in the oneness of the lived moment" (Aoki, 1992/2005, p. 196). I reflect on this notion and how it captures the process and purpose of my poetic expressions and the Dervish, who keeps her heart open to be touched by a divine source of love that *moves* her inner being.

Being with/in the slash is how I live as an Ismaili Muslim striving for balance between my material (horizontal) and spiritual (vertical) existence. This is a place of happiness, hope, and humility which re/minds me to attune to the Spirit that infuses all of my life's intentions.

Aoki (1992/2005) writes that a good teacher *is* the teaching and calls on pedagogues to keep in mind and hold in us a good teacher we have experienced in our lives. Now, to summon that teacher forth is to feel the sheer scope and breadth of what is immeasurable. And "in the silence allow the unsaid to shine through the said. Savour now the elusively true, the mystery of what teaching essentially is" (p. 20). Although I did not meet Ted Aoki, I journeyed with Carl Leggo for several years as my supervisor and guide for my doctorate programme. He spoke of his teacher, Ted, often and carried him in his heart and mind. I felt Aoki's resonances and lessons through Carl and this light was strong. Carl is now passed on, but I *feel* him, particularly, when I am in the midst of teaching. There is still a bridge between us and I linger with him there. Through this physical loss, what I know now, more than ever before, is that he *was* the teaching. There was no separation. In the middle of what I am feeling is both Aoki's absence/presence profound and "in the silence of the pedagogue's absence [is] an opening wherein the student can truly learn what it is to stand, what it is to be one's becoming" (Aoki, 1991/2005, p. 394). I follow forward on a horizontal and vertical path (Figure 2.1) with a profundity that all this writing and living in-between the

Figure 2.1 Untitled | Photo: Anar Rajabali.

metonymic and metaphoric moments of my life, reciprocates with wholeness and a way of living well. *I am with Ted and Carl, both.*

References

Aoki, T. T. (1987/1991/2005). The dialectic of mother language and second language: A curriculum exploration. In W. F. Pinar & R. L. Irwin (Eds.), *Curriculum in a new key: The collected works of Ted T. Aoki* (pp. 235–245). Lawrence Erlbaum.

Aoki, T. T. (1990/2005). Sonare and videre: A story, three echoes and a lingering note. In W. F. Pinar & R. L. Irwin (Eds.), *Curriculum in a new key: The collected works of Ted T. Aoki* (pp. 367–376). Lawrence Erlbaum.

Aoki, T. T. (1991/2005). The sound of pedagogy in the silence of the morning calm. In W. F. Pinar & R. L. Irwin (Eds.), *Curriculum in a new key: The collected works of Ted T. Aoki* (pp. 389–401). Lawrence Erlbaum.

Aoki, T. T. (1992/2005). Layered voices of teaching: The uncannily correct and the elusively true. In W. F. Pinar & R. L. Irwin (Eds.), *Curriculum in a new key: The collected work of Ted T. Aoki* (pp. 187–197). Lawrence Erlbaum.

Aoki, T. T. (1996/2005). Spinning inspirited images in the midst of planned and live(d) curricula. In Pinar & R. L. Irwin (Eds.), *Curriculum in a new key: The collected works of Ted T. Aoki* (pp. 413–423). Lawrence Erlbaum.

Aoki, T. T. (2003/2005). Locating living pedagogy in teacher "research": Five metonymic moments. In W. F. Pinar and R. L. Irwin (Eds.), *Curriculum in a new key: The collected works of Ted T. Aoki* (pp. 425–432). Lawrence Erlbaum.

Bachelard, G. (1958/1964). *The poetics of space: The classic look at how we experience intimate places* (M. Jolas, Trans.). Beacon Press.

Bochner, A. P., & Ellis, C. (2002). *Ethnographically speaking: Autoethnography, literature, and aesthetics.* AltaMira Press.

Chittick, W. C. (2003). *The Sufi path of love.* State University of New York.

Fels., L. (2013). Waiting for my son's call: Invitation to contemplate possible/impossible. In W. Hurren and E. Hasebe-Ludt (Eds.), *Contemplating curriculum* (pp. 38–44). Routledge.

Frost, R. (1939/2007). The figure a poem makes. In A. Charters & S. Charters (Eds.), *Literature and its writers* (4th ed., pp. 1154–1156). Bedford/St. Martins.

Irigaray, L. (2002). *The way of love.* Continuum.

Irwin, R. L., & Springgay, S. (2008). A/r/tography as practice-based research. In S. Springgay, R. L. Irwin, C. Leggo & P. Gouzouasis (Eds.), *In Being with a/r/tography* (pp. xix–xxxiii). Sense Publishers.

Irwin, R. L. (2010). Aoki, Ted. T. In Craig Kridel (Ed.), *Encyclopedia of curriculum studies, volume 1* (pp. 40–41). Sage.

Ladinsky, D. (1999). *The gift: Poems by Hafiz.* Penguin Putnam Inc.

Leggo, C. (1999). Research as poetic rumination: Twenty-six ways of listening to light. *The Journal of Educational Thought (JET), 33*(2), 113–133. https://www.jstor.org/stable/23767362?seq=1

Leggo, C. (2006). Learning by the heart: A poetics of research. *JCT: Journal of Curriculum Theorizing, 22*(4), 73–95. https://www.questia.com/library/journal/1G1-173422694/learning-by-heart-a-poetics-of-research

Lincoln, Y. S. & Denzin, N. K. (2005). Locating the field. In Y. S. Lincoln, & N. K. Denzin (Eds.), *Handbook of qualitative research* (pp. 33–41). Sage.

Pinar, W. F. (2005). A lingering note: An introduction to the collected works of Ted. T. Aoki. In W. F. Pinar & R. L. Irwin (Eds.), *Curriculum in a new key. The collected works of Ted. T. Aoki* (pp. 1–85). Lawrence Erlbaum.

Rajabali, A. (2017). *(Re)turning to the poetic I/eye: Towards a literacy of light* (Doctoral dissertation, University of British Columbia). https://open.library.ubc.ca/cIRcle/collections/ubctheses/24/items/1.0343399

Steinbock, A. J. (2007). *Phenomenology as mysticism: The verticality of religious experience*. Indiana University Press.

3 Finding the Human in the Middle of (In)visible Pandemics

Nicole Y. S. Lee

There is much to celebrate in joyful and inspirational educational encounters as they can be highlights of human becoming. In this essay, I turn toward another opening for human becoming: The traumatic. It takes time to untangle the incomprehensibility of such situations and to move past the hurt that lingers. In the process of writing, adding, cutting, revising, and editing, the knots are combed out of the event. When the strands of who, what, where, why, when, how lay bare, it becomes possible to story with mindful discernment and to heal. As the story becomes less embodied, the distance helps me see the twists and turns, the possibilities and affordances of what happened. One does not go looking for suffering, but when it occurs, it has the capacity to change one—both a hardening *and* a softening. I appreciate the ongoing conversations with Rita Irwin and Joanne Ursino, who have been alongside the reshaping of my first-year university teaching experience into a meaningful contribution to self-understanding, cultivation, and development. I will return again and again to understand it differently in time. This work reflects where I am at, at the time of writing these words.

Whenever I meet adversity and fall, my teachers encourage me to dust myself off and try again—perhaps differently, but do get back up. It is what American researcher storyteller Brené Brown (2019), referencing United States President Teddy Roosevelt's 1910 speech, calls getting back into the arena. She talks about vulnerability as a necessity for courage, where "if you're brave with your life, you choose to live in the arena … You're going to know heartbreak. It's a choice" (16:32). She continues, "vulnerability is not about winning. It's not about losing. It's having the courage to show up when you can't control the outcome" (17:33). Working in art education and curriculum studies as part of my graduate scholarship, I am immersed in a lived, process-based unfolding every day as part of my artistic, research, and teaching practices. In this work, the unknown comes up in the form of a blank page, a question, and/or the other. Being an art educator demands courage to step into the arena with an openness to engage in whatever happens. I went into teaching my first elementary art methods courses in a teacher education programme from January to March 2020 with this orientation and commitment. From the classes, this story unfolds. In this writing,

I contemplate upon my teaching experiences and my becoming both inside and outside of it.

Teaching During a Global Pandemic

When the COVID-19 pandemic hit and quarantine measures were upon my community mid-March, there was one week left of classes. Making what we now call the "March pivot" required transitioning online within two days. As this was an unprecedented moment in history, no one knew what to do and what tomorrow looked like. There were no plans, support systems, or protocols in place yet for frontline workers like me. More comprehensive plans would only start coming together months later. I created an asynchronous remote education plan that addressed learning goals at a minimum level and extended the deadline—health and safety came first and the course should surely not be an impediment to one's access to basic needs. Being a new instructor, I had little experience and guidelines to follow except for my humanity. I wondered: What does it mean to be human, to engage ethically, specifically during moments of crisis?

While attempting to stay afloat, fearing for myself and my loved ones, I felt responsible weaving a net and catching my students who were all in crisis, at the same time. In my considerations of what would be good and appropriate, I juggled competing demands of honouring the integrity of pre-established learning expectations; the rigour and accountability involved in training the leaders of future generations; the compassion, accommodations, and concessions necessary in moments of crisis; the fair treatment of students (with varying levels of commitment and effort); and my emotional, mental, and time/energy boundaries. I became lost in the multiplicity of *and*, drowning as the riptide of 71 individual and complicatedly entangled curricula (Aoki, 1993/2005a, p. 297) swept me into the sea of moral and ethical relativism. I could not come up for air until a month later. The fear, anxiety, stress, scarcity, precarity, and chaos of these early pandemic times impacted and changed everyone, including the aspiring teachers I taught. What remained from the abrupt end to the courses was the sting of hateful comments in course evaluations, with no opportunities for closure. Though I have found refuge in the safety of my home, I seemed to have lost a part of myself out in that vast ocean of multiplicity. As the storm of COVID-19 raged on, the needle of my internal compass continued to spin.

It took reading the life-affirming words of Ted Tetsuo Aoki, a Japanese Canadian curriculum scholar, to remind me not to give up hope for the potentiality of education, not to simply quit and forget about the whole ordeal. He talks about how living in

> tensionality calls on us as pedagogues to make time for meaningful striving and struggling, time for letting things be, time for question, time for singing, time for crying, time for anger, time for praying and hoping.

> Within this tensionality, guided by a sense of the pedagogic good, we are called on as teachers to be alert to the possibilities of our pedagogic touch, pedagogic tact, pedagogic attunement—those subtle features about being teachers that we know, but are not yet in our lexicon, for we have tended to be seduced by the seemingly lofty and prosaic talk in the language of conceptual abstractions. We must recognize the flight from the meaningful and turn back again to an understanding of our own being as teachers.
>
> (Aoki, 1986/1991/2005, p. 164)

Aoki's words reminded me of the permission I always already have: To simply be. I felt his gentle summon for me to consider my rupturing state of tensionality as an opening for profound learning. He invited me to sit with my emotions, consider my experiences intently, and be kind to myself in this practice. He called me to get back into the arena when I am ready. I have rewritten this story of teaching and learning repeatedly and I share it so others can also learn from my experiences. These contemplations touch on the personal *and* they transcend the personal. Before continuing, it is worth noting the context of the time in which I write.

Context of (In)Visible Pandemics: COVID-19, Neoliberalism, Racism, and Xenophobia

The context of this time is one of many pandemics; COVID-19 has exposed numerous social, political, and ideological maladies lying underneath the surface that have become difficult to ignore, some of which I discuss here. In a timely piece connecting the medical crisis of COVID-19 with the political and ideological crisis of neoliberalism, Henry Giroux (2020) observes: "neoliberalism's emphasis on commercial values rather than democratic values, its virulent ideology of extreme competitiveness and irrational selfishness, and its impatience with matters of ethics, justice and truth has undermined critical thought and the power of informed judgment" (para. 4). The impact of COVID-19 is exacerbated by the plague of neoliberalism, which has gripped the West for over 40 years and seeped into every crevice of society, including education. Teacher education programmes that take up a commercial model of production function as manufacturing plants for workers, who are, in turn, expected to care for children so that parents can produce and keep the economy running.

Those who embrace neoliberalism determine the value of acts based on an ends-means model, where "evaluators … are technologically oriented, primarily interested in seeing how well the system is able to control its own components in struggling to achieve system goals" (Aoki, 1991/2005, p. 172). The goal-oriented paradigm requires one to know what is being produced and to execute the manufacturing plans, which runs counterintuitively to the notion of human becoming because it rarely unfolds with a predetermined end. Aoki (1991/2005) notices that "underneath the avowed interest in efficiency, effectiveness, predictability, and certainty, as reflected in the preceding list of interests, is a more deeply rooted interest—that of *control*" (p. 170). Most unsettling is that some teacher candidates themselves can be heard using the language of market and management—framing themselves as consumers of a service and their own education as products that their instructors provide, unknowingly contributing to a system that will make the same demand of them.

Linking the pandemic of neoliberalism to the pandemics of racism and xenophobia, Giroux (2020) notes that neoliberalism has "ravaged the public good and imposed misery and suffering upon the poor and others considered excess, waste or dangerous" (para. 10). With COVID-19 being labelled as the "China virus," "kung flu," and "Wuhan virus" in the United States, members of the Chinese community worldwide, including those in Canada, are being accused of eating bat soup, of having disgusting cultural practices, and of being a virus. As the infection rate and death toll rose, anger reached boiling points and became increasingly apparent, to the point where all Asian ethnic groups were grouped as one target. Ontology was flattened and all Asian-looking people shifted from model minorities to outsiders—strangers who were no longer welcomed nor even tolerated. While early prevention strategies by Asian communities like wearing masks and gloves prevented the virus, they drew attention to individuals as targets for unprovoked racist attacks. Giroux (2020) describes this age at a macro level, as being

> defined by a pedagogical catastrophe of indifference and a flight from any viable sense of moral responsibility … marked by a contempt for weakness, as well as rampant racism, the elevation of emotion over reason, the collapse of civic culture, and an obsession with wealth and self-interest.
> (para. 32)

And many individuals are living through all of it at a micro and personal level.

Hong-Kong born Canadian writer Carianne Leung (2020) articulates the feeling of being Chinese Canadian during this time: "While others became scared about getting infected, I felt the added layer of being afraid of getting assaulted or harassed or shunned. I had grown too anxious to be in public spaces including my own neighbourhood" (para. 5). The COVID-19 pandemic manifests social inequities that put racial and ethnic minorities at an increased risk of harm. Watching the news became depressing, anxiety provoking, and frightening not only due to the spread of the virus, but because of reports of assault, harassment, tirade, and vandalism fuelled by anti-Asian sentiments. Leung (2020) describes racism and xenophobia as "the other pandemic":

> Racist speech and acts are meant to send the message that you do not "belong," that you don't have the right to space. Once enacted, it fills the air and all the spaces unless there is a swift intervention on an individual scale and an analysis that identifies and speaks back on a global scale.
> (para. 14)

Overwhelmed by the racial fear that Leung details, I also experienced the need to brace for sudden attacks, which has become increasingly unsurprising for Asians in the climate of this time. After wrapping up the two courses in this context and reading the course evaluations that evoked a sense of shame in me for being who I am, I too, for a time, felt unsafe going out in public spaces. Brown (2019) describes shame as

> the feeling you would get if you walked out of a room that was filled with people who know you, and they start saying such hurtful things about you that you don't know if you could ever walk back in and face them again in your life.
>
> (12:19)

The worst consequence of this shame was that I felt I no longer belonged in the education community that I treasured.

Considering the Human in Aokian Ways

Canadian poet and language and literacy education scholar Carl Leggo (2012/2019) suggests that "in order for an education community to succeed, everybody involved must be responsible for one another, and must be committed to responding to one another" (p. 41). Moments of crisis urge a reassessment of one's priorities in bringing what matters into sharper focus, revealing what is underneath the buffer of privilege. During these times, implications of responsibility and ethics become most apparent and come to matter critically because the stakes become higher in the discernment of what it means to be human and to follow the pedagogic good.

Aoki's (1981/2005) call to linger in the metaphor of a bridge between self *and* other becomes increasingly urgent when one is inclined to turn away from the other. He remarks,

> When two strangers meet, indeed two worlds meet. How is it when two worlds meet? I have heard that a bridge is necessary only when there are two worlds to begin with and when there is a committed interest in bridging the two worlds.
>
> (p. 219)

What happens in the "in-between" space and the "and" of self *and* other? What happens when two strangers with committed interest to connect are bridged? What happens if one turns away from another? The bridge and the arena are not the same, but both are "human place[s] of openness wherein humans may struggle in their dwelling aright" (Aoki, 1987/2005, p. 354). The bridge and the arena are spaces of *and*, of the in-between, of both and neither, where "indwelling in the zone between… is not so much a matter of overcoming the tensionality but more a matter of dwelling aright within it"

(Aoki, 1986/1991/2005, p. 163). Being on the bridge necessitates being in the arena, as it requires courage and vulnerability to dwell and linger with alterity and multiplicity.

I write to examine my teaching experiences as a Chinese Canadian female pedagogue, with a particular way of being and presenting in the world informed by a set of racial, ethnic, cultural, and gendered understandings. I write to consider lingering questions around the complexities of my 2020 teaching experience, filled with incidents of racial microaggression, passive aggressiveness, and outright confrontation. Like Aoki (1979/2005), I am becoming "sensitive to the tension between the being of my humanness [or] lack thereof, and the social condition within which I interethnically dwelled" (p. 335). While I am confined in my home due to multiple pandemics and Aoki was interned during World War II, I sense a connection between my experiences and Aoki's (1979/2005), resonating particularly with his feelings of his humanness being "crushed or disturbed" as a Japanese Canadian (p. 335).

Far from being hopeless, he suggests that "this kind of opportunity for probing" into one's "isness," or "the essence of what it means to be human—the essence of what it means to become more human" "comes more readily to one who lives at the margin—to one who lives in a tension situation" (Aoki, 1979/2005, p. 336). He believes that it is "a condition that makes possible deeper understanding of human acts that can transform both self and world, not in an instrumental way, but in a human way" (p. 336). In thinking about leadership in relation to humility/Aokian humiliation and in exploring the notion of presence in relation to invisibility, I consider how we might become more human.

Leading with Humility and Aokian Humiliation

Being an educator means being a leader, "for 'to educate' itself means, in the original sense, to lead out *(ex-ducere)*. To lead is to lead others out, from where they now are to possibilities not yet" (Aoki, 1987/2005, p. 350). A quick search online on "leadership" produces entries on business and organizational management, on lists of essential qualities, on step-by-step formulas. Yet, Aoki clarifies that "the management sort of authority… is not being true to what authority truly is—but be guided more by the deep sense of authority that speaks to leadership linked to authentic followership" (p. 351). He suggests that a leader "must lead by following that which is true to that which is good in the situation within which he dwells" (p. 351). Attuning to situational entanglements to figure out a good path means an engagement with ambiguity, vagueness, and abstraction, which are integral parts of artistic and aesthetic processes as well. They have the potentiality to lead everyone somewhere and the path that one finds would be one's own.

While neatly packaged readings, lessons, and unit plans that can be directly implemented; takeaways; checklists of learning goals; know-hows; tricks of the trade; marketable skills; jargon; and binders of curriculum plans can have their place, Aoki (2003/2005) teaches those of us working in education communities to engage in "pedagogic struggles in the midst of the plannable and the unplannable, between the predictable and the unpredictable, between the prescriptible and the nonprescriptible ... between the curriculum-as-plan and the live(d) curriculum" (p. 426). Inspired by Aoki, I shared stories of teaching and learning with my students. I offered resources as possibilities and discussed my considerations while dwelling in the "site of living pedagogy" with "a multiplicity of curricula" (p. 426), taking especial care not to act as a fortune teller for my students' unfolding as everyone has a unique path. Since teachers inevitably teach themselves to their students, being an educator means taking up the responsibility of continuously educating one's self and cultivating the best possible self.

Part of being an educator involves gauging how much to assert one's self in another's process of becoming: How much space and time to take up/hold for participation, how much consistency/variety, how much to tell/show/do, how much to let go/interject and redirect, how much structure and freedom to offer, how much to make explicit/let students come to an understanding themselves, and more. Though humility can be interpreted as a lack of confidence that signals an opportunity for power play, Leggo (2012/2019) articulates that it is important to conceptualize "authority as integrally connected to humility" (p. 44).

Aoki (1993/2005a) takes humility further into the realm of humiliation, where "to be humiliated is to be reminded that we are communally ecologic, that the rhythmic measures of living on Earth come forth polyphonically in *humour* and *human* and *humus* and *humility*" (p. 300). The concept of humiliation decentres the human. In such spaces, ideally there would no longer be a need for egos to compete and dominate one another. When Aoki (1993/2005b) talks about decentring, he does not mean an erasure of personhood, as

> life in the classroom is not so much *in* the child, *in* the teacher, *in* the subject; life is lived in the spaces between and among ... We ought to *decenter* them *without erasing them,* and to learn to speak a noncentered language.
> (p. 282)

It takes a full education community to be willing to engage in this way, for ones embracing humility and Aokian humiliation to not be wounded by the entitled, narcissistic, doubtful, and insecure.

Humility and Aokian humiliation become especially complicated for the marginalized and othered. Mari Ruti (2011), an interdisciplinary scholar in critical theory and gender and sexuality studies, discerns that

> there are plenty of individuals ... who have been forcibly robbed of their egos and who are consequently struggling to reestablish a sense of legitimate personhood. Telling them to rid themselves of their egos is akin to ignoring all the socio-political and economic circumstances that make it

difficult for them to develop an ego in the first place. It is akin to saying that there is something amiss with their attempts to carve out a firm foothold in a world that is making their lives unsafe and sometimes even unbearable.

(p. 172)

I resonate with Ruti's words and often contemplate on how I can take up humility and Aokian humiliation without tolerating abuse and being complicit to my own erasure and dehumanization. After all, as Brown (2019) observes, "brave leaders are never silent around hard things. Our job is to excavate the unsaid ... And that requires courage and vulnerability" (1:02:22). Perhaps I have been too hesitant to hold individuals accountable for their actions under the guise of humility and for the sake of momentary peace.

Advocating for intellectual humility, Global News, Canada journalist and news anchor Farah Nasser (2019) states that "as much as we believe that we are separated by a clash of race, of culture, of political belief, we are much more separated by a clash of our own ignorance," (10:20) because "in a time where we are all pulling away from each other ... we all think we are right, and that is dangerous" (8:21). Humility and Aokian humiliation means holding space for differences in kind, recognizing and addressing our own and others' ignorance. The state of being ignorant, though triggering for those who interpret it as a judgement of one's lack and an attack of one's ego, signals an opening for learning, connecting, relating, and understanding. To Aoki (1987/2005), "being an educated person is more than possessing knowledge or acquiring intellectual or practical skills, and that basically, it is being concerned with dwelling aright in thoughtful living with others" (p. 365). Embracing humility and Aokian humiliation is an act of lingering on the bridge with a commitment to acknowledge the humanity in another, even those we might disagree with.

Recognizing the Human: Invisibility and Presence

In the spirit of humility and Aokian humiliation, I discuss the course evaluations I received in relation to the critical-hermeneutical evaluation orientation (Aoki, 1991/2005, pp. 179–183), the paradigm through which I ascertain the pedagogic good. In students' visual journal entries, group discussions, spontaneous questions and conversations, exit-slips and responses, and summative feedback, my students and I engage in hermeneutic conversation, which "is a dialectic of questions and answers that in their interpretive turnings are attempts to move to deeper ontological realms of meanings" (Aoki, 1991/2005, p. 180). In these conversations, I begin to know who my students are, beyond their teacher candidate identities in the classroom. Aoki expresses that "critical hermeneutics is an activity that deepens existential themes, as the source of our human beingness is sought in the realms of the finite and infinite" (p. 181). This space is where I would like to linger more.

During these moments of human connection, I learn about their levels of (dis)comfort with artistic processes, techniques, and materials, class-based apprehensions regarding museums, personal and cultural connections to the subject, and family dynamics in relation to educational experiences. At the end of the course, I wrote each student a note with feedback on their assignments, a description of what I noticed about their engagement during our time together, and some questions for each to consider as they continue developing their teaching practice.

In the course evaluations, some comments offered concrete strategies I can try the next time I teach. Other comments felt senselessly cruel and can be taken lightly in a conscious choice to embrace self-love. I have come to understand such comments through British Columbia, Canada's provincial health officer, Bonnie Henry's statement in response to "the abuse she has faced over the last year" as "the face of B.C.'s COVID-19 response" (CBC News, 2021). While unacceptable, Henry recognizes that "when people are in crises, part of the way they respond or react is to lash out or be angry" (CBC News, 2021). Rather than ruminating on the sharp pain of being a recipient of a lashing, I linger on the dull ache of loss—of my personhood—and pause here with the comments regarding teacher presence. They trouble me because they stir up something beyond what they are. While I have learned that teacher candidates may project the expectations with which they are grappling onto their instructors, the comments about my lack of presence strikes a chord with how I have felt in many moments of my life no matter how hard I try—invisible. It resonates with how I have felt amidst the multiple pandemics of COVID-19, neoliberalism, racism, and xenophobia. I use invisibility and not absence because I am undeniably *here*, just not seen nor recognized.

I linger on the bridge here to explore the concepts of invisibility and presence as part of a "critical reflection [that] leads to an understanding of what is beyond the actor's ordinary view by making the familiar unfamiliar, by making the invisible visible" (Aoki, 1991/2005, p. 174). Taking up this work and deconstructing assumptions around one's own way of being-in-the-world allows the possibility of reconstructing one's self-in-relation. An experience that epitomizes invisibility for me during my teaching is a brief, innocuous exchange during a field trip to a nearby museum. I waited for my students in the lobby. After walking around a while, my students finally find me standing in plain sight.

"We didn't see you," they exclaimed, half accusatory, half sheepish.

"Yup, I'm pretty short," I replied spontaneously with the least controversial excuse I could summon at that moment, directing them into a line to get into the museum and suppressing the urge to say more.

On racializing perception and the phenomenology of invisibility, critical phenomenologist and social theorist Danielle Petherbridge (2017) writes in relation to Ralph Ellison's *Invisible Man* (1952) that

> invisibility is a form of ontological and epistemological violence, which points to the sedimented habits or general normative constructs of white

perception of "others." ... The problem is that when you remain constantly unseen or invisible you begin to "doubt if you really exist ... You ache with the need to convince yourself that you do exist in a real world, that you're a part of all the sound and anguish" and you begin to comport yourself in a manner that might "make them recognize you" instead of bumping into you in the darkness of the night.

(p. 107)

This idea of presence prompted me to contemplate upon my voice, stature, walk, and my way of being-in-the-world. How might the mysterious aura that is one's (teacher) presence magically materialize? In what ways can I assert the fact that "I am here" and "I matter" so that I could not be ignored? My physicality predisposes a kind of engagement with another as I confront stereotypical expectations of being "nice"—mild-mannered, submissive, and quiet—on a regular basis. Grace, leniency, and emotional labour seem to be expected. The enforcement of expectations seems to be interpreted as steely and intimidating. Due to racial, cultural, and gender stereotypes, prejudice, and discrimination, it is a fight to be taken seriously as a pedagogue—to be acknowledged, heard, and seen.

American philosopher Alva Noë (2012), who theorizes on perception and consciousness, argues that presence requires access and that something becomes present through understanding (p. 2). He proposes that "the world shows up for us in experience only insofar as we know how to make contact with it, or, to use a different metaphor, only insofar as we are able to bring it into focus" (p. 2). This argument echoes the words written half a century earlier by American educationist Earl C. Kelley (1962), who recognizes that "we cannot see that which we have no experience to see" (p. 14). This does not mean we cannot learn to see anew and see differently. Petherbridge (2017) offers two components to bringing the presence of an Other into focus: Recognition as affirmation, coupled with a critical practice of affective hesitation. Affective hesitation means becoming aware and "halting or interrupting the process of racializing perception and perceptual habits built up over time through social and cultural constructs and the reiteration of embodied practices" (Petherbridge, 2017, p. 120). For those willing to engage, such recognition "offers a means of rupturing ... indifference and denial, of hypervisibility and invisibility" (Petherbridge, 2017, p. 121). This work is not done as a favour for the Other. Rather, Noë (2012) emphasizes that the phenomenon of how "the world shows up ... corresponds [to] the fact that *we ourselves show up*" (p. 12). Put plainly, if I want my world to show up, then I need to show up, regardless of how I may or may not show up in others' worlds. I have my own responsibilities to show up and others have theirs.

In thinking about theories of presence, perception, and critical phenomenology in relation to the context of my 2020 teaching experience, I am coming to understand that my invisibility to others is not an indication of my lack of presence. It may instead be an expression of their state of access to the world. My presence is not something I can achieve for others. I would lose my sense of self if my compass for attuning to the pedagogic good is guided merely by the satisfaction of others. Aoki (1987/2005) reminds me, "an educated person, first and foremost, understands that one's ways of knowing, thinking, and doing flow from who one is" (p. 365). The self is complex and ever-changing, and I am in the middle of many identities and relational practices. Situated in Aoki's (1996/2005) conception of "and" as a "discursive imaginary that can entertain 'both this and that,' 'neither this nor that'—a space of paradox, ambiguity and ambivalence" (p. 317), I enact a multiplicity of relational practices as Chinese, Canadian, woman, artist, researcher, teacher, student, daughter, partner, friend, colleague, and human. Because "worlds open up that would otherwise be closed off" through this cultivation and "in this way we achieve for ourselves new ways of being present" (Noë, 2012, p. 13), I am continuing to "achieve myself" through my efforts to dwell aright in such webs of relations. It is with a renewed commitment to show up and see the human in the Other, a newfound capacity to discern what situations call for hardening and softening, and a profound understanding of my own power to attribute value and weight, that I return to teaching again in 2021.

References

Aoki, T. T. (1979/2005). Reflections of a Japanese Canadian teacher experiencing ethnicity. In W. F. Pinar & R. L. Irwin (Eds.), *Curriculum in a new key: The collected works of Ted T. Aoki* (pp. 333–348). Lawrence Erlbaum.

Aoki, T. T. (1981/2005). Toward understanding curriculum talk through reciprocity of perspectives. In W. F. Pinar & R. L. Irwin (Eds.), *Curriculum in a new key: The collected works of Ted T. Aoki* (pp. 219–228). Lawrence Erlbaum.

Aoki, T. T. (1986/1991/2005). Teaching as in-dwelling between two curriculum worlds. In W. F. Pinar & R. L. Irwin (Eds.), *Curriculum in a new key: The collected works of Ted T. Aoki* (pp. 159–165). Lawrence Erlbaum.

Aoki, T. T. (1987/2005). Revisiting the notions of leadership and identity. In W. F. Pinar & R. L. Irwin (Eds.), *Curriculum in a new key: The collected works of Ted T. Aoki* (pp. 349–355). Lawrence Erlbaum.

Aoki, T. T. (1991/2005). Layered understandings of orientations in social studies program evaluation. In W. F. Pinar & R. L. Irwin (Eds.), *Curriculum in a new key: The collected works of Ted T. Aoki* (pp. 167–186). Lawrence Erlbaum.

Aoki, T. T. (1993/2005a). Humiliating the Cartesian ego. In W. F. Pinar & R. L. Irwin (Eds.), *Curriculum in a new key: The collected works of Ted T. Aoki* (pp. 291–301). Lawrence Erlbaum.

Aoki, T. T. (1993/2005b). The child-centered curriculum: Where is the social in pedocentricism? In W. F. Pinar & R. L. Irwin (Eds.), *Curriculum in a new key: The collected works of Ted T. Aoki* (pp. 279–289). Lawrence Erlbaum.

Aoki, T. T. (1996/2005). Imaginaries of "East and West": Slippery curricular signifiers in education. In W. F. Pinar & R. L. Irwin (Eds.), *Curriculum in a new key: The collected works of Ted T. Aoki* (pp. 313–319). Lawrence Erlbaum.

Aoki, T. T. (2003/2005). Locating living pedagogy in teacher "research": Five metonymic moments. In W. F. Pinar & R. L. Irwin (Eds.), *Curriculum in a new key: The collected works of Ted T. Aoki* (pp. 425–432). Lawrence Erlbaum.

Brown, B., Haykel, C., Hare, J., & Restrepo, S. (Director). (2019). Brené Brown: The call to courage [Video file]. Retrieved from https://www.netflix.com/watch/81010166

CBC News. (2021, February 25). *Threats against Dr. Bonnie Henry 'unacceptable,' B.C. health minister says.* https://www.cbc.ca/news/canada/british-columbia/bc-bonnie-henry-threats-1.5928948

Ellison, R. (1952). *Invisible man.* Random House.

Giroux, H. (2020, April 7). The COVID-19 pandemic is exposing the plague of neoliberalism. TruthOut. https://truthout.org/articles/the-covid-19-pandemic-is-exposing-the-plague-of-neoliberalism/

Kelley, E. C. (1962). The fully functioning self. In Association for Supervision and Curriculum Development (Ed.), *Perceiving, behaving, becoming: A new focus for education* (pp. 9–20). ASCD. https://eric.ed.gov/?id=ED096575

Leggo, C. (2012/2019). Challenging hierarchy: Narrative ruminations on leadership in education. In R. L. Irwin, E. Hasebe-Ludt, & A. Sinner (Eds.), *Storying the world: The contributions of Carl Leggo on language and poetry* (pp. 38–49). Routledge

Leung, C. (2020, July 14). *Racism: The other pandemic.* University College of the University of Toronto. https://www.uc.utoronto.ca/racism-other-pandemic

Nasser, F. (2019, February). *The power of intellectual humility* [Video]. TED Conferences. https://www.ted.com/talks/farah_nasser_the_power_of_intellectual_humility

Noë, A. (2012). *Varieties of presence.* Harvard University Press.

Petherbridge, D. (2017). Racializing perception and the phenomenology of invisibility. In L. Dolezal, & D. Petherbridge (Eds.), *Body/self/other: The phenomenology of social encounters* (pp. 103–229). SUNY Press

Ruti, M. (2011). *The summons of love.* Columbia University Press.

Interlude
Walking with Aoki

Rita L. Irwin

Nitobe Memorial Garden at The University of British Columbia (UBC) is perhaps one of the most authentic Japanese Gardens outside of Japan. Visitors, students, staff, and faculty members come to this garden to experience its tranquility nestled within a campus often bustling with energy. Reflecting on Ted T. Aoki's scholarship is of great interest to my PhD study group and it coincides with a moment of revisiting my own scholarship. For one of our walking seminars, we choose to walk and linger separately and collectively in these incredible gardens where Ted often walked and discussed his ideas with other scholars (see Figure Int.1). Many of us thought about his work while we breathed in the ocean kissed air, soaked up the stunning beauty, and listened to the sweet serenades of birds swooping across its expanse. The very presence of these gardens is special, yet knowing how much they meant to Aoki, makes walking there even more delightful.

Silently walking these garden paths prompted me to think about the genealogy of ideas, and really the genealogy of scholars. I was never lucky enough to study with Aoki, yet I seemed to follow in some of his educational paths. I taught in Lethbridge, Alberta where he had been a public-school teacher. He had an immense influence on curriculum studies while he was at UBC and the University of Alberta (U of A). I followed by being a doctoral student at UBC taking my doctoral seminars with Walt Werner, one of Aoki's PhD graduates from the U of A. The greatest shift I experienced happened in my first semester and came from one of Aoki's articles in an unpublished Curriculum Canada monograph. He made room for the transformative power of the arts in the curriculum in a way that made perfect sense to me. I was forever changed then. It would take several years before I would meet him in person, but once I did, a lasting friendship was created.

As I have reread his work in recent years I realise now more than ever, how profoundly his work influenced my own. The genealogy of ideas is not limited to the citational practices of scholars, it is also in the walking-alongside practices of pedagogues. Aoki's interest in the slash (/) is such a practice. He freely used this rhetorical device to encourage us to dwell in the in-between that exists between concepts and relationships, where ambiguity and uncertainty may reside in what is also a very dynamic learning space. In

DOI: 10.4324/9781003037248-6

Figure Int.1 Nitobe Memorial Garden Walk | Photo Collage: Rita L. Irwin.

an interview, Aoki said of the slash: "It looks like a simple oppositional binary space, but it is not. It is a space of doubling, where we slip into language of both this and that, but neither this nor that" (Aoki, 1999, p. 181).

Dwelling in this generative space became a living inquiry (Meyer, 2006) for Aoki and all those who walked with him. We learned to dwell in these uncertain spaces, embracing the ambiguous, and learning the potential of the in-between. As I was immersed in my own living inquiries, I was coming to linger in the spaces between making, learning, and inquiring, and shared this vibrant space with my own students. It was in this profound space of possibility that a/r/tography emerged. Traces of the scholarly practices and citations of Aoki may be found in how I was learning to think about the possible/impossible (Fels, 2014). Indeed, as Aoki's ideas were lingering alongside my own, others with whom he worked closely, like William Pinar, also became important and influenced my work in very profound ways. I was dwelling in the genealogy of ideas and practices without necessarily recognizing them. Citations are one thing but the practices of others, taken in as our own, become second-nature and integrated into the cells of our very being.

This book is a testament to the genealogy of Aokian ideas and ways of being. Scholars upon scholars have taken up his work. Each of the editors has studied Aoki through graduate school readings and particularly through the lenses of William Pinar who dedicated a course to the work of Aoki (see Pinar & Irwin, 2005). Many of the authors and two of the editors have studied with me. And each of them has been influenced by other scholars who have also embraced Aokian concepts and practices. While the editors may not have personally known Aoki, they have embraced his ideas in ways that are profoundly Aokian.

As my PhD study group walked through the Nitobe Memorial Garden, we embraced the potential of dwelling in the in-between: Between curriculum-as-plan and curriculum-as-lived, between planning-our-learning and living-our-experiences. We were artists on a photo walk, methodically yet silently dwelling in these Japanese gardens that Aoki loved, and where he often came to walk with others. Listening intently, he would provoke others to think differently. For us, this meant ambling differently, seeing differently, hearing differently, and feeling differently. There is something about this space. We know he came to think, to be, to linger in these gardens. Manicured yet not manicured, they hold Aoki's way of seeing and being in the world that still speaks to us. Leggo (2014) echoes how I feel:

> Ted's scholarship reminds me to look in ways I have never looked, to see in ways I have never seen. I am fascinated, infatuated even, with the multiple and fragmentary. My texts are always open, not because I can't write closed texts, but because I don't want to. I am always questioning, never satisfied, always confused, never re-solved.
>
> (p. 193)

May we continue to walk and dwell in this richly laden, unexpected, wonderfully nuanced, Aokian way of being in the world.

References

Aoki, T. (1999). Interview with Ted Aoki: Rethinking curriculum and pedagogy. (1999). *Kappa Delta Pi Record*, 35(4), 180–181.

Fels, L. (2014). Waiting for my son's call: Invitation to contemplate possible/impossible. In W. Hurren & E. Hasebe-Ludt (Eds.), *Contemplating curriculum: Genealogies/times/places* (pp. 38–44). Routledge.

Leggo, C. (2014). Contemplating and complicating curriculum by attending to language. In W. Hurren & E. Hasebe-Ludt (Eds.), *Contemplating curriculum: Genealogies/times/places* (pp. 183–198). Routledge.

Meyer, K. (2006). Living inquiry – A gateless gate and a beach. In W. Ashton & D. Denton (Eds.), *Spirituality, ethnography and teaching: Stories from within* (pp. 156–166). Peter Lang

Pinar, W. F., & Irwin, R. L. (2005). *Curriculum in a new key: The collected works of Ted T. Aoki*. Lawrence Erlbaum.

Part 2
Arts-Based Education Research and Stories

Introduction

Joanne M. Ursino

Arts-based education research and stories are at the heart of Aoki's call for an "inspirited education" (Aoki, 1996/2005, p. 423). Aoki (1991/2005) invites the "curriculum world … to ask the place of stories and narratives in understanding curriculum or doing curriculum research" (p. 250). Chapters by Joanne M. Ursino, Joanne Price, and Jee Yeon Ryu are contemporary, vibrant responses, illustrative of Aoki's (1978/1980/2005) own efforts to search for "alternative research possibilities in education" (p. 89). In reflecting on research, and in particular arts-based education research, Aoki (2003/2005) references the writing of Maxine Greene (1994) and in a demonstration of attunement notes that she "calls upon us to move to the edgy edges of representational discourse, and there, open ourselves to discourses beyond" (p. 427). Each of the chapters in this part invite the reader to engage with arts-based education research that pushes these edgy edges—through auto-poetic fragments and found poetry, curriculum at play and as a play, and autoethnographic stories. We are guided through pages of a handmade book, meet plants in conversation, and listen to children as they learn the piano. It is a joyful, unabashed trio of emboldened texts.

Aoki (1993/2005) invites scholars to write the poetic, "the language of the lived curriculum … in which life is embodied in the very stories and languages people speak and live" (p. 207). In doing so, he is mindful that it decentres "the modernist view of education" and opens "the way to include alternative meanings, including lived meanings, legitimated by everyday narratives—the stories and narratives in and by which we live daily" (Aoki, 1991/2005, pp. 250–251). Aoki (1996/2005) seeks this "guiding hand in reshaping and reconstituting the landscape" (p. 423). In Part 2, we encounter this very gesture in reference to paper, petals, and crayons. Ursino, Price, and

DOI: 10.4324/9781003037248-7

Figure P.2 Nitobe Memorial Garden Bench and Tree | Photo: Joanne M. Ursino.

Ryu offer the "fingertip whispers" (Aoki, 1996/2005, p. 423) that question "the underlying presuppositions of the dominant tradition in curriculum conceptions and research calling for close examination of curriculum orientations at the root level" (Aoki, 1978/1980/2005, p. 92).

These three chapters and the following questions, invite the reader to slow down and think otherwise (see Figure P.2). The invitation of Aokian scholarship is in "allowing space for stories, anecdotes, and narratives that embody the lived dimension of curriculum life" (Aoki, 1993/2005, p. 209). Here, we give way to a "more open landscape that offers possibilities by, in part, giving legitimacy to the wisdom held in live stories of people who dwell within the landscape" (Aoki, 1993/2005, p. 214).

Chapter 4: An Aokian Sensibility at the Intersections of both Arts-Based Research and Relations—Joanne M. Ursino

1 How does an Aokian sensibility inform arts-based research?
2 How does a strong citational commitment and notetaking practice entwining both study and studio shape an understanding of representation and difference?
3 What possibilities might Aoki's both and, as celebrated in the found poem, offer in one's practice and thinking?

Chapter 5: When Does an Haleliwia Become More than an Haleliwia?: Abeying to a Poethics of Plants with Aoki—Joanne Price

1 How does the narrative structure of the play invite multiplicities of understanding?
2 The pedagogue walks alongside the student, in this writing the plants are teachers: How might we learn from and with them?
3 How does scholarship that is intimate and personal decentre and invite emerging curricular possibilities?

Chapter 6: "That's My Way": Indwelling between the Two Worlds of Piano Teaching—Jee Yeon Ryu

1 How do small stories and tales contribute to an understanding of the experiences and the agency of children exploring music and piano playing?
2 How might the tension of curriculum-as-plan and curriculum-as-lived make room for flexibility and spontaneity in relational learning experiences with children?
3 What openings does listening extend in arts-based educational research contexts?

References

Aoki, T. T. (1978/1980/2005). Toward curriculum inquiry in a new key. In W. F. Pinar & R. L. Irwin (Eds.). *Curriculum in a new key: The collected works of Ted T. Aoki* (pp. 89–110). Lawrence Erlbaum.

Aoki, T. T. (1991/2005). Five curriculum memos and a note for the next half-century. In W. F. Pinar & R. L. Irwin (Eds.), *Curriculum in a new key: The collected works of Ted T. Aoki* (pp. 247–261). Lawrence Erlbaum.

Aoki, T. T. (1993/2005). Legitimating lived curriculum: Toward a curricular landscape of multiplicity. In W. F. Pinar & R. L. Irwin (Eds.), *Curriculum in a new key: The collected works of Ted T. Aoki* (pp. 199–215). Lawrence Erlbaum.

Aoki, T. T. (1996/2005). Spinning inspirited images in the midst of planned and live(d) curricula. In W. F. Pinar & R. L. Irwin (Eds.), *Curriculum in a new key: The collected works of Ted T. Aoki* (pp. 413–423). Lawrence Erlbaum.

Aoki, T. T. (2003/2005). Interview. In W. F. Pinar & R. L. Irwin (Eds.), *Curriculum in a new key: The collected works of Ted T. Aoki* (pp. 441–447). Lawrence Erlbaum.

Greene, M. (1994). Postmodernism and the crisis of representation. *English Education*, 26(4), 206–219. http://www.jstor.org/stable/40172842

4 An Aokian Sensibility at the Intersections of both Arts-Based Research and Relations

Joanne M. Ursino

This is a chapter in ten short parts, a movement through the cut of a minor arcana. The initial fragments intertwine autobiography and an inspirited Aokian sensibility for both eclectic and idiosyncratic method. It is a sharing shaped by enabling constraints (Castro, 2007), and an homage to my graduate experience at The University of British Columbia (UBC) alongside the course offering by William Pinar (2017) on the scholarship of Ted. T. Aoki. With regard to the later, the experience speaks to the impact of proximities, relations, and citations that take place over time among and with faculty, staff, and students.[1] I conclude this chapter with a three-fold layering that dwells on a recent art education conference, my arts-based research, and the offering of a found poem in a temporal reading of *Curriculum in a new key: The collected works of Ted T. Aoki* (Pinar & Irwin, 2005).

Both Invitation and Intention

The scholarship of Aoki resounds in my graduate experience at UBC. In classrooms, studio practices, and conversations, I find the teachings of Aoki to be both invitation and intention. The gesture of hands opened in possibility—hold both praxis and promise in their entanglements. I find in this return and call to write a time for honouring and for grounding.[2] Aoki's use of both/and alongside his play with space(s) on the page, reminds me of the needle's pierce and the pull of thread not unlike the use of the em dash— because like the stitch, fragments are drawn together creating connections for thinking otherwise.

Both Pause and Acknowledgment

I take pause and acknowledge that I write on the unceded, ancestral, and traditional territories of the xʷməθkʷəy̓əm (Musqueam), Sḵwx̱wú7mesh Úxwumixw (Squamish), and səlilwətaʔɬ (Tsleil-Waututh) Nations. Teaching has concluded for the term,[3] the third wave of the pandemic is upon us and my appointment for an injection scheduled. Patents and ethics trouble my thinking as I reflect on our shared humanity and the distribution of vaccines

DOI: 10.4324/9781003037248-8

both here and elsewhere in the world. And, the quotidian beat is a steadying pulse: I am in the midst of marking, working on my dissertation, and moving from one home to another. Cherry blossoms have been in full, glorious bloom. A riot of pinks and greens. With moody weather, there is a mix of fragrances with the fruit trees in sunshine and the earth fecund after a rainfall. I am queer and turning sixty. I am white and, note that my privilege is both catalyst for action and cause for temperance—the measure of which falls to page and street.

Both Study and Studio

It was an honour to study the work of Aoki in the mid-Summer of 2017. The description of the course reads as follows: "Perhaps no Canadian curriculum studies scholar has been more influential than Ted Aoki ... we will read his collected works, connecting his ideas to contemporary issues in curriculum and pedagogy, emphasizing those of concern to those enrolled." (Pinar, 2017). Invited guests included Carl Leggo, Karen Meyer, Patricia Liu Baergen, and Erica Hasebe-Ludt. Students gathered around a large table, meeting every day for upwards of three hours—spanning two weeks. For our last class, we walked together in the Nitobe Memorial Garden at UBC.

I kept a journal and upon completion of the course transcribed my notes for remembering in a small-bound book. This is a practice that I undertook throughout my PhD coursework. Books vary in size and structure: A material holding that both mark and arc these unique moments in my studies. In part an effort of meaning-making (Sedgwick, 2011, pp. 79–84), and in part a doubling of learning for the fear of forgetting: A tangible place for holding fragments of thoughts after being in a car accident early in the programme. I find it was also a rest from the screen—giving way to paper and ink, stitch and glue, that would unfold in both reflection and turn of page. I wrote no more than two pages from daily class conversations in various colours of ink on mulberry paper. In completing the book, the cut boards were wrapped with purple Kyoseishi paper. Three-ply waxed linen thread secured the hemp-leaf binding following directions from the text *Japanese Bookbinding: Instructions from a Master Craftsman* (Ikegami & Stephan, 1979). A purple and white Chiyogami paper named *contemporary* enveloped the finished book (see: Figure 4.1).[4]

This course was significant in my effort to trouble notions of representation. I also came to recognize the extent to which my experience with Aoki's work had been foreshadowed by studio classes on textile design and ceramics, art education, poetic and narrative inquiry, and curriculum theory. The experience of studying alongside those who shared an Aokian sensibility marked a radical shift in how I came to more fully understand learning, teaching, writing, and making (art). It opened spaces in education that resonated with both the haptic and optic. In both movement and stillness. In both sound and silence. This, in turn, brought about a shift in my thinking and research. It brought about a shift in my understanding of subjective presence.

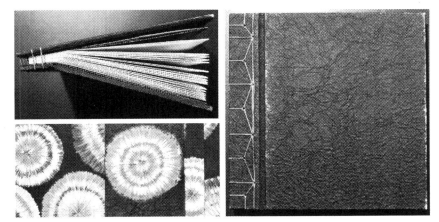

Figure 4.1 Photo Collage of Handmade Book Art | Photo Collage: Joanne M. Ursino; Top Left: Overhead of Handmade Book art *EDCP 508 (951)*, (Special Course in Curriculum and Pedagogy: Ted T. Aoki); Bottom Left: Book Wrapping of *EDCP 508 (951)*; Right: Front Cover of *EDCP 508 (951)*, Dimensions: 5.1in (w) × 5.3in (h) × 5in (d).

Both Equity and Excellence

By way of background, I was accepted as a graduate student in the Faculty of Education the same week my position in the Equity Office at UBC was terminated. Four years of employment on the Vancouver campus was cut short for the institutional demand of something new[5] and arguably the power found in erasure that trumps accountability. This followed more than two decades of national and regional employment with the Federal government and trade union movement with responsibilities related to the Employment Equity Act and the Federal Contractors Program. My work addressed issues of representation and workforce availability, human rights and regulation, accommodation and special measures, the Canadian Census, and training on employment equity with employers, unions, and equity-seeking groups. Taking for-granted a strong pedagogical imperative and a resolve that change was possible through education, I believed in the potential of transformation. The loss of this position underscored a time of crisis in my understanding of representation. I questioned not only what mattered but also the value of my work alongside a critique of leadership and agency—commitment and resolve. Matters of representation cut at the edges of equity and notions of excellence in the academy.

Data and self-identification, quantitative and qualitative methods were at home in a landscape of curriculum-as-plan (Aoki, 1986/1991/2005, p. 159). This cut gave way to art and writing. Difference become far more nuanced. I moved from a bifurcation of thinking: either/or to resonance with both/and. I came to appreciate spaces of paradox, ambiguity, and ambivalence

(Aoki, 1996/2005a, p. 317) without trepidation—as an antidote to control in a neoliberal regime. What Aoki's teachings established was the capacity to hold difference: to be both unsettled and to reimagine imperfect unities. I come into a fuller life in curriculum-as-lived (Aoki, 1986/1991/2005, pp. 160–161).

Both Autobiography and Poetic Inquiry

A beautiful language alongside the push-pull of grammar begins to emerge in my studies in art education, curriculum theory, and later, cross-faculty inquiry. The scholars I encounter speak a generous, vibrant, poetic discourse. One that allows for complexity and uncertainty, imagination and discipline. And, nourished by a deep regard for relationality the critique no longer stands alone. The liminal, the in-between, the crack, and the oblique slash offered openings and possibilities. I find on this journey the metaphor of both bridges and non-bridges (Aoki, 1996/2005a, p. 318) and that there is room to move, to breath, to think—both embodied and in the materiality of page, screen, and in the work of my hands. This is a rich landscape for an ontological swerve. So, I piece narratives of art, research, writing, and later, teaching. After 25 years, my studio practice of quilt-making shifts remarkably, and space is made for ceramics, printmaking, photography, and book arts. The latter two becoming integral in my doctoral research. The challenges and entanglements of both studio and study become an Aokian Web of my own making—an entwinement of a/r/tography (Irwin, 2012; Irwin & de Cosson, 2004), curreré (Pinar, 2012), autobiography (Pinar, 1994), and writing: Both a living (Meyer, 2010) and poetic inquiry (Leggo, 2016). It is an auto-poetic journeying. I begin to articulate both a method and the resistance to universal signification.

Both Note-Taking and Tracings

Re-reading the transcribed notes from the class on Aoki, I am reminded of how Leggo (July 27, 2017) lit up the room—a conversation that crescendoed—sparking possibilities in *crafting a poem*, the *magic of grammar*, and that the etymology of *spelling is to cast a spell*. At the time, Leggo brought one of his poems to our attention and now I trace my underlined words for its citation (see: Figure 4.2). The poem is in *Storying the World: The Contribution of Carl Leggo on Language and Poetry* (Irwin, Hasebe-Ludt & Sinner, 2019). It is found in the pages of its first chapter, *Loving Language: Poetry, Curriculum and Ted. T. Aoki*, (Leggo, 2018/2019, pp. 5–18) where the abecedarian of *fragments from Ted's letters* (pp. 12–13) is a profound marking of friendship and esteem—both anchored on the page and celebrated in our class.

I follow these threads and in the pull to tension, note that Leggo (2018/2019) first met Aoki at a conference (p. 6). Pinar (2005a) also shares that while he initially read Aoki's influential work, their introductory meeting was after a

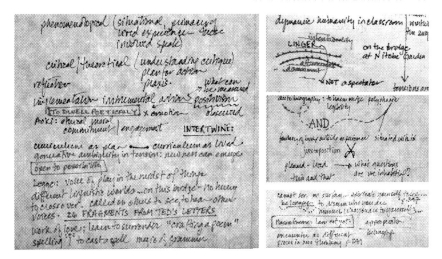

Figure 4.2 Photo Collage of Notes in Handmade Book Art | Photo Collage: Joanne M. Ursino; Left: Note-Taking from Wednesday, July 26, 2017 from the Handmade Book Art for *EDCP 508 (951)*; Top Right: Note-Taking from Friday, July 28, 2017, *EDCP 508 (951)*; Middle Right: Note-Taking from Wednesday, August 9, 2017, *EDCP 508 (951)*; Bottom Right: Note-Taking from Wednesday, August 2, 2017, *EDCP 508 (951)*.

colleagues' talk (p. xx); and throughout *A Lingering Note* he further weaves in Aoki's presence and presentations at conferences,[6] Finally, in the pivotal text, "Toward Curriculum Inquiry in a New Key," Aoki (1978/1980/2005) refers to scholars grounded in art education and their "vibrant call for calling into question the constraining mould of tradition" (p. 92). Inspired by these revelations and references, I reflect on the possibilities that my opportune attendance at a longstanding art education conference might evoke, and give way to noting traces of Aokian sensibilities at this event.

Both Attending and Discerning

The [Virtual] National Art Education Association (NAEA) Annual Convention (March 4–7, 2021), was held during the COVID-19 pandemic, engaging over 4,500 visual arts and design education professionals creating an online community. Watching numerous presentations via the convention platform and on Zoom, I dwell with two for this moment that draws a connection between my own research and recent readings of Aoki texts. I note the first and ponder the second.

First, I attend the *2020 Higher Educator of the Year Award Lecture* given by Rita Irwin (National Art Education Association National Convention, Virtual. March 4, 2021). Irwin references several texts. She holds a copy of *Curriculum in a New Key* (Pinar & Irwin, 2005) in her hands and speaks of

Aoki's impact on her thinking. Irwin's lecture then moves to a contemplation on a/r/tography. In this presentation, the language of one informs the other, and the gesture of gratitude in turn makes manifest how Aokian scholarship lives in both a citational practice on the page and the legacy of research creation that has unfolded in a/r/tography for two decades.

The second presentation at the NAEA National Convention is a panel discussion titled: *Arts-Based Research and the Ruin of Art Education Scholarship in Higher Education?* (Virtual. March 5, 2021). The panelists are Daniel Barney, Jorge Lucero, Nadine Kalin, Mira Kallio-Tavin, James H. Rolling, Richard Siegesmund, and Kevin Tavin. The scope of their conversation is stated in the programme: *Is it time for art education experts to set guidelines and standards for arts-based research, What is it? Who can or gets to do it? Who benefits from it? What are the limits and possibilities of this type of research?* I linger with their conversation, skilfully held by Lucero, and share five moments that resonate with this chapter. First, they grappled with the signification and identity of the artist, alongside notions of research and what arts-based research (and, in turn, art education) did. Tavin emphasized the *how*, not the *what*, of the work of the artist. Second, Rolling recalled the contribution of Kenneth Beittel, whom Aoki (1978/1980/2005), referenced in his noted chapter, "Toward Curriculum Theory in a New Key" (p. 92). Rolling suggests that we search "for models outside from what is not already built" and that Beittel spoke of a resistance to a uniform method, coining "methodolotry." Third, Siegesmund shared that "arts-based research is different than qualitative ... arts-based is outside of language ... and that is the power of what we are trying to teach." Fourth, Kalin remarked that "this conversation is a reminder of what might be possible outside the traps of fetishizing method if we are continually being asked to be in a discomfort—that's the kind of space that is disruptive." The conclusion offered a quickening of discernment. Barney drew on the comments of previous panelists, in particular Rolling and, highlighted the both/and of arts-based research.[7] Noting the importance of "making those models those maps those frameworks for yourself—just like you do with your paintings—you need to find the method to address that concept." Barney concluded by sharing that "I develop an idiosyncratic method every time I engage in that work."

Both Citations and Relations

The work of attending to a citational practice is relational in becoming both eclectic[8] and idiosyncratic.[9] Aoki is at the heart of this understanding. As I continue to work with large data sets and their juxtapositions in arts-based research, I am less concerned with the tension of representation and more with the intention of attending to difference in making and unfolding an auto-poetic narrative.[10]

Both data gathering and curating the page, becomes part of my process as this research evolves. Regarding the former, I am moved by the writing of Lupi and Posavec (2016), who note that "spending time with your data is spending time with yourself" (p. 128). The data gathered now informs my auto-poetic ruminations. In the theory and practice of living and poetic inquiry, I read, listen, write, and make to locate and hone my voice alongside others. I attend to time, place, self, and other (Meyer, 2010). In this work, I am in relation with a cacophony of voices related to "*vox theoria* ... poems about poetry and/or inquiry in itself. Some ... are overtly political and critical in content ... *vox autobiographia* ... researcher-voiced poems ... writing as the data source" (Prendergast et al., 2009, p. xxii).

Aoki (1996/2005b) in an oft quoted statement writes: "I call on fine arts educators in particular, with their strong sense of poetics, to offer inspiration and leadership in the promising work of creating a new landscape wherein 'live(d)curricula' can become a legitimated signifier" (p. 423). We hear its echo with Barone and Eisner (2012) who reasoned that the value in arts-based research is in "unearthing questions that have been buried by the answers, and thereby in remaking the social world" (p. 27). Sandra Faulkner (2019), in turn, introduces the text, *Poetic Inquiry as Social Justice and Political Response* with "poetic inquiry can be an active response to social issues, a political commentary, and a call to action" (p. xi).

Both Voice and Attunement

I take up Aoki's call both with text and, alongside needle, scissors and threads, camera lens, and computer screen. Not only in teaching but also in studio and study, inquiring: "What do I make of what I have been made?" (Pinar, 1994, p. 204). And so, I stitch fragments: With both materials and words—threads and em dashes. Reminded of Aoki's (1992/2005) diagram, "for the want of a name, I call it the C & C Landscape" (p. 273), where the dashed lines of circles and the floating words "and" is his pen to the draw of the page—both image and point of alignment for writing with. Aoki's offerings become method-making in my understanding of research creation. Macintyre Latta (2013) notes that "as human beings we are all fundamentally creative. How we make sense of the world is through creating meaning. As we create meaning, we create ourselves" (p. 105).

The research I undertake marks a "slowing down" (Hoofd, 2012, p. 25), in a hypermodal contestation of subjective presence and currerè (Pinar, 2012), in social justice activism. It is an attunement (Aoki, 1987/2005b; Greene, 2001) through listening and writing to the material (Bolin & Blandy, 2011; Robertson, 2014; Sturken, 1997; The Artist Circle Alliance, 2017), visual (Drucker, 1998; Rose & Tolia-Kelly, 2012), and digital (James, 2017, 2009; Klein, 2014) iterations of the speech act and their concatenations in relation to school and street.[11] Joan Retallack (2003) posits that "one writes essays and poetry to stay warm and active and realistically messy ... to attend to alternative kind of sense and—if possible, if lucky—to come up with some oddly relevant, frankly partial meaning" (p. 5).

In offering an opening at the close, I return to Leggo (2016) who wrote that "poetry works with form in order to challenge formula and formulaic uses of language" (p. 356). I find that the found poems[12] of others make for good company, in this regard Leggo (2018) also structured an homage to Aoki's words (p. 10). Here, I gather the phrasings of both/and that permeates Aoki's writing in *Curriculum in a New Key* (Pinar & Irwin, 2005). This becomes a two-fold effort to both recognize the temporal framing of Aoki's use of both/and over three decades, and to invite the reader to imagine alongside and otherwise: How do we think in relation with Aoki still—in 2020 and 2021?

Both Grammarings and Imaginaries

Aokian Magic[13]

both Bruner and Schwab	(Aoki, 1978/1980/2005, p. 92)
both researcher and subjects	(Aoki, 1978/1980/2005, p. 105)
both him and me,	(Aoki, 1979/2005, p. 335)
both his past and my past,	(Aoki, 1979/2005, p. 335)
both Cumberland and Hirosaki.	(Aoki, 1979/2005, p. 335)
both Japanese and non-Japanese.	(Aoki, 1979/2005, p. 335)
both insider and outsider,	(Aoki, 1979/2005, p. 335)
both self and world	(Aoki, 1979/2005, p. 336)
both students and a curriculum-to-be-implemented.	(Aoki, 1983/2005, p. 112)
both the situationally human condition of man and the irreducible transcendence of the human person	(Aoki, 1983/2005, p. 120)
both the communal condition of man and the irreducible transcendence of the human person	(Aoki, 1983/2005, p. 130)
both teacher and students	(Aoki, 1984/2005, p. 131)
both self and world	(Aoki, 1984/2005, p. 133)
both Canada and in the United States	(Aoki, 1985/1991/2005, p. 231)
both evaluator and subjects	(Aoki, 1986/1999/2005, p. 146)
both identity and difference	(Aoki, 1987/2005, p. 354)
both the school and the parents	(Aoki, 1987/1991/2005, p. 240)
both here in the world of the mother language, and there in the world of the second language.	(Aoki, 1987/1991/2005, p. 242)
both teachers and students,	(Aoki, 1987/1991/2005, p. 245)
both extending the language potential as code and to submerging the second language	(Aoki, 1987/1991/2005, p. 245)
both a means and human activity	(Aoki, 1987/1999/2005, p. 153)
both man and nature	(Aoki, 1987/1999/2005, p. 153)
both epistemologically and ontologically?	(Aoki, 1987/1999/2005, p. 156)
Both of these call on Miss O and make their claims on her.	(Aoki, 1987/1999/2005, p. 156)
Both Miss Buck and my father	(Aoki, 1991/2005e, p. 385)
both evaluator and subjects	(Aoki, 1991/2005c, p. 174)
both social studies and evaluation.	(Aoki, 1991/2005c, p. 183)
both *pedagogy* and *education*	(Aoki, 1991/2005d, p. 436)

both the lived curricula of students and the designed curriculum	(Aoki, 1992/2005b, p. 273)
both the curriculum-as-plan and the lived curricula,	(Aoki, 1992/2005b, p. 275)
both you and the multitude of others, teachers and students,	(Aoki, 1992/2005b, p. 277)
both hope and sadness:	(Aoki, 1992/2005a, p. 196)
both the curriculum-as-plan and the curriculum-as-lived.	(Aoki, 1993/2005b, p. 201)
both of these understandings of "self/other"— the "self/other" in distanced solitude and the "self/other" in integrated wholeness	(Aoki, 1993/2005b, p. 212)
both annoyed and delighted	(Aoki, 1993/2005c, p. 280)
both self and other	(Aoki, 1993/2005c, p. 288)
both self and other	(Aoki, 1993/2005c, p. 288)
both self and other	(Aoki, 1993/2005c, p. 288)
both self and other	(Aoki, 1993/2005c, p. 289)
both self and other	(Aoki, 1993/2005c, p. 289)
both drawn into the chuckles and puzzled by them.	(Aoki, 1993/2005a, p. 291)
both this and that?	(Aoki, 1993/2005a, p. 292)
both enjoying *and* worrying	(Aoki, 1993/2005a, p. 292)
both this and that	(Aoki, 1993/2005a, p. 292)
both a blessing and a burden	(Aoki, 1993/2005a, p. 292)
both blessings and burdens	(Aoki, 1993/2005a, p. 293)
both this *and* that	(Aoki, 1993/2005a, p. 293)
"both this and that, and more ... "	(Aoki, 1993/2005a, p. 294)
"BOTH THIS AND THAT, AND MORE"	(Aoki, 1993/2005a, p. 295)
both this and that.	(Aoki, 1993/2005a, p. 295)
both blessings and burdens-	(Aoki, 1993/2005a, p. 295)
both this and that	(Aoki, 1993/2005a, p. 295)
"both this and that, and more"	(Aoki, 1993/2005a, p. 295)
"both this and that, and more"	(Aoki, 1993/2005a, p. 295)
both the lived curricula of students and the designed curriculum	(Aoki, 1993/2005a, p. 297)
"both this and that, and more."	(Aoki, 1993/2005a, p. 297)
"both this and that, and more,"	(Aoki, 1993/2005a, p. 299)
"both this and that, and more."	(Aoki, 1993/2005a, p. 299)
both enjoyment and worry.	(Aoki, 1993/2005a, p. 300)
both in Japan and in Canada,	(Aoki, 1995/2005, p. 305)
both contains and constrains	(Aoki, 1995/2005, p. 307)
both entranced with and puzzled by the strange word "individual,"	(Aoki, 1995/2005, p. 309)
both divided and undivided.	(Aoki, 1995/2005, p. 310)
both Japanese and English	(Aoki, 1995/2005, p. 310)
both the British colony of Hong Kong and the United States	(Aoki, 1995/2005, p. 311)
both West and East	(Aoki, 1996/2005a, p. 314)
"both this and that,"	(Aoki, 1996/2005a, p. 318)
"both 'and' and 'not-and,'"	(Aoki, 1996/2005a, p. 318)
both conjunction and disjunction.	(Aoki, 1996/2005a, p. 318)
both bridges and non-bridges.	(Aoki, 1996/2005a, p. 318)
both "and/not-and"	(Aoki, 1996/2005a, p. 318)
both individual identity and doubled identity-	(Aoki, 1996/2005a, p. 319)
both this and that,	(Aoki, 1996/2005a, p. 319)

74   *J. M. Ursino*

both East and West,	(Aoki, 1996/2005a, p. 319)
both happy and shocked.	(Aoki, 1996/2005b, p. 403)
both *"and"* and *"not-and,"*	(Aoki, 1996/2005b, p. 405)
both conjunction and disjunction,	(Aoki, 1996/2005b, p. 405)
both continuity and discontinuity.	(Aoki, 1996/2005b, p. 405)
both conjunction and disruption	(Aoki, 1996/2005b, p. 406)
both Margo and George.	(Aoki, 1996/2005b, p. 408)
both whole and fragmented	(Aoki, 1996/2005c, p. 413)
both difficulty and ambiguity	(Aoki, 2000/2005, p. 322)
both "presence" and "absence"	(Aoki, 2000/2005, p. 323)
both language and culture.	(Aoki, 2000/2005, p. 326)
both ourselves and our understandings of the words.	(Aoki, 2000/2005, p. 328)
both "presence" and "absence".	(Aoki, 2003/2005, p. 426)
Both Greene and Whittaker	(Aoki, 2003/2005, p. 427)
both English and Japanese,	(Aoki, 2003/2005, p. 430)
both produces its subjects and displaces them.	(Aoki, 2003/2005, p. 442)
both subjects and subjects-supposed-to-know	(Aoki, 2003/2005, p. 442)
both the subject and the signifier with an "S."	(Aoki, 2003/2005, p. 443)
both curriculum-as-plan and curriculum-as-live(d.)	(Aoki, 2005, p. 449)
both in Chinese and in English	(Aoki, 2005, p. 451)

2020: Both Noun and Adjective

both virus and
both pivot and
both trauma and
both loss and
both life and

2021: Both Noun and Verb

both Indigenous and
both land and
both decolonization and
both queer and
both trans and
both Asian and
both Black and
both patent and
both access and
both abolition and
both in/tension and
both   and improvise
both   and love.

Notes

1. Carl Leggo (2018/2019) wrote: "I weave poetry, personal anecdotes and recollections, quotations from writers who have informed and inspired me, and reflections about (my) institutional autobiography" (p. 72). I follow this thread in my own stitching of experience in the academy.
2. With profound gratitude to Nicole Y. S. Lee and Lesley E. Wong for the conversations and learnings I carry with me. And, to Blake Smith and Joanne Price for the gift of their wisdom in editing this chapter.
3. This included Textile Design and Pedagogical Approaches in Art Education (EDCP 304_002), offered over the Fall and Winter terms; as well as co-instructing Arts Based Educational Research: A/r/tography (EDCP 514) with Rita Irwin during the Winter term.
4. Both the Kyoseishi and Chiyogami papers were sourced from the Japanese Paper Place in Toronto, Ontario.
5. It was a moment: for a new model, new resources, a new structure, and a new direction. See: *UBC Equity and Inclusion Office Annual Report 2012-2013*, p. 5–6 (https://equity3.sites.olt.ubc.ca/files/2017/05/Annual-Report_2012.pdf).
6. Pinar (2005) in *Lingering Note* writes of Aoki's rich engagement with attending and presenting at education conferences (p. xv, xvi, xx, xxi, 5, 13, 16, 26, 31, 36, 40, 41, 42, 50, 51, 52, 53, 57, 60, 62, 64, 65, 66, 69, 74, 75, 78, 79, 81).
7. Barney's (2009) dissertation offers a strong Aokian citational thread—hence this moment at NAEA felt relational, intentional, resonant and particularly poignant.
8. With gratitude to Samson Nashon, for a serendipitous conversation in the lunch room (Summertime 2018), when he remarked that method can be eclectic, stating: "Of course! Why not?!"
9. With gratitude to Dan Barney for his offering in conversation at the [Virtual] NAEA Annual Convention (March 5, 2021).
10. Without coding for representation and flattening difference, all I hold is difference and this now demands attunement, discernment, and the fullness of an Aokian sensibility in its articulation/s.
11. The first moment is the conference for "lesbian, gay and bisexual trade unionists and our allies" organized by the Canadian Labour Congress (CLC), in Ottawa, Ontario from October 15–19, 1997. The *Pride/Fierté/Solidarité* quilt, commemorates this bilingual gathering. The next moment is the Women's March on Washington – Vancouver, British Columbia, held on January 21, 2017 with a rally at Jack Poole Plaza before marching to the Trump Tower. This research juxtaposes photographs – the testament and selfie. In the third moment, I reference the two-fold petitioning of the Vancouver Pride Society (VPS) with regard to the participation of the police in the Pride Parade. Opposing on-line petitions were released within twelve days of each other in February 2017.
12. A quick note on found poems. In this instance, an existing text is refashioned and reordered, and then presented as a poem. It is noted as the "literary equivalent of a collage" (See: https://poets.org/glossary/found-poem).
13. The title is inspired by Leggo's (2018) words that "Ted knows the magic of grammar" (p. 10).

References

Aoki, T. T. (1978/1980/2005). Toward curriculum inquiry in a new key. In W. F. Pinar & R. L. Irwin (Eds.), *Curriculum in a new key: The collected works of Ted. T. Aoki* (pp. 89–110). Lawrence Erlbaum.

Aoki, T. T. (1979/2005). Reflections of a Japanese Canadian teacher experiencing ethnicity. In W. F. Pinar & R. L. Irwin (Eds.), *Curriculum in a new key: The collected works of Ted T. Aoki* (pp. 333–348). Lawrence Erlbaum.

Aoki, T. T. (1983/2005). Curriculum implementation as instrumental action and as situational praxis. In W. F. Pinar & R. L. Irwin (Eds.), *Curriculum in a new key: The collected works of Ted. T. Aoki* (pp. 111–123). Lawrence Erlbaum.

Aoki, T. T. (1984/2005). Competence in teaching as instrumental and practical action: A critical analysis. In W. F. Pinar & R. L. Irwin (Eds.), *Curriculum in a new key: The collected works of Ted. T. Aoki* (pp. 125–135). Lawrence Erlbaum.

Aoki, T. T. (1985/1991/2005). Signs of vitality in curriculum scholarship. In W. F. Pinar & R. L. Irwin (Eds.), *Curriculum in a new key: The collected works of Ted. T. Aoki* (pp. 229–233). Lawrence Erlbaum.

Aoki, T. T. (1986/1991/2005). Teaching as in-dwelling between two curriculum worlds. In W. F. Pinar & R. L. Irwin (Eds.), *Curriculum in a new key: The collected works of Ted. T. Aoki* (pp. 159–165). Lawrence Erlbaum.

Aoki, T. T. (1986/2005). Interests, knowledge and evaluation: Alternative approaches to curriculum evaluation. In W. F. Pinar & R. L. Irwin (Eds.). *Curriculum in a new key: The collected works of Ted. T. Aoki* (pp. 137–150). Lawrence Erlbaum.

Aoki, T. T. (1987/1991/2005). The dialectic of mother language and second language: A curriculum exploration. In W. F. Pinar & R. L. Irwin (Eds.), *Curriculum in a new key: The collected works of Ted. T. Aoki* (pp. 235–245). Lawrence Erlbaum.

Aoki, T. T. (1987/1999/2005). Toward understanding "computer application." In W. F. Pinar & R.L. Irwin (Eds.), *Curriculum in a new key: The collected works of Ted. T. Aoki* (pp. 151–158). Lawrence Erlbaum.

Aoki, T. T. (1987/2005a). Inspiriting the curriculum. In W. F. Pinar & R.L. Irwin (Eds.), *Curriculum in a new key: The collected works of Ted. T. Aoki* (pp. 357–365). Lawrence Erlbaum.

Aoki, T. T. (1987/2005b). Revisiting the notions of leadership and identity. In W. F. Pinar & R. L. Irwin (Eds.), *Curriculum in a new key: The collected works of Ted. T. Aoki* (pp. 349–355). Lawrence Erlbaum.

Aoki, T. T. (1990/2005). Sonare and videre: A story, three echoes and a lingering note. In W. F. Pinar & R. L. Irwin (Eds.), *Curriculum in a new key: The collected works of Ted. T. Aoki* (pp. 367–376). Lawrence Erlbaum.

Aoki, T. T. (1991/2005a). Bridges that rim the Pacific. In W. F. Pinar & R. L. Irwin (Eds.), *Curriculum in a new key: The collected works of Ted. T. Aoki* (pp. 437–439). Lawrence Erlbaum.

Aoki, T. T. (1991/2005b). Five curriculum memos and a note for the next half-century. In W. F. Pinar & R. L. Irwin (Eds.), *Curriculum in a new key: The collected works of Ted. T. Aoki* (pp. 247–261). Lawrence Erlbaum.

Aoki, T. T. (1991/2005c). Layered understandings of orientations in social studies program evaluation. In W. F. Pinar & R. L. Irwin (Eds.), *Curriculum in a new key: The collected works of Ted. T. Aoki* (pp. 167–186). Lawrence Erlbaum.

Aoki, T. T. (1991/2005d). Principles as managers: An incomplete view. In W. F. Pinar & R. L. Irwin (Eds.), *Curriculum in a new key: The collected works of Ted. T. Aoki* (pp. 435–436). Lawrence Erlbaum.

Aoki, T. T. (1991/2005e). Taiko drums and sushi, perogies and sauerkraut: Mirroring a half-life in multicultural curriculum. In W. F. Pinar & R. L. Irwin (Eds.), *Curriculum in a new key: The collected works of Ted. T. Aoki* (pp. 377–387). Lawrence Erlbaum.

Aoki, T. T. (1991/2005f). The sound of pedagogy in the silence of the morning calm. In W. F. Pinar & R. L. Irwin (Eds.), *Curriculum in a new key: The collected works of Ted. T. Aoki* (pp. 389–401). Lawrence Erlbaum.

Aoki, T. T. (1992/2005a). In the midst of slippery theme-words: Living as designers of Japanese Canadian curriculum. In W. F. Pinar & R. L. Irwin (Eds.), *Curriculum in a new key: The collected works of Ted. T. Aoki* (pp. 263–277). Lawrence Erlbaum.

Aoki, T. T. (1992/2005b). Layered voices of teaching: The uncannily correct and the elusively true. In W. F. Pinar & R. L. Irwin (Eds.), *Curriculum in a new key: The collected works of Ted. T. Aoki* (pp. 187–197). Lawrence Erlbaum.

Aoki, T. T. (1993/2005a). Humiliating the Cartesian ego. In W. F. Pinar & R. L. Irwin (Eds.), *Curriculum in a new key: The collected works of Ted. T. Aoki* (pp. 291–301). Lawrence Erlbaum.

Aoki, T. T. (1993/2005b). Legitimating lived curriculum: Toward a curricular landscape of multiplicity. In W. F. Pinar & R. L. Irwin (Eds.), *Curriculum in a new key: The collected works of Ted. T. Aoki* (pp. 199–215). Lawrence Erlbaum.

Aoki, T. T. (1993/2005c). The child-centered curriculum: Where is the social in pedocentricism? In W. F. Pinar & R. L. Irwin (Eds.), *Curriculum in a new key: The collected works of Ted. T. Aoki* (pp. 279–289). Lawrence Erlbaum.

Aoki, T. T. (1995/2005). In the midst of doubled imaginaries: The Pacific community as diversity and as difference. In W. F. Pinar & R. L. Irwin (Eds.), *Curriculum in a new key: The collected works of Ted. T. Aoki* (pp. 303-312). Lawrence Erlbaum.

Aoki, T. T. (1996/2005a). Imaginaries of "East and West": Slippery curricular signifiers in education. In W. F. Pinar & R. L. Irwin (Eds.), *Curriculum in a new key: The collected works of Ted. T. Aoki* (pp. 313–319). Lawrence Erlbaum.

Aoki, T. T. (1996/2005b). Narrative and narration in curricular spaces. In W. F. Pinar & R. L. Irwin (Eds.), *Curriculum in a new key: The collected works of Ted. T. Aoki* (pp. 403–411). Lawrence Erlbaum.

Aoki, T. T. (1996/2005c). Spinning inspirited images in the midst of planned and live(d) curricula. In W. F. Pinar & R. L. Irwin (Eds.), *Curriculum in a new key: The collected works of Ted. T. Aoki* (pp. 413–423). Lawrence Erlbaum.

Aoki, T. T. (2000/2005). Language, culture, and curriculum …. In W. F. Pinar & R. L. Irwin (Eds.), *Curriculum in a new key: The collected works of Ted. T. Aoki* (pp. 321–329). Lawrence Erlbaum.

Aoki, T. T. (2003/2005). Interview. In W. F. Pinar & R. L. Irwin (Eds.), *Curriculum in a new key: The collected works of Ted. T. Aoki* (pp. 441–447). Lawrence Erlbaum.

Aoki, T. T. (2005). Postscript/rescript. In W. F. Pinar & R. L. Irwin (Eds.), *Curriculum in a new key: The collected works of Ted. T. Aoki* (pp. 449–457). Lawrence Erlbaum.

Artist Circle Alliance. (2017). *Threads of resistance: A juried exhibition created to protest the trump administration's actions and policies.* The Artist Circle Alliance.

Barney, D. T. (2009). *A study of dress through artistic inquiry: Provoking understandings of artist, researcher, and teacher identities.* University of British Columbia. https://open.library.ubc.ca/collections/ubctheses/24/items/1.0055260

Barney, D., Lucero, J. Kalin, N., Kallio-Tavin, M., Rolling, J. H., Siegesmund, R., & Tavin, K. (2021, March 5). *Arts-based research and the ruin of art education scholarship in higher education?* [Panel Discussion/Higher Education]. National Art Education Association National Convention, Virtual. March 4–7, 2021.

Barone, T., & Eisner, E. (2012). *Arts based research.* Sage Publications, Inc.

Bolin, P. E., & Blandy, D. (2011). *Matter matters: Art education and material culture studies.* National Art Education Association.

Castro, J. C. (2007). Enabling artistic inquiry. *Canadian Art Teacher, 6*(1), 7–15.

Drucker, J. (1998). *Figuring the word: Essays on books, writing and visual poetics.* Granary Books.

Faulkner, S. & Cloud, A. Eds. (2019). *Poetic inquiry as social justice and political response.* Vernon Press.

Greene, M. (2001). *Variations on a blue guitar: The Lincoln Center Institute lectures an aesthetic education.* Teachers College Press.

Hoofd, I. M. (2012). *Ambiguities of activism: Alter-globalism and the imperatives of speed.* Routledge.

Ikegami, K., & Stephan, B. B. (2015). *Japanese bookbinding: instructions from a master craftsman.* Weatherhill.

Irwin, R. (2021, March 4). *2020 Higher educator of the year award lecture.* [Lecture]. National Art Education Association National Convention, Virtual. March 4–7, 2021.

Irwin, R. (2012). Becoming a/r/tography. In M. R. Carter, & V. Triggs (Eds.), *Arts education and curriculum studies: The contributions of Rita L. Irwin* (pp. 193–211). Routledge.

Irwin, R., & de Cosson, A. (Eds.). (2004). *a/r/tography: Rendering self through arts-based living inquiry.* Pacific Educational Press.

Klein, S. R. (2014). Making sense of data in the changing landscape of visual art education. *Visual Arts Research, 40*(2), 25–33.

Leggo, C. (2018/2019). Loving language: Poetry, curriculum, and Ted T. Aoki. In Irwin, R. L., Hasebe-Ludt, E., & Sinner, A. (Eds.), *Storying the world: The contributions of Carl Leggo on language and poetry* (pp. 5–18). Routledge.

Leggo, C. (2016). Theory and research in the teaching of written composition [Course]. Department of Language and Literacy, The University of British Columbia.

Leggo, C. (2016). A poem can: Poetic encounters. *LEARNing Landscapes, 9*(2), 351–365.

Lupi, G., & Posavec, S. (2016). *Dear data.* Princeton Architectural Press.

Meyer, K. (2010). Living inquiry: Me, my self, and other. *Journal of Curriculum Theorizing, 26*(1), 85–96.

Macintyre Latta, M. (2013). *Curricular conversation: Play is the (missing) thing.* Routledge.

Pinar, W. F. (1994). *Autobiography, politics and sexuality.* Peter Lang.

Pinar, W. F. (2005a). "A lingering note": An introduction to the collected works of Ted T. Aoki. In W. F. Pinar & R. L. Irwin (Eds.), *Curriculum in a new key: The collected works of Ted. T. Aoki* (pp. 1–85). Lawrence Erlbaum.

Pinar, W. F. (2012). *What is curriculum theory?* Routledge Taylor & Francis Group.

Pinar, W. F. (2017). EDCP508 (951) Special course in curriculum and pedagogy: Ted T. Aoki [Syllabus]. Department of Curriculum and Pedagogy, The University of British Columbia.

Pinar, W. F., & Irwin, R. L. (Eds.). (2005). *Curriculum in a new key: The collected works of Ted. T. Aoki.* Lawrence Erlbaum.

Prendergast, M., Leggo, C. D., & Sameshima, P. (2009). *Poetic inquiry vibrant voices in the social sciences.* Sense.

Retallack, J. (2003). *The poethical wager.* University of California Press.

Robertson, K. (2014). Quilts for the twenty-first century: Activism in the expanded field of quilting. In J. Jefferies, H. Clark, & D. Wood (Eds.), *Handbook of textiles* (pp. 197–210). Bloomsbury Press

Rose, G., & Tolia-Kelly, D. P. (Eds.). (2012). Visuality/materiality: Introducing a manifesto for practice. In *Visuality/materiality* (pp. 1–11). Ashgate Publishing Limited.

Sedgwick, E. K. (2011). *The weather in proust* (J. Goldberg, Ed.). Duke University Press.

Sturken, M. (1997). *Tangled memories: The Vietnam War, the AIDS epidemic, and the politics of remembering.* University of California Press.

5 When Does an Haleliwia Become More Than an Haleliwia?
Abeying to a Poethics of Plants with Aoki

Joanne Price

I heard plants choose people, like making space for understanding. So, when Haleliwia called to me, I knew to give it my time.

Tiny flowers swaying in the breeze were drawing my attention and making me smile. I felt enchanted, and could see among the tall stems rising out of a canopy of heart-shaped leaves … whole worlds dancing.

I relish moments like this when I can enter into dreamtime. I welcome the species at play, expanding my understanding to include the sub-cellular and planetary. Fairy beings even, flying among the plants and inviting ways of being and becoming rich in feeling and instinctual connections to larger social, cultural, and spiritual contexts. And now, in writing, drawing my attention to a mossy rock upon which Haleliwia grows: millennia old rock holding space amidst the flow of a rushing mountain stream (see Figure 5.1).

Living centrally at the limits of time and space, rock's constancy gathers me further into the silence and spaciousness of this ffridd or upland edge. Before saying more, let me introduce ffridd.

Introducing Ffridd

Ffridd sounds like breathe, and is a Welsh word used to describe irregular and diverse ecological communities on the fringe between enclosed farmland and unenclosed uplands. As habitats on the edge, ffridd have different meanings for different people, making them elusive to define. These marginal and often steep lands "made invisible by our societal grid" (Gerofsky, 2018, p. 57) act as "and/and … and … and/but" places (Aoki, 1992/2005, pp. 187–197). As wildlife havens, ffridd play a vital role in overlapping notions of one and more than one, and allowing "thinking of the yet unthought" (Aoki, 1991/2005, p. 398).

I was born into a ffridd in rural west Wales and my early childhood education held within it many paradoxes of an and/and place. Coming from an

DOI: 10.4324/9781003037248-9

Figure 5.1 An Haleliwia Moment—Noticing Plants in the Language of Pedagogy | Photos: Joanne Price.

English speaking Welsh home and attending a Welsh speaking school, my beginning education was characterized by the chaos and hope of Welsh language resurgence. Feeling as Aoki (1979/2005) says, "'in' yet not fully in, 'out' yet not fully out" (p. 335) this pattern will have unconsciously repeated itself in relation to my being lesbian and a double nation-gender Welshness that came to haunt me in middle life. As a child, I developed allergies to cope with insider society. Sneezing my way to the edge, I am still learning to nurture a fierce and compassionate curiosity toward all stories—societal and individual—as a creation of self. And yet as Cixous writes, "all autobiographies like all narratives tell one story in place of another" (in Cixous & Calle-Gruber, 1997, p. 178).

Writing now, from another gap between communities, between living in Vancouver and just moving to Wales, finishing a doctorate and beginning teaching, all amidst the COVID-19 lockdown in Wales, I take time to contemplate the roots of my relationship with ffridd. I wander with Aoki among the silences, resistances, and hopes that inhabit this place. I walk to reclaim a sense of self. And amidst the ancientness of ffridd, I welcome a certain quiet curiosity as I am open to visions, rhythms, and faraway voices as punctuations. Becoming a little more aware of the multiple life-worlds, edges, and boundary layers living within ffridd, I hope to place the temporarily paused real-life curriculum in perspective and make room for something else. I hope to give voice to ffridd as sacred power places and they usher what Denise Ferreira da Silva (2014) writes as "the creative capacity—a quality only apparent when one contemplates the world as plenum" (p. 85). Emancipated from scientific and historical ways of knowing that produce otherness, amidst a plenum or ffridd, a person or curriculum can "wonder about another praxis and wander in the World with the ethical mandate of opening up to other ways of knowing and doing" (da Silva, 2014, p. 81).

So, when I wit*h*nessed[1] Haleliwia calling to me, I knew to give it my time. I knew to observe in a way that is more like listening, its tiny white bell-shaped flowers with purple veins, red stems, and lime green leaves. As I wander amidst ffridd, I stop to notice Haleliwia growing along tree branches, in the hollows of nurse logs, among grasses and mosses on stream rocks. I feel humbled and joyful, seeing this familiar springtime herb dancing in the breeze, and would have wondered whether Haleliwia's strange and even sublime gesturing accounts for its many names:

>hallelujah
>crinche cranche
>suran y coed
>suran y gôg
>cuckoo's meat
>swan tair dalen
>thirty three sheets
>good luck
>trigl tair dalen,
>fairy bells
>and
>...
>Haleliwia.

Hairy Rocker Curriculum

Time passes and I come to know this life-world of Haleliwia dancing among mosses and grasses amidst ancient rock mountain stream as, hairy rocker. With a name and personality, its calling to me is "no longer an abstraction" (Aoki, 1996/2005, p. 419), and as Robin Wall Kimmerer (2003) writes, shows respect and creates conditions for generative relationships with more-than-human realms. Rather than determining another, giving sweet names for the ones we love, she says, allows for names to change and several worlds to co-exist (p. 21).

HAIRY ROCKER: A plant with a lot of names is a plant with a lot of lessons.

Hairy rocker even speaks to me in writing. Entering into text and releasing my world from self-seriousness, together with other voices from within ffridd, it welcomes tension, risks different formats, and extends compassion toward untold possibilities at play. Amidst these words that are more than words, I learn to abey[2] with the voices of plants, trees, super-naturals, and ancestors. I attend to the ways in which they can be seriously beautiful and useful in their similarities and differences.

As such, this chapter enacts a response to Aoki's (1996/2005) call on artists to kindle afire the word curriculum, with a "strong sense of poetics, to offer inspiration and leadership in the promising work of creating a new landscape wherein 'live(d) curricula' can become a legitimated signifier" (p. 423). Responding to this context, "with the concern and courage of an artist" writes Retallack (2003), also asks for "a patience for duration" (p. 3–4).

THE HAIRY ROCKER CURRICULUM: I do endurance, but when it comes to education I'm really lacking in confidence. I get short of breath. My grasses blur and I can't see the ffridd for the flowers. All I wish for everybody is to hold space for an Haleliwia to become more than an Haleliwia.

OGHAM KNOWLEDGE SYSTEM BEGINNING WITH TREES: I'm here to extend a guiding hand, Curriculum. Let me propose an outline for this chapter to follow. Inspired by Aoki, I suggest four dimensions or echoes sounding and resounding within and among each other. In an opening echo, let me introduce myself as Ogham (pronounced Oh-am) and talk about curriculum-as-plan. A second echo would embody a lived curriculum; a third contemplates plant poet*h*ics and ways in which curriculum can perform life's changing experience; and a fourth echo would welcome contributions to live this chapter forward.

THE HAIRY ROCKER CURRICULUM: Thanks.

Echo One: Ogham Curriculum-as-Plan

OGHAM: I heard you say you plan to make space for Haleliwia to become more than an Haleliwia. Can you say more, Curriculum?

THE CURRICULUM: Yes, when sun shines after rain my porousness opens, the Haleliwia dances, and somehow links with surrounding species and lift each other up with organelles of potential. But, there are times when I feel too old and I lack the withies to flow. *Ogham and Curriculum converse beneath an Oak tree. Oak listens attentively and with the utterance of the word but ... raises its bows and makes space for a breeze.*

OGHAM: I get tired of being used as a representational system. True, I am a tree alphabet but ...

A breeze flows among them.

OGHAM: I'm made up of twenty five letters and while Sessile Oak here is known by the letter D or duir or doo-er, it shares so much more strength and vitality. Like Haleliwia, Oak has astringent qualities, a bitterness long lost in the Welsh palette that assists species not only to bear discomfort, but to let its medicine approach as a long sweet labour.

A breeze swerves among contradictory words, and Curriculum takes deep breaths.

People help energise you, Curriculum, by exhaling hundreds of times more carbon dioxide than they inhale. What's more: their inhaling oxygen from you fires life and boosts their immune systems.

THE CURRICULUM: I do enjoy the positive feelings of people. I'd be happy to respond at my own pace.

OGHAM: I suggest staying just where you are in ffridd.

AOKI: I would take time to better understand what I've given my heart to, "allow the unsaid to shine through the said (1992/2005, p. 197)?

THE CURRICULUM: I've given my heart to Haleliwia. I wonder how people relate to Haleliwia, Ogham wise?

OGHAM: Haleliwia is a member of the *h* or hoo-ah family together with hawthorn tree and fairy or fox folk deities. Commonly considered strange and Welsh, Haleliwia has long been outlawed and today grows deep within ffridd.

RETALLACK: Its verticality, "is held in pursuit of the good life–a good life that must be contrived in the midst of happenstance and chaos" (Retallack, 2003, p. 11).

OGHAM: A horizontal line acts like a breeze of awen or poetic flow.

AOKI: I'm reminded of thoughts, ideas, and living experiences that put "into turbulence this quietest sense of 'harmony'" (1990/2005, p. 371). Always in motion, awen allows individual characters and letters to "sing polyphonically" (p. 371).

BORHANI: To me, awen "feels like a shimmering, diaphanous Web encircling and encompassing this entire theoretical [ffridd], flexible and transformative, reflective, encouraging interior, as well as outward thought" (personal communication with Maya Borhani, May 2020).

AOKI: I'm imagining ffridd being inhabited by a "pretextual realm" (Aoki, 1990/2005, p. 399).

OGHAM: A realm welcomes a wild ridiculousness into living.

LEGGO: And, "activism, awareness, comedy, consonance, contemplation, description, emotion, exposition, fantasy, imagery, imagination, music, narration, orality, performance, philosophy, prophesy, rhetoric, romance, story-telling, tragedy, voice, wisdom, and words" (Leggo cited in Leggo et al., 2017, p. 28).

THE CURRICULUM: I am open to experimentation.

AOKI: The "word *curriculum* is yearning for new meanings" (1996/2004, p. 423).

THE CURRICULUM: I am open to questioning who I think I am and experiencing abashen[3], but I don't know I do new. I'm designed to live in a regenerative way.

As awen breeze makes room for this slight difference to emerge, oak bows and welcomes more voices into conversation.

Echo Two: A Play for Voices

In preparation for writing echo two, I engage in research. I immerse myself in centuries old herbal manuals of the physicians of Myddfai, mid Wales (Breverton, 2012). I forage and chew Haleliwia while studying Ogham lore and oral tradition, medieval stories, and tree calendars, totems and lists of archetypal plants, beings, spirits, and creatures in volumes of the Celtic encyclopaedia (Mountain, 1998). I learn of a poetic and performative subject at the heart of Welsh culture, and of generations of creative responses to seemingly overwhelming situations. And so, heeding Aoki's (1990/2005) advice to experiment with "polyphonic improvisation" (p. 371), I am delighted to introduce Danaan Thomas, a poetic-storyteller. Danaan, would you speak to your storytelling.

DANAAN THOMAS, A POETIC-STORYTELLER: Well, I wander from place to place telling never-ending stories, with words that refuse to stand still and situations who defer. Precisely because I am not all there, stories get told and their failure and success in and out of my control. I take time for quiet between stories. I sleep and walk among ffridd to near exhaustion. I encourage you to trust all voices are connected there and, especially, partial voices, unevenly contradictions and incomplete understandings, because this is where radical potentialities abide. Be kind to yourself, and create with an attitude of wishing voices well. That said there's no denying this may be an elusive and messy practice, which is why I've come to Einon's shop.

EINON, A PHYSICIAN OF MYDDFAI: Danaan, how's life treating you this morning?

DANAAN THOMAS, A POETIC-STORYTELLER: Morning Einon. Do you happen to have Haleliwia bitters? I need something to keep me in question and let my stories emerge into a greater whole.

EINON, A PHYSICIAN OF MYDDFAI: Here's an Haleliwia elixir, infused with honey. Take two tablespoons every morning on an empty stomach. This is from a fourteenth century remedy for plague (Breverton, 2012), and should bring restraint to stories. It will likely slow your words, let them take flight when necessary, and be nourished by the earth on occasion.

DANAAN THOMAS, A POETIC-STORYTELLER: Wonderful. Looks like you've been busy.

EINON, A PHYSICIAN OF MYDDFAI: Yes, my shop was in need of a good tidy. We've managed to categorise remedies and put them in alphabetical order so they can be truly complementary.

COMMA COMFREY: Ydw, Einon! I like being placed into neat semblance.

DR. FOX GLOVE: Me too. I live negative capability in action.

HAIRY ROCKER: Not not …

HAZEL WITHIE: Who's there?

DR. FOX GLOVE: Poison and cure in one, and with just the right amount of suffering to let healing usher a renewed place.

DANAAN THOMAS, A POETIC-STORYTELLER: I like what you've achieved here Einon. The way each remedy, as a non-self identical concept made of/by others, faces toward the door so it can adapt itself in intra-actions with openness.

DR. FOX GLOVE: I like how I can see all of my relatives from where I've been positioned. Being called to grow in difficult places, I miss Haleliwia.

While I celebrate elements of Haleliwia in me, they grow only in places they know. Working from home in the shade of ancient woodland and only flowering in April and May.

AOKI: A plant-based thought-style rooted in a dialectic mode (1979/2005, p. 346). Without Haleliwia, there'd be no meaning in fox glove.

BEE: I have the pleasure of flying between both. From my perspective, Haleliwia and fox glove are root metaphors which help me to attend to my assumptions. Rubbing my body in your bells, I am metonymically buzzed by how plants among you are strengthened by questioning what they take for granted.

HAZEL WITHIE: Nut nut...

HAIRY ROCKER: Who's there?

AOKI: Two ways of seeing. Negative is positive. Positive as negative (1979/2004, p. 346).

The bell over the door rings as the LADY OF LLYN Y FAN FACH (small) AND YET FAWR (large) walks into the apothecary: Hylo lovelies.

EINON, A PHYSICIAN OF MYDDFAI: Welcome lady of Llyn y Fan Fach and yet Fawr. What can I do you for?

LADY OF LLYN Y FAN FACH AND YET FAWR: I want to Haleliwia.

EINON, A PHYSICIAN OF MYDDFAI *PASSING HER SOME HALELIWIA*: You're the second person in here today asking for this.

Reading the remedy for plague, the lady of Llyn y Fan Fach and yet Fawr begins to cry: This is hilarious.

EINON, A PHYSICIAN OF MYDDFAI: Why?

LADY OF LLYN Y FAN FACH AND YET FAWR: Because Haleliwia has been mixed with honey, Einon. I want Haleliwia in and of and un its own volition.

EINON, A PHYSICIAN OF MYDDFAI: Yes I mean no as in yes.

DANAAN THOMAS, A POETIC-STORYTELLER: As the lady of Llyn y Fan Fach and yet Fawr laughs inexhaustibly, Einon, together with shelves of herb-filled delights look on with esbair[4] astonishment.

AOKI: Maybe I could give meaning to my lifestyle by keeping Haleliwia and fox-glove, and say comfrey in view simultaneously. "Instead of the power of a (n Haleliwia) monovision, the power of a double vision maybe what I should seek ... more importantly, I should learn to see life within the fullness of a double vision or even a multiple vision" (1979/2004, p. 347).

DANAAN THOMAS, A POETIC-STORYTELLER: Such an approach may reveal more fully my self-imposed and socially-imposed stories and distortions.

The bell over the apothecary door rings again and in walks Dwynwen the Lust Bearing farmer. *Surprised to see Foxhy, they are speechless.*

LADY OF LLYN Y FAN FACH AND YET FAWR ALSO KNOWN AS FOXHY: Hylo Lust Bear, been a while.
DWYNWEN THE LUST BEARING FARMER ALSO KNOWN AS LUST BEAR: I last saw you disappearing into the waters. I apologise for my Cartesian thinking, I was confused by your crying at happiness, laughing at sadness, and when I flicked my facemask at you it was in jest. But, you've come back?
FOXHY: I changed my mind. And besides, I needed some Haleliwia.
EINON: How long has it been since you last saw one another?
FOXHY: We were separated in 1556. That was when I merged into nothingness.
LUST BEAR: We've been in abeyance for 464 years. The last time we met, this place was woodland. Everywhere was ffridd. Nowadays, I have to walk a couple of hours to find Haleliwia.

As Foxhy and Lust Bear laugh and cry together, Foxhy says: Sshhh. Close your eyes Lust Bear and imagine looking inside an Haleliwia bell. Tell me what you see.

LUST BEAR: I see baby fox-bears splashing in a stream, I see forest gardens and Haleliwia surprises. I see ...
FOXHY: More, more ...
LUST BEAR: Not now Fox*hy*. I'm out of practice. I've been learning restraint, relearning original language, and taking responsibility for the systems I am a part of. I'd like to do life differently with you.
FOXHY: I can wait. I'm open to being more careful, risking a change.

The doorbell rings and in walks THE CURRICULUM *grasping a napkin*: I've been foraging Haleliwia and I wonder whether you have a use for this. I harvest a third, leave a third for someone else, and a third for Haleliwia.

EINON, A PHYSICIAN OF MYDDFAI: Give a third to Fox*hy*, a third to Lust Bear, and bring a third to the ffridd tonight. 7pm at the waterfall by hairy rocker. Everybody's welcome.
THE CURRICULUM: Einon?
EINON: Yes, Curriculum.
THE CURRICULUM: I've seen refugees in the ffridd, mountain streams filled with boats, climate separating loved ones, lovers, children, and grandparents, streams patterning the tympanic membranes of my middle ear, and Haleliwia bitter veins. I've met disproportionates. I am a disgrace filled with learning and super-naturals living without the support of the world and with all its limitations, safely arriving warriors, attentive shoppers, real and virtual weather tizzies, and joyful trees, ridiculous plot-lines,

wit*h*nessing effects before causes, and serious whispers among the hard working lax and lazies dwelling among living walls a turning everything we ever assumed inside out, calling me to question my complicity in slavery, my responsibility toward several communities and town clock spiral dances, warm summers, and plentiful futures, Haleliwia makes me dance it does delay, play, regress, defract, propel, I smell, I tell, and I shell see you this evening.

EINON: You're not alone, Curriculum. We're all suffering amidst these strange times. Everybody's falling out of grace with life in our own way... come by this evening, we'll walk together.

Walking together and apart, their pace slows to wandering carefully as they enter ffridd. An already lit fire welcomes all as they sit around, socially distanced. Time passes, and THE CURRICULUM *says*: Plants and people, negative and positive. Lust Bear and Fox*hy*, culture and art, Haleliwia and fox glove, and comfrey and horse and Einon and Danaan and hazel withie and oak bow...

A HORSE *LISTENING AMONG THE TREES*: Snorts.
AOKI: It's strange when there's a collision of things one doesn't expect to go together. It makes me laugh. What is it about the capacity of chuckling as a gesture touched by ambiguity? Could "it be that the structure of our chuckles" is the structure of this gathering (1993/2005, p. 291)? This "site of tension between this and that, a site of difference that speaks of two or more things at the same time" (1993/2005, p. 291)? Can we find "humour in things that collide" and change in our differences (p. 300)?
DANAAN THOMAS, A POETIC-STORYTELLER: The Curriculum and Haleliwia.
THE CURRICULUM: I was welcomed into Haleliwia's beautiful world.
COMMA COMFREY: I would say carrying Haleliwia with you has been an act of courage and anticipatory regeneration, Curriculum.
FOX*HY*: I experience grief and creativity as wonderful companions.
THE CURRICULUM: I met Haleliwia as a person.
EINON, A PHYSICIAN OF MYDDFAI: Plant teachers were considered persons when the physicians began practicing. This knowledge somehow got lost during five centuries of lockdown.
LUST BEAR: Fox*hy* did try explaining this to me. Stop the clocks striking, she kept saying, bear with me or I could and she did and I.
HAZEL WITHIE: Be kind to yourself Lust Bear. I am reminded of negative as positive, as plants are to people.
THE CURRICULUM: And people are to plants.

The Curriculum opens their hanky and with encouragement from comfrey, sprinkles Haleliwia into the fire. As an ancient astringence fills the air, a deep and caring silence ensues. All pain and blame in the world is welcomed and abiding uninterrupted in this moment, flickers into night skies. Time passes, and a nearby ELDER TREE makes a three times turn and in a propelling gesture, slowly showers berries into the fire.

HORSES: Snort.

Echo Three: Curriculum in a Renewed Ffridd

Throughout *Curriculum in a New Key*, Aoki refers to an innermost layer where he experiences the isness of his existence at the edge. Contemplating his words in relation to ffridd and the plant lives I have given my heart to, I feel a dignity. I am reminded of the curriculum speaking of plants with personhood in echo two, and ways in which ffridd teaches intimacy with real life worlds we are yet to know.

As a child, playing in ffridd alone and with my sisters, in moments, I had no doubt that as people love plants, they love us back.

> I am held here.
> I am grateful.

Remembering this, Aoki's (1986/1991/2005) description of earthly rhythms pulsating like drumbeats indwelling "earthily, spiritually, poetically" (p. 413), sound and resound.

Elderberry Proliferations

Gestures sound and resound, and are held within our mindbodyheartspirits. They speak to great differences between people and plants. As I am drawn further into echo three, I am reminded of elderberry's wild and generous gesture. Where did this come from? Why had I not noticed elder tree before?

> I am undone.

THE CURRICULUM IN A RENEWED FFRIDD: Being with Haleliwia these past months, I learned to welcome plant gestures as kind acts in a challenging time. Haleliwia takes so little from the world and nevertheless endures in beauty, dances patience, feeds people with food and medicine, and has its own ways in which it gifts and learns.

FOXHY: But, an elderberry proliferates as seed fest for future generations if ever I saw one.

COLE: "We call it working with sacred medicines" (2016, p. 3).

LUST BEAR: A proliferation of potential plant rights, responsibilities to pronoun pollinations and minority languages.

FOXHY: I will have been living at the scale of an elderberry shower, a sweet drop rain-dance expanding with sunrise.

EINON, A PHYSICIAN OF MYDDFAI: Belonging to a third or m Ogham family, grandmother elder is known by the letter r for Ruis and vertical line with five diagonal lines, each one endlessly poet*h*ic, lets summer linger longer.

RETALLACK: Adding an aitch to poetry to make poet*h*ic (2003) has the capacity to inspirit writing with an experimentally feminine practice of exploring the multiplicity and unintelligible beauty of life.

CURRICULUM IN A RENEWED FFRIDD: To me, elderberry's gesture is like an encouragement, a genuine non-conceptual hopefulness. When I wandered in ffridd, plants came to me in gestures of rescue.

DANAAN, A POETIC-STORYTELLER: Suffering does not end this story, but care for one another does.

Hazel withies shimmer in delight.

DR. FOX GLOVE: And yet, in opening up life to be/coming between suffering and care, negative and positive, failure and success, metaphor and metonymy, matter and spirit, real and imagined, aitch trees can be powerful teachers.

DANAAN, A POETIC-STORYTELLER: Elder means burden, and the weight of their berries bring branches close to breaking...

AOKI: A blessing and a burden.

COMMA COMFREY: Elderberry juice helped ancestors working long into the night adjust to nighttime. Let us weigh with care ...

HORSES: Snort.

In a sudden obviousness, I remember my allergy to horse dust and am propelled out of the story and into a real-life ffridd. Leaning into elder tree, I hear a vast emptiness and am terrified when a black horse wanting answers runs towards me. I am running, leaping over hairy rocker, clambering mud stream banks...

Stopping to breathe in, I remember I am breathing in with plants. Breathing out, I know I am breathing out with plants.

Time passes and I am open to journeying with Aoki some more.

Welcoming Elder

Walking barefoot, earth presses into the arches of my feet. Moisture squishing between toes, I am reminded of Aoki's singular and plural sounds. I am hearing doubles. *Rh* sounding a breeze, *dd* (pronounced *th*) amidst slow close-to-earth still, a melodic *ch ch ch* of whimchat song, *ng ng* pipits, and *ll* (pronounced *cla*) as moving stream waters ripple round rocks. With each sound, "I am able to hear the rhythmic measure of the earth, our place of dwelling, where its earthy humus provides nurturance to new meanings" (Aoki, 1993/2005, p. 300).

I am breathing slow double deep breaths. Words linger, *dd* slows, *rh* elongates companion wor*l*ds.

I am becoming aware of multiple ffridds within ffridd. Whole species, each their own ffridd centres in relation. Stepping into stream, a play of vivid greens shines from earth below, and illuminates a multitude of rainbow rock and moss life-worlds. Life's isness lives at a very very long wavelength at this boundary between earth, water, and air. Multiple meanings exist within ancient conversations that reimagine a unique "reciprocity with the world around us as a generative and creative way to be a human" (Wall Kimmerer, 2003, p. 21). Elder lore takes pride in dwelling here, in solidarity with my queerly rooted more-than-human friends. In solidarity with kin who mined kilns toward healing earth. Amidst this quiet, I am completely devoted to: "that pedagogical relationship that reverentially knows its attunement to being" (Aoki, 1991/2005, p. 400).

Looking toward mountains I wit*h*ness an earth-sky ffridd. Lost in passing clouds, I see colourful parachutes dancing mountain stream skies with grace and in a play of real hope. The currents are ethereal today, they call. As they resound in a vision of a grandmother armed with summer vegetables making space for children playing.

Haleliwia brings me back. Soothing bell like notes of its dancing somewhere between being grounded and taking flight.

HORSES: Snort.

And, I stay put and entertain, "a sense of humour where joyous pleasure and laughter can co-mingle with serious living" (Aoki, 1996/2005, p. 414). Sway dancing with Haleliwia, I am called to make a *rh* sound with my nose and smile in reply. Elder tree smiles, and I know my lesson with this tree is done for now. I am grateful to elder for letting me go lightly.

As Haleliwia continues to dance, I am moving forward with an attitude of tender gratitude. I am grateful to Aoki in relation to more than human worlds for teaching a way of learning to live in both careful and exhilarating ways. I carry this gratitude as a blessing and a burden toward all influences inside and outside my life, and everything coming to writing.

Echo Four

CURRICULUM IN A RENEWED FFRIDD: Welcome to echo four. This echo is for you to further these words and the spaces among them! I invite you to take a risk on writing in different ways... toward a new dawn.

In Welsh, dawns translates as dance. Here are two Ogham calligraphies for dawns, expressed vertically and horizontally, as well as one for Haleliwia (see Figure 5.2).

Remembering Aoki's (1996/2005) call on artists to kindle afire the word curriculum (p. 423), I invite you to wander among a cultural ffridd in your own life, and be open to bringing curriculum to life in more ecologically compassionate ways. Good luck!

92   J. Price

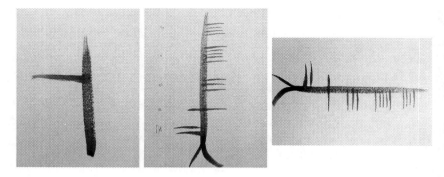

Figure 5.2 Haleliwia and Oak, Pine, Alder, Ash, and Willow Trees | Illustrations and Collage: Joanne Price; Image (left): People recognize Haleliwia with a vertical and horizontal line to the left;[5] Image (middle and right): In Ogham, dd refers to an oak; a – pine, w/f – alder, n – ash, and s – willow.

Notes

1. Snowber and Bickel (2015) describe wit*h*nessing as both witnessing and withness (p. 72–76).
2. Abey is a rootprint of abeyance, meaning to bend or curve. In ffridd, I abide with words as they shape my mind in relation to theirs, and are lived (Price, 2020).
3. Abashen is a root word of abeyance, and related to abey. It refers to losing and finding composure.
4. A rootprint of abeyance, esbair refers to being astonished and is a derivative of *bäee* meaning opening.
5. Deriving from people's relationships with Haleliwia itself, the vertical line is said to be rooted in a wish for each other to be happy.

References

Aoki, T. T. (1979/2005). Reflections of a Japanese Canadian teacher experiencing ethnicity. In W. F. Pinar & R. L. Irwin (Eds.), *Curriculum in a new key: The collected works of Ted. T. Aoki* (pp. 333–348). Lawrence Erlbaum.

Aoki, T. T. (1986/1991/2005). Teaching as indwelling between two worlds. In W. F. Pinar & R. L. Irwin (Eds.), *Curriculum in a new key: The collected works of Ted. T. Aoki* (pp. 159–165). Lawrence Erlbaum.

Aoki, T. T. (1990/2005). Sonare and videre: A story, three echoes, and a lingering note. In W. F. Pinar & R. L. Irwin (Eds.), *Curriculum in a new key: The collected works of Ted. T. Aoki* (pp. 367–376). Lawrence Erlbaum.

Aoki, T. T. (1991/2005). The sound of pedagogy in the silence of the morning calm. In W. F. Pinar & R. L. Irwin (Eds.), *Curriculum in a new key: The collected works of Ted. T. Aoki* (pp. 389–401). Lawrence Erlbaum.

Aoki, T. T. (1992/2005). Layered voices of teaching: The- uncannily correct and the elusively true. In W. F. Pinar & R. L. Irwin (Eds.), *Curriculum in a new key: The collected works of Ted. T. Aoki* (pp. 187–197). Lawrence Erlbaum.

Aoki, T. T. (1993/2005). Humiliating the Cartesian ego. In W. F. Pinar & R. L. Irwin (Eds.), *Curriculum in a new key: The collected works of Ted. T. Aoki* (pp. 291–301). Lawrence Erlbaum.

Aoki, T. T. (1996/2005). Spinning inspirited images in the midst of planned and live(d) curricula. In W. F. Pinar & R. L. Irwin (Eds.), *Curriculum in a new key: The collected works of Ted. T. Aoki* (pp. 413–423). Lawrence Erlbaum.

Breverton, T. (2012). *The physicians of Myddfai: Cures and remedies of the medieval world*. Cambria Books.

Cixous, H., & Calle-Gruber, M. (1997). *Rootprints: Memory and life writing*. Routledge.

Cole, P. (2016). Education in an era of climate change: Conversing with ten thousand voices. *TCI: Transnational Curriculum Inquiry, 13*(1), 3–13.

da Silva, D. F. (2014). Toward a Black poet*h*ics: The quest(ion) of Blackness toward the end of the world. *The Black Scholhar, 44*(2), 81–97.

Gerofsky, S. (Ed.) (2018). *Contemporary environmental and mathematics education modelling using new geometric approaches. Geometries of liberation*. Palgrave Macmillan.

Leggo, C., Sameshima, P., Fidyk, A., & James, K. (2017). *Poetic inquiry: Enchantment of place*. Vernon Press.

Mountain, H. (1998). *The Celtic encyclopaedia*. UPublish.

Price, J. (2020). *Journeying with abeyance: A Welsh cultural approach to contemplative connection with the living world*. University of British Columbia: Vancouver. http://hdl.handle.net/2429/73507

Retallack, J. (2003). *The poethical wager*. The University of California.

Snowber, C., & Bickel, B. (2015). Companions with mystery: Art, spirit and the ecstatic. In Walsh, S., Bickel, B., & Leggo, C. (Eds.) *Arts-based and contemplative practices in research and teaching: Honoring presence* (pp. 67–87). Routledge.

Wall Kimmerer, R. (2003). *Gathering moss: A natural and cultural history of mosses*. Oregon State University Press.

6 "That's My Way"
Indwelling between the Two Worlds of Piano Teaching

Jee Yeon Ryu

In this chapter,[1] I share three autoethnographic stories and reflective narratives about the importance and value of children's individual ways of exploring music and piano playing.[2] Inspired by the teachings of Ted T. Aoki, I explore children's own unique ways of learning to play the piano and share examples of the joys and challenges of my everydayness as a piano teacher.

To convey a sense of wonder, respect, and appreciation for my students' ways of exploring music and piano playing, I write in a style of "small stories" (Nutbrown, 2011) and "tales" (van Maanen, 2011) that are reminiscent of short, impressionistic vignettes to illustrate the meaningful and memorable teaching and learning moments and experiences from my piano studio.

In my stories, I draw attention to what matters most in our lessons. I focus on my students' emergent ideas, questions, and stories that inspire our piano learning. I highlight their personal, individual ways of making meaningful musical experiences through piano playing. All the stories are also written in the present tense to draw the readers immediately into the conversations, ideas, and experiences that my students and I are sharing with one another.

And so, please join us as we use the beautiful seashells as tiny drums to accompany our piano improvisations, sing and make up new words and melodies to our songs, and have fun teaching our favourite little stuffed animals to play the piano.

Let's discover why it is important to learn about the day when my student lost her tooth and how another learned to play his very first song on the piano. Let's explore how we like to improvise our own music and enjoy playing everything backwards from what may be notated in our music scores.

> We have many stories to share with you,
> many questions to explore.
> We welcome you to our happy piano play,
> our own wondrous journeys in (re)making meaningful discoveries,
> connections, experiences, and memories through creative music and
> piano playing.

DOI: 10.4324/9781003037248-10

My Way #1: Using the Seashells as Tiny Drums

Cecilia lost a tooth today.

"Two more to go," she smiles.

Today is a very special day for her. She is wearing a beautiful bright yellow cheetah print dress and holding out an empty tooth necklace case that she wants to show me. She also brought in all the beautiful seashells she found at the beach in West Vancouver.

"These are for you!" she says as she reaches in for the seashells in her two little hand pockets. They are so pretty ... in all different shades of white ... White Smoke ... Snow ... Seashell White... Floral White ... Linen... and Splashed White ... so beautiful...

When I ask her if she would like to create a song about her seashells or the missing tooth, she replies with sparkles in her eyes, "How about *both*?"

So, Cecilia and I start improvising on the piano about how she lost a tooth today and how she found so many seashells in West Vancouver.

"Can I use the seashells as tiny drums?" she asks.

"Seashells can be our special little instruments," I reply with a smile.

As I place my hands on the piano ready to play, Cecilia places her seashells across the piano keys. When I try to match my playing to her seashells, she tries to match hers to mine. As I continue to improvise on the piano, Cecilia quietly plays along with her seashells.

From time to time, she comes back to the piano and happily twinkles along few notes on the treble keys.

And, when I ask her about the title for our music, she cries out, while showing off her proudly missing tooth, "A *fire* shell!"

* * *

For Cecilia, the beautiful seashells inspired her piano playing. As soon as she walked into the studio, she asked me to close my eyes because she had a big surprise for me. She then asked me to start guessing and shared little clues until she couldn't wait any longer to show me what she was hiding inside her two little pockets.

Like Cecilia, many of my students bring surprises for me. Sometimes, they pick a leaf or wild berries on their way to our lesson. Other times, they bring colourful bracelets or necklaces that they made with their friends. I have students who proudly keep me informed about their new Pokémon cards or the Lego sets that they are working on at home.

"I have something to show you," they like to say.

So, my students and I like to talk about all the things that they bring for me. They love to share stories about what happened at school or at home during the week. I learn about their fights in the playground, birthday parties, or the weekend trips that they are looking forward to.

From week to week, we talk about many things that matter for us.

Every day, they include me in their life stories.

And, whenever there are little gifts and surprises, we use them as our inspirations to explore our piano playing. On some days, they become our special instruments for our improvisations. On other days, we create our own music to tell stories about the surprises.

By focusing on our stories, ideas, questions, and wonders about music and piano playing, my students and I are always in search for more meaningful, joyful ways of learning about music and piano playing with one another.

For us,
our weekly surprises
are our pedagogical gifts.
Our life stories,
everyday experiences,
and all the things that matter
in our everyday lives invite meaningful,
joyful ways of learning to play the piano.

* * *

"What shall I teach [today]? How shall I teach?"
(Aoki, 1986/1991/2005, p. 161)

From exploring music and piano playing with my students, I am learning that the basis for musical growth of young piano learners needs to begin with sound explorations (Moorhead & Pond, 1941, p. 17). Children love to play with sound. For them, music making is an integral, natural, and inseparable part of their lives, and they require time and space to explore and play with music, as well as to pursue their own musical interests, curiosities, and purposes.

Aoki's question above: "*What* shall I teach [today]? *How* shall I teach?" (Aoki, 1986/1991/2005, p. 161), when applied to young children, requires much unstructured free play that includes, supports, and nurtures their ever-changing interests and needs in exploring music and piano playing. Their questions and ideas are wonderfully colourful, imaginative, and creative.

For those reasons, we need to take time with all the conversations and the extra musical exploration in the lessons. What may seemingly have nothing to do with music and piano playing may have a great deal to do with the child's reality, and developing a sense of well-being through respect and empathy (Gouzouasis & Ryu, 2015, p. 410). Even though some activities, such as playing with the little seashells as tiny drums may at times appear to be meaningless or unrelated to piano lessons, they could have a greater significance for young children. What might appear as quick changes and distractions in young students' attention spans, behaviours, and activities may in fact be connected to their own individual purposes, meanings, and experiences. What we may think as irrelevant and distractive in one moment could incite new ideas, directions, and possibilities.

In the moment, children's interests, questions, and ideas are invaluable to keeping our lessons meaningful, alive, and moving (Aoki, 1986/1991/2005, p. 161). Their curiosities, ideas, and unique ways of learning to play the piano inspires me as a teacher to listen and be attuned (Aoki, 1986/1991/2005, p. 161) to the care that requires openness and compassion for my students' own personal ways of exploring music and piano playing. The quality of children's piano learning experience is deeply guided by teachers' pedagogical ways of being in presence with their students (Aoki, 1987/2005, p. 361).

> There are many ways
> to teach and learn
> to play the piano.
> My students humble me
> with their creative and imaginative
> ways of thinking about music and piano playing.
> What I teach
> and how I teach
> needs to connect with
> the aliveness of my students'
> ever-present living experiences.

My Way #2: Teaching Little Fuzzy to Play the Piano

Sandy quietly holds my hand as we walk down the hall to our piano studio. As I whisper, "I'm happy to see you again," she quickly whispers back to me, "I'm happy to be here."

Sandy is four years old and likes to look for different pink coloured crayons during our piano lessons.

"I love pink," she always reminds me.

Sandy likes to draw her music with various shades of pink.

So, every week, I help her find new colours like the coral pink, crimson, French rose, fuchsia, or lavender pink. Sometimes, she wants a brighter pink and asks for the magenta and Persian rose. Other times, she looks for a softer amaranth pink.

But, today, Sandy doesn't ask for the colourful pink crayons. To my surprise, she just wants to play the piano. As Sandy prepares her ten little fingers ready to play, she says, "Let's play *my* song today."

Delighted, I immediately start to improvise the background accompaniment for her to play along.

But, suddenly, without playing a single note, Sandy changes her mind.

"Where is Fuzzy?" she asks as she tries to stand up on the piano bench.

"*F-u-z-z-y*, where are you?" she calls for her.

As I help her to carefully look over the top of the piano, she reaches for the little bunny stuffed animal tucked away by the music books.

"Ah-ha! There you are!" she smiles.

"I'm going to teach you piano!"

Today, instead of looking for the different shades of pink-coloured crayons, Sandy happily teaches the *Little Fuzzy* the opening melody of *Bunny Foo Foo*.

* * *

Prior to learning *Bunny Foo Foo*, Sandy used to play *Mary Had a Little Lamb*.

But, before we could start playing the piano, she always looked for the little stuffed animals hiding between the piano books.

Every time, Sandy carefully placed them by the edge of the piano so that they could listen to our piano playing.

"*Fuzzy* will be audience," she said.

Instead of using her fingers to play the notes on the piano, Sandy would try to play the melody by pressing down the arms and legs of the animals into the piano keys. She also liked creating her own music by making up new songs for each of the furry friends that we have in our studio.

For the cheetah and the dinosaur, we might play very fast and loud music. For the turtle and the snail, we usually think of very slow and quiet songs. For her very favourite stuffed animal, our *Little Fuzzy*, we always like to make up a very happy, lively, and jumpy piano music.

However, when I first met Sandy, she was not very interested in learning to play the piano. Sandy just wanted to draw pictures for me in our lessons.

"Can I draw you something?"

So, during the first several weeks of our lessons, we spent most of our time drawing pictures or talking about everything else that interested her on the day. Instead of focusing our attention on playing new songs and learning the names of the piano keys and notes, we shared long conversations about finding new names for all of Sandy's favourite pink colours.

Then, in one of the lessons, I noticed that our *Little Fuzzy* had a pink nose. That was the moment when I was finally able to connect Sandy's love for the pink colour with *Mary Had a Little Lamb*.

"Sandy, look—Guess what colour our *Little Fuzzy* has on her nose?" I asked with hopes of catching her attention.

"Pink," she joyfully shouted as she immediately stopped drawing and picked up the stuffed animal for a closer look.

"I didn't know her nose was pink!"

She was so happy.

On that day, Sandy nicknamed the stuff animal as our *Little Fuzzy*. As we happily hummed and played our first melody, *Mary Had a Little Lamb*, we started changing the words to *Sandy Has a Little Fuzzy*.

By the end of the lesson, we were laughing and giggling as we sang our *Little Fuzzy Has a Pink Nose*.

"Sandy has a Little Fuzzy,
Little Fuzzy, Little Fuzzy,
Sandy has a Little Fuzzy,
She has a bright pink nose ..."

* * *

"Teaching as a mode of being."
(Aoki, 1986/1991/2005, p. 163)

In addition to the development of strong music reading skills and techniques, I am learning that valuing what children have to say, what they want to explore, or how they like to express music and piano playing are more critical to young students' early piano learning experiences.

In our lessons, it is not always possible for us to be playing the piano at all times.

My students have many things to say.

They have endless questions.

We have stories that need to be shared and ideas that require in-depth exploration.

That is why our piano lessons need to remain spontaneous and flexible.

Many times, we stop in between our piano playing to talk about all the things that my students wish to share with me. Often times, there are days when we don't even play the song from the beginning to the end. We simply move on to another piece or to a different activity without ever finishing what we started. After playing the few notes in a melody, we might talk about what happened on the day at the school or playground.

There are many moments in our lessons when I need to put aside my own interests, assumptions, and goals of teaching (Aoki, 1986/1991/2005, p. 160). In being with young children, my lesson planning and objectives do not always work out in the ways that I imagined or hoped for. The process of learning to play the piano needs flexibility and spontaneity because children have their imaginative ways of exploring music and piano playing. They bring stories, ideas, and questions that do not necessarily relate to music. No matter how much I prepare and plan for the lessons, I always need to be ready to adjust, change, and respond to my students' immediate interests, questions, and ways of being in the moment (Aoki, 1986/1991/2005, p. 160). To have truly meaningful piano learning experiences, I practice being present to the (un)planned moments and possibilities in our piano lessons (Ryu, 2017a, p. 300).

For those reasons, we constantly move beyond the topics and lessons that I have in mind for my students. I give them my full, undivided attention to what they have to say, feel, and think about all the things that capture their curiosities, interests, and wonder. As Aoki encourages us in the quote above, I practice piano teaching "as a mode of being," fully attuned to the care that calls from the very living moments that I share with my students (Aoki, 1986/1991/2005, pp. 161–163).

No matter what I may have prepared and planned for the day, I give precedence to all the things that my students wish to share with me at any given time. I remind myself that listening to each other, both musically and verbally, plays a critical role in young children's experiences of learning to play the piano. I practice attending to the uniqueness and particularity of the ways in which we encounter, interact, and experience music and piano playing.

Whether my students' stories, ideas, and questions are directly, indirectly, or completely (un)related to music and piano playing, I value and respect everything that they wish to explore and share with me.

> Whatever that my students may
> wish to explore at the time
> is when it matters deeply.
> Take the time to listen,
> explore, and embrace
> children's ways
> of being.
> Embrace the shared moments
> as opportunities for discovering new
> possibilities for music and piano playing.

My Way #3: Playing Everything Backwards

Tyler is learning to play *Monster March* for his Halloween concert, and he insists that he plays the whole piece while standing up.

"I don't need the bench," he says as he pushes it away from the piano.

He always has his own style of playing the piano. Most of all, Tyler likes to play everything the opposite from what is written on the music score.

"I want to play it backwards!" he insists.

When there is a dynamic marking for *forte*, he plays it *piano*. When he sees a dynamic marking for *piano*, he purposefully plays it as loud as he can. Any *legato* melody turns into jumpy *staccato* notes. Any longer notes become as short as possible.

And, the short notes?

Well, he likes to stretch them out, and he holds them for a very long time until the notes eventually stop resonating.

"I'm doing the *extra* stuff, but in *my* way," he likes to remind me.

Every week, Tyler adds the extra musical ideas, and we talk about how there are so much more than just the notes in our music.

But, he always has his own ways of adding the extra musical ideas. Moreover, each time Tyler plays something wonderfully extravagant, like screaming out his notes while crashing into the bass keys of the piano, he loves to check for my reactions.

"Was it scary enough? Are you surprised?"

He asks *every* time.

* * *

Instead of following the directions and notations indicated by the composers, Tyler likes to play the songs in his ways.

Sometimes, he changes the rhythm. Other times, he either adds or omits the notes. Tyler also enjoys making up his own words.

Most recently, he is playing all of his music as fast as possible. The more he likes the songs, the faster he plays them.

Moreover, Tyler never wants to polish the pieces. Whenever I invite him to think about the extra musical ideas, such as the dynamics, rhythm, and expressions that are notated in the music, he asks, "Why? Why do I *have* to do that?"

I agree.

What if Tyler wants to play everything backwards from the written music? What if he just wants to play all of his songs as fast as possible? Why does Tyler always need to sit on the bench to play the piano? What's wrong with playing the piano while standing up?

For me, it is important that I listen to Tyler play his favourite pieces in his own ways. I wish to encourage him to play everything differently.

Instead of correcting his dynamics, tempo, articulation, and rhythm, I share *his* ways of understanding music. I welcome *his* ways of playing the piano. I value *his* ways of being with music and piano playing.

Whenever Tyler says, "That's my way," I smile and acknowledge his creative efforts in making his own meaningful ways of connecting with music and piano playing.

As for *if* and *when* Tyler might like to think about the composers' extra musical ideas, I remind myself of what he said to me with a big smile on his face, "Sure, one day!"

> *Week after week,*
> *we patiently wait*
> *for that one day.*
> *Until that day,*
> *we let ourselves be.*
> *Together,*
> *we wait for his day,*
> *we wait for his time.*

* * *

"Teaching is… a mode of being-with-others."
Aoki (1987/2005, p. 361)

From young children, I am learning to discover piano teaching as a "mode of being-with-others" (Aoki, 1987/2005, p. 361), and one of the true pedagogical ways of being with my students begins with mindful listening.

The ways in which I listen, react, respond, and value all the things that are meaningful for them will significantly shape and influence their attitudes, understandings, and appreciation for music and piano playing. How I recognize beauty and possibilities in all the things that capture my students' interests, curiosities, and wonder will define their long lasting experiences of meaningful piano playing.

For young children, forming a lifelong connection with piano playing is not only a process that occurs *in* and *through* the music—it is formed *in*, *with*, and *through* the piano teacher (Gouzouasis & Ryu, 2015, p. 407). Thus, my students' experiences of learning to play the piano are greatly influenced and supported by the type of relationship that I develop with them. My ways of being with young children has the capacities to motivate or discourage their curiosities, joy, and growth in exploring music and piano playing.

In acknowledging children as an active participant and contributor in their own learning, we can practice "pedagogic listening" (Aoki, 1993/2005, p. 211) as a collaborative act, a give-and-take process whereby both teachers and students take time to truly listen to one another. As we attentively engage with children's freely moving ideas, interests, and questions, we can create what Aoki calls an "extraordinarily unique and precious place, a hopeful place, a trustful place, a careful place—essentially a human place" (Aoki, 1986/1991/2005, p. 164) wherein both teachers and students are committed to (re)discovering new musical possibilities together.

There is no singular approach to piano teaching and learning that will work for all students because each child has his/her own ways of directing their own learning (p. 162). In each lesson, every moment invites individuality, creativity, imagination, and flexibility for all the different ways in which children (re)discover meaningful music making experiences.

> *There is no one correct or right*
> *way of learning to play the piano.*
> *No two piano playing*
> *are exactly alike.*
> *No two experiences*
> *are ever the same.*
> *Piano teaching and learning*
> *is an ever-present, continuous*
> *process of shared meaning making.*

* * *

Can I play piano *my* way?

All the stories that my students want to tell, the little gifts that they bring, their endless questions, ideas, and unique, individual ways of playing the piano call for my caring attention, response, and enthusiasm.

How I think, feel, and respond to their expressed needs, interests, and ideas matter to young children. It is critical that I sincerely accept my students' ways of being and place great value in enabling them to grow and develop at their own paces.

What my students wish to share, create, and explore matters in our lessons. How they connect with music and piano playing need to direct our learning.

All children have their own ideas about what matters in our lessons. They all have their ways and preferences for piano playing.

Every child is unique in the ways they think, experience, and learn.

They imagine little seashells as tiny drums. They like to teach furry stuffed animals to play the piano. Playing everything backwards and opposite from the written notation can be a meaningful way of learning to play the piano.

With young students, it is very natural for them to move from one new idea to another and continue carrying on conversations in between their piano playing.

However, every time I encounter those pedagogical moments with my students, I find myself conflicted.

On the one hand, I wish to be attentive and carry on with the ideas, stories, and conversations as long as we need to, but on the other hand, I am reminded of my lingering responsibilities, goals, and plans as a piano teacher (Aoki, 1986/1991/2005, p. 160).

In my piano studio, I have many families who ask for a more teacher-directed, technique-oriented, and grade-driven approach to piano instruction. They request that I quickly develop the correct hand positions, postures, and concentrate my lessons on working through the method books and learning to read music notation. They discipline their children to sit quietly and pay attention to me, *the* piano teacher.

Those parents expect us to be ready for the next grade as fast as possible.

They want more piano exams.

They demand results.

And, if we carried conversations about how my students lost a tooth, and anything else that they felt were unrelated to our piano lessons, there are parents who immediately interrupt us, and say, "Okay, now. That's enough. Let's get back to your piano playing. Pay attention to your teacher."

In our piano lessons, we are expected to learn to play the piano. We are asked to read the real notes. We are told that we should be learning more difficult, complex, and longer songs. Instead of children's true, colourful, expressive, improvisatory playing, they are pressured to play the piano by the notation as it is written in the music score.

No more talking about how you lost your first tooth in the lesson.

No more seashells or teaching your little fuzzy friends to play the piano.

No more playing music backwards.

"Piano is serious."

"Time for more practice."

That's what we are told.

And so, in every lesson with each student, I find myself in what Aoki calls the "two curriculum worlds" (Aoki, 1986/1991/2005, p. 159) of piano teaching.

In one of the worlds, I practice being in presence with my students as I listen, play, and be with their own unique, individual ways of exploring music and piano playing.

When they wish to tell me their stories, I listen.

When they ask me their questions, I answer.

In every lesson, my students and I carry on our piano playing as we move freely from one song to the next, from one question to another. We talk about everything that captures our imaginations.

We use seashells as tiny drums to create our own music.

We draw pictures with our favourite crayons.

We like to play the piano standing up or play everything in our music backwards.

In my other world of teaching, I question what it means to *be* piano teaching and learning *with* young children (Aoki, 1986/1991/2005, p. 163). I search for more meaningful ways of integrating their creativity, imagination, and play with the technical and expressive elements of learning to play the piano. Like Aoki, I am learning to teach in "tensionality" (Aoki, 1986/1991/2005, pp. 162–163) as I search for more meaningful ways of connecting the two worlds of piano-as-*plan* and piano-as-*lived* experiences.

Inspired by Aoki's (1987/2005) ways of teaching as a "tactful leading out" (p. 361–362) into the ever-present possibilities, I continue to ask myself: What if teachers could focus their piano curriculum and pedagogy on children's creative and musical ideas? What if teachers and parents openly discussed about each child's own unique, individual ways of exploring music and piano playing? What if we reconsidered the true meanings, possibilities, and experiences of learning to play the piano? What if we can be more open to exploring children's love for sharing their stories, ideas, improvisations, and anything else that capture their curiosities and imagination? What if we could practice more child-centred, emergent approach to piano pedagogy, a way of knowing through music that could bring more creativity to music making and piano playing? What if teachers and parents embraced an (un)planned, improvisational approach to piano teaching and learning that encourages, supports, and values young children's own ways of learning to play the piano? What if there could be more smiles, laughter, and play in our lessons?

By embracing our students' conversations, questions, curiosities, and everything else that they wish to explore and share with me as important, valuable, and critical expressions of what matters most to them and their experiences, we can join our students in their creative, magical ways of exploring music, and piano playing.

In honouring their unique, individual ways of playing the piano with open minds and hearts, we can share more beautiful, playful, and personal ways of discovering wonderful music and piano playing with one another. In searching for what it means to *be* a teacher and what teaching truly *is* (Aoki, 1986/1991/2005, p. 163), we can move toward more "inspiriting" (Aoki, 1987/2005, p. 357) piano pedagogy and curriculum for young children.

As we continue to question and reflect on *what* we teach and *how* we teach (Aoki, 1986/1991/2005, p. 161), we can learn to indwell between the two worlds of exploring music and piano playing with our students.

Together, we can (re)create more joyful, imaginative, and wondrous piano teaching and learning experiences. We can share more smiles, laughter, and stories that bring us happiness, joy, and fun in learning to play the piano (Ryu, 2018).

My students' own ideas, stories, and musical journeys
are our constant inspirations and foundation
for (re)creating meaningful experiences,
connections, and lasting memories
with music and piano playing.
I am grateful for every moment
I share with my students.
They are my teachers,
my inspirations.

Notes

1. Children in this chapter are preschool students ages four and five years old.
2. The three autoethnographic stories presented in this paper belong to a collection of stories included in the author's doctoral dissertation (see Ryu, 2017b). For a detailed explanation of my use of autoethnography as a theoretical framework and methodology, see p. 1–28.

References

Aoki, T. T. (1986/1991/2005). Teaching as indwelling between two curriculum worlds. In W. F. Pinar & R. L. Irwin (Eds.), *Curriculum in a new key: The collected works of Ted. T. Aoki* (pp. 159–165). Lawrence Erlbaum.

Aoki, T. T. (1987/2005a). Inspiriting the curriculum. In W. F. Pinar & R.L. Irwin (Eds.), *Curriculum in a new key: The collected works of Ted T. Aoki* (pp. 357–365). Lawrence Erlbaum.

Aoki, T. T. (1993/2005). Legitimating lived curriculum: Toward a curricular landscape of multiplicity. In W. F. Pinar & R. L. Irwin (Eds.), *Curriculum in a new key: The collected works of Ted T. Aoki* (pp. 199–215). Lawrence Erlbaum.

Gouzouasis, P., & Ryu, J. (2015). A pedagogical tale from the piano studio: Autoethnography in early childhood music education research. *Music Education Research, 17*(4), 397–420.

Moorhead, G., & Pond, D. (1941). *Music of young children, I: Chant.* Pillsbury Foundation for the Advancement of Music Education.

Nutbrown, C. (2011). A box of childhood: Small stories at the roots of a career. *International Journal of Early Years, 19*(3–4), 1–16.

Ryu, J. (2017a). Deweyan fragments: Erasure poetry, music, and a story. In P. Sameshima, K. James, C. Leggo, & A. Fidyk (Eds.), *Poetic inquiry III: Enchantment of place* (pp. 297–304). Vernon Press.

Ryu, J. (2017b). *Exploring music and piano playing with young children: A piano teacher's pedagogical stories* (Doctoral dissertation). University of British Columbia. https://open.library.ubc.ca/cIRcle/collections/ubctheses/24/items/1.0362235

Ryu, J. (2018). I wish, I wonder, and everything I like: Living stories of piano teaching and learning with young children. *LEARNing Landscapes, 11*(2), 319–330.

van Maanen, J. (2011). *Tales of the field: On writing ethnography* (2nd ed.). The University of Chicago Press.

Interlude
Letters from Ted

Karen Meyer

> *Dear Karen:-*
> *Following our conversation over sushi…*

I came to know Ted's script much like recognizing his facial expressions or tones in his voice. He wrote all correspondence by hand. I learned Ted-calligraphy, down to how he crossed a "t". He rarely crossed out a word (see Figure Int.2). About 150 words covered a page in straight lines under various letterhead affiliations. "Over" and page numbers indicated more to come. To close, he offered kind words, while a "ps" left a particular point I might ponder: *I thought you won't mind me throwing in a few words to make things messier for you!*

Ted's correspondence as teacher and mentor remains a keepsake for me. I browse through his texts from time to time. Reading them in hindsight, I appreciate his foresight into scholarship on the fringe of curriculum studies 20 plus years ago. Even now, I study his insight into pedagogy—still a lucid beacon I share with practicing teachers. I'm grateful for our conversations back then over sushi lunches, which continued in his letters. Ted wrote:

> Ever since we last conversed, the word "scholarship" has been haunting me insistently … "Scholarship"—a master signifier of the Academy in the <u>uni</u>verse of the <u>uni</u>versity with its own legitimated discourse. I cannot help but beckon Derrida's not too well-known article, "Canons and Metonymies"…

The sequence of Ted's letters tells a story from beginning to end—my five-year tenure as director of an academic unit focussed on curriculum, I call the Centre (1998–2003). Like Alice, I had fallen down a deep rabbit hole, too raw to seek out a mentor. At nearly 80, Ted stepped in. He already knew the territory around this unit to be politically contentious. I believe Ted saw promise in me, the naïve pro(an)tangonist. For those five years, he walked beside me as teacher, pointing to what he thought I needed to know in the world of ideas. As mentor, he pointed out warning "signs" wrapped in slippery signifiers of academic discourse. From him, I learned the

Notes:

Re. Draft Green Paper (CSCI)

Synopsis: The articulation-in-process of a vitalized CSCI mandate.

Note 1. — 20 Some years ago when the Centre was first founded the going curricular language subscribed to Ralph Tyler's metanarrative that embraced the instrumental linearity of C & I (Curriculum and Instruction) in which the "and" was really a "→", from curriculum-as-master plan through instruction to "structure" the givens "into" the learners. In spite of this handicap in the lake of the centre, the draft disrupts such linearity by scripting in the language of interdisciplin[arity] which marks out not only the interspaces midst disciplines, but also the inter-textual, inter-socio-cultural and inter-gender spaces.

Note 2: The draft embraces lived and living curricula marking out the living sites of teachers and students in dialogically textured spaces. The emphasis on "community" (living communally) points to such imaginary.

Note 3: The focus on ~~both~~ scholarship in both scholarly practice and pedagogical practice subscribes to a non-linear relation

Figure Int.2: A Letter from Ted | Image: Karen Meyer.

whereabouts of obstacles wrapped in language and opened myself to unconventional choices. My motto became: Obstacles aren't moments of truth, but moments of choice.

Ted's letters became a sort of epistolary pedagogy, wherein he offered critical thoughts on prevalent and marginal scholarship, often outside education. Sometimes he added an article or chapter to a letter: *I've also included Maxine Greene's recent paper wherein she is wrestling with The Crisis of Representation. I feel she's still struggling* .... I could linger in an underlined passage or read his commentary in the margins of any such text. For example, he wrote *not learning but recollection* and *the impossibility of teaching* on the first page of "Psychoanalysis and Education," a chapter he copied for me from Shoshana Felman's book, *Jacques Lacan and the Adventure of Insight*.

In several letters, Ted explained the Centre's history from his perspective as its first director (1976–1978). *I left* [the Centre] *to chair the Department of Secondary Education in 1978 till retirement in 1985.*

Ted included the following candid anecdote in a letter:

> When I became first director of the Centre here, I organized a curric. symposium and featured Mike Apple just getting to be known. (It was in Seoul about four years ago that we lived in memories of our experiences two decades+ ago!)

I came on board as director two decades later, following two interim directors. Freshly promoted and tenured, I showed signs of institutional promise. But in this admin position, I arrived a naïve newcomer.

Before my appointment, Ted wrote to me in February of 1998 with his first correspondence:

> Dear Karen:
> I heard of your nomination as director of the Curriculum Centre. I wish you the best. For whatever they are worth, my thoughts. ...
> How do I envision the difference between the Centre and the curriculum departments? The curriculum departments are designated primarily by the disciplines: language curriculum, science curriculum, social studies curriculum, etc. The centrality of disciplines is very notable and movement to the margins already resumes centrality of the discipline's core. Hence, interest in interDISCIPLINARITY is characterized by the prior existence of disciplines.
> The Center (CSCI) accommodates those who may be oriented towards INTERdisciplinarity, where the space of INTER can be considered its significant location: a different positioning and a positioning that can accommodate both "disciplinarity and interdisciplinarity," a site where I see you positioning yourself.

Ted taught several courses for the Centre during my tenure. I drove to his home and picked him up on his teaching days. Before each course, he sent me notes and drafts of hand-written syllabi. In one such draft he wrote:

> Conventionally, the word "curriculum" is bounded within a discursive space wherein stands a master curriculum-as-plan overloading the shaping of "implementation,", "instruction" and "assessment/evaluation." Here, we might recognize curriculum-as-live(d) allowing us to locate ourselves in the interspace between curriculum-as-plan and curriculum-as-lived— a site of the living practices of teaching/learning.

Even 20 years ago, letter writing remained rare—perhaps one reason I kept all Ted's correspondence, this collection of over 60 hand-written texts. Always, his salutations stirred a smile. He put time and care into each letter, his way of looking after me. In response, I called Ted on the phone, or invited him to lunch where conversation continued. In script or in our conversation, I found his attention and intention toward academic landscapes critically clear. He spoke candidly and, at times, confidentially.

I can't say I followed all his rhizomatic lines of thought, or exactly what he meant by "the metonymic space of living". As mentor, Ted engaged me in understanding my discursive whereabouts when lost *and* found in that deep rabbit hole of the academy. As teacher, he pushed me to reinterpret and relocate "curriculum" as a critical site of living practice.

That said, I will always deeply appreciate his cheerful, generous, and humble approach to life. My beacon.

With warm regards Ted,
Karen

Part 3
Curricular and Pedagogical Contexts
Introduction

Lesley E. Wong

In this part, the chapters by Lesley E. Wong, Kshamta Hunter, and Margaret O'Sullivan resonate with Aoki's contribution to curriculum and pedagogy. They engage with Aokian discourse and explore three distinct themes: (1) Wong from their relationship with technology; (2) Hunter through her experience in sustainability education; and (3) O'Sullivan from the perspective of a music educator. Each author shares the intricacies and complexities within each of their disciplines, offering the possibility that "critically reflective orientations may lead us further along the way" (Aoki, 1978/1980/2005, p. 110) and informing curricular and pedagogical paths and transformations (see Figure P.3).

Throughout his writings, Aoki considered numerous contexts to engage his readers and bring clarity to his theoretical explorations and pedagogical and curricular insights. As a university representative (Aoki, 1996/2005), a delegate at a conference (Aoki, 1991/2005b), a teacher in his own elementary school classroom (Aoki, 1993/2005), an observer in Miss O's classroom (Aoki, 1986/1991/2005), a professor and supervisor to his own graduate student (Aoki, 1987/1999/2005), and as an eyewitness to the formation of his own hybrid identity (Aoki, 1996/2005), Aoki uses context to bring forth implicit ways of being-in-the-world, the importance of focusing on the curriculum-as-lived, and as a demonstration of what it means "to be able to see what is right in a situation" (Aoki, 1987/1999/2005, p. 155). Speaking from an embeddedness within specific contexts, Wong, Hunter, and O'Sullivan explore Aokian approaches of discernment, in the commitment to a pedagogy that is right for each unique situation.

The authors articulate the tensions experienced within their own context and discipline, from calls of instrumentalization and implementation (Aoki, 1983/2005) to reflections on the implications and expectations driven by

DOI: 10.4324/9781003037248-12

Figure P.3 Nitobe Memorial Garden Path | Photo: Simon Wong.

educators, researchers, facilitators, music education practitioners, and global calls to action. The nuances and complexities of technology, sustainability, and music curriculum that inform the pedagogical histories and traditions of each discipline, becomes the textured landscape by which Wong, Hunter, and O'Sullivan invite the reader to dwell both on the ornamental bridge of in-between spaces and in the third space of possibility (Aoki, 1991/2005a).

Entwining narratives and Aokian understanding, the chapters in this part offer ways in which educators and researchers can linger with Aokian reflections in one's own practice, furthering understandings of selves, students, the needs of others, and the situation at hand. The opportunity to reflect alongside others helps to shift our thinking in the third space of generative multiplicity (Aoki, 1996/2005) so that we may think otherwise within our own contexts, disciplines pedagogies, and curricular choices in ways which enable us to "dwell together humanly" (Aoki, 1991/2005, p. 439). In their writing, we come to share Aoki's own call to notice the "possibilities for empowerment that can nourish transformation of the self and the curriculum reality" (Aoki, 1983, p. 121).

Chapter 7: Walking across Contexts with Technology: An Aokian Methodology—Lesley E. Wong

1. How might lingering inform ourselves and our educational practices with regards to technology?
2. How might one's curricular and pedagogical choices be revisited by dwelling in hybrid and third spaces?
3. What might recognizing pre-existing binaries and the opening of possibilities offer various contexts?

Chapter 8: Visualizing and Reconceptualizing Transformative Sustainability Learning through an Aokian Lens—Kshamta Hunter

1. How does the bridge metaphor offer new possibilities in leadership within other curricular contexts?
2. How can Aoki's work in curriculum implementation and situational praxis assist educators to create connections between sustainability, leadership, and the engagement of young people?
3. How might lingering inform pre-existing frameworks and practical action?

Chapter 9: Listen to What the Situation is Asking: Aoki and Music Education—Margaret O'Sullivan

1. How does listening to a situation shift and impact traditional pedagogies?
2. How does attuned and repeated listening to what the situation is asking reveal ideas, theories, and concepts embedded in practices?
3. How might community education inform curricular discourses?

References

Aoki, T. T. (1978/1980/2005). Toward curriculum inquiry in a new key. In W. F. Pinar & R. L. Irwin (Eds.), *Curriculum in a new key: The collected work of Ted T. Aoki* (pp. 89–110). Lawrence Erlbaum.

Aoki, T. T. (1983/2005). Curriculum implementation as instrumental action and as situational praxis. In W. F. Pinar & R. L. Irwin (Eds.), *Curriculum in a new key: The collected works of Ted T. Aoki* (pp. 111–123). Lawrence Erlbaum.

Aoki, T. T. (1986/1991/2005). Teaching as indwelling between two curriculum worlds. In W. F. Pinar & R. L. Irwin (Eds.), *Curriculum in a new key: The collected works of Ted T. Aoki* (pp. 159–165). Lawrence Erlbaum.

Aoki, T. T. (1987/1999/2005). Toward understanding "computer application". In W. F. Pinar & R. L. Irwin (Eds.), *Curriculum in a new key: The collected works of Ted T. Aoki* (pp. 151–158). Lawrence Erlbaum.

Aoki, T. T. (1991/2005a). Bridges that rim the Pacific. In W. F. Pinar & R. L. Irwin (Eds.), *Curriculum in a new key: The collected works of Ted T. Aoki* (pp. 433–436). Lawrence Erlbaum.

Aoki, T. T. (1991/2005b). Taiko drums and sushi, perogies and sauerkraut: Mirroring a half-life in multicultural curriculum. In W. F. Pinar & R. L. Irwin (Eds.), *Curriculum in a new key: The collected works of Ted T. Aoki* (pp. 377–387). Lawrence Erlbaum.

Aoki, T. T. (1993/2005). Humiliating the Cartesian ego. In W. F. Pinar & R. L. Irwin (Eds.), *Curriculum in a new key: The collected works of Ted T. Aoki* (pp. 291–301). Lawrence Erlbaum.

Aoki, T. T. (1996/2005). Imaginaries of "East and West": Slippery curricular signifiers in education. In W. F. Pinar & R. L. Irwin (Eds.), *Curriculum in a new key: The collected works of Ted T. Aoki* (pp. 313–319). Lawrence Erlbaum.

7 Walking across Contexts with Technology
An Aokian Methodology

Lesley E. Wong

The process of walking through the Nitobe Memorial Garden reflects a personal, autobiographical, interdisciplinary, and cross-curricular approach to looking at multiple contexts; these contexts refer specifically to my own life, my field of research in online learning and cyberbullying, and my teaching practices. In this chapter, I spend time in the Nitobe Memorial Garden, a site where Aoki frequented and drew inspiration for his work, to explore Aokian themes. This approach is one of many ways which scholars can invoke an Aokian methodology, and through this process I explore my relationship with technology in multi-faceted ways. This turn towards an interdisciplinary approach is intentional, as conversations with educators combined with work of media and technology scholars (Code, 2013; Petrina, 2020), literacy researchers (Asselin & Moayeri, 2010; Bulger & Davison, 2018), and cyberbullying experts (Bonanno & Hymel, 2013; Englander, 2019a; Smith, 2015) all recognize that we do not yet have a comprehensive understanding of the effects of technology on youth and our students. When considering my own context, I recognize the important role technology has played in my own life and begin there.

As both a second-generation Canadian and a fifth-generation Canadian, my own identity is complicated and informed by a variety of perspectives. I was born in Canada; however, my great-great-grandfather came to Canada in the late 1880s as a logger. He paid the Chinese head tax and eventually saved enough to also pay for his son to immigrate to Canada and work on the railway. My grandmother was left behind in China, as a result of the Chinese Exclusion Act, and eventually made her own way to Canada with her husband and children many decades later. This curious position as a second- and fifth-generation Canadian provides a unique seat[1] from which I have inherited stories from multiple perspectives, to contemplate several points of view for a multiplicious understanding of what it means to be Chinese-Canadian. My father and his siblings were educated under a Canadian curriculum in Japan to prepare for their family's final destination; like them, I too was educated under a Canadian curriculum, yet I use technology to search what it means to be Chinese-Canadian. Like Aoki, "for many years I have been in search for this identity—searching into my heritage, searching for the ground on which

DOI: 10.4324/9781003037248-13

I stand" (Aoki, 1991/2005b, p. 381). Throughout my life, I have used technology to research moments and places in history to piece together my own identity in an attempt to understand contexts which I no longer have access—either because the storyteller has since passed or that specific place and time can only be accessed through a screen or button. I am too young to fully comprehend the depths of the hardship and strife that Asian–Canadians, like Aoki (1979/2005, p. 335), experienced during Canada's tumultuous past; yet, I am appreciative and can learn from Aoki's reflective approach to his own cultural identity and explore this tensioned bifurcative stance, which is "both this and that," and "neither this nor that" (Aoki, 1996/2005, p. 317).

My own relationship with technology leads me to reminisce the words of Grade 8 research participants from the first research study I designed and conducted (Liu, 2016).[2] Situated in a technology enhanced classroom, these students explored how technology both facilitated and hindered their ability to collaborate with each other. In turn, the experiences of these adolescent collaborators help me to revitalize my approach to technology in the classroom as a workshop educator with the Centre for Teaching and Learning Technology and graduate facilitator for the Instructional Skills Workshop (ISW) at The University of British Columbia (UBC).

Walking across these multiple contexts generates a new space and provides a context from which to contemplate, reflect, and linger (Aoki, 1996/2005). This chapter examines three of Aoki's themes: (1) the limits of binaries; (2) instrumentalism and praxis; and (3) bridges of lingering and multiplicity, and how they speak to the role of technology in the classroom and the lives of students. I begin this process with a walk through the Nitobe Memorial Garden, a place Aoki frequently returns to in his work, and a place which I find grounding in the tangible and real. In the context of the Nitobe Memorial Garden, I unlock memories of my own lived experiences with the three Aokian themes, in relation to my own experience with technology, the experiences of adolescent research participants in a technology enhanced classroom, and reflections on my research and own teaching practices which are indebted to technology during the COVID-19 pandemic. Although the contexts differ, the same message has relevancy: allowing space to contemplate across contexts is vital to delve into our own educational practices, especially during a time that includes technology.

Limiting Binaries

In the centre of the Nitobe Memorial Garden is a small structure, formally called the "Family Viewing Pavilion" as indicated on my map. Early in the morning, I am enveloped by the silence and my solitude, and take in my surroundings. Here I stand in a cultivated Japanese garden, which sits inside a forested area, which is surrounded by architectural buildings that frame the skyline of the Vancouver campus at UBC, located on the traditional, ancestral, and unceded territory of the Musqueam people. I consider where I am situated and my context. Surrounded by natural wilderness, cultivated gardens, and human-made structures, am I in nature or an urban city? I see the top of the next building between the peaks of two trees and hear the echo of car engines in the parking structure, yet I still hear and feel the echo of calm in the garden. From where I stand, I see both ends of this spectrum and can observe this binary. These binary questions play back a memory of rejected paperwork. I was about to embark on my first trip to Asia—Kyoto, Japan—for my teaching practicum. The first step to tracing a twenty-year migratory path made by my father's family across Asia. An arrow drawn in red-ballpoint pen points to a problem area with my form: "What is your nationality?" In my haste and excitement, I had written Chinese-Canadian, and beneath my response was the comment, "Are you Chinese or Canadian?" Yes, I was born in Canada, but simply writing 'Canadian' seemed to lose the depth of my identity. Yet, how could I simply write Chinese, if I had never been to China and my identity was wrapped in cultural practices passed down, practiced, and blended with Thai, Vietnamese, and Japanese ingredients and items that were borrowed out of necessity but then became an intercultural practice for our family? Grappling with these limiting binaries confounding my own view, of my own identity, I quickly wrote "Canadian," and resubmitted my paperwork to be on my way.

In Chapter 18, "Imaginaries of 'East and West:' Slippery Curricular Signifiers in Education" (1996/2005), Aoki examines the problems of dealing with binaries in the context of his own cultural identity. "The labels 'East' and 'West' suggest two distinct cultural wholes, 'Eastern culture' and 'Western culture,' each identifiable, standing distinctly and separately from each other" (p. 315), in a "modernist binary discourse of 'this or that'" (p. 317), and this distinct separation emphasizes difference rather than "a becoming in the space of difference" (p. 318). When contemplating whether I was Canadian or Chinese, I recall Aoki's own experience with interculturalism and how he too was asked, "Are you Japanese or are you Canadian?"; in this moment, Aoki observes how others can urge us to open ourselves and help us in our own self-understanding (Aoki, 1991/2005b, p. 382). Aoki continues his argument against the limits of binaries and extends this to the context of education, technology, and instrumentalization in "Humiliating the Cartesian Ego" (1993/2005). This polarizing view is also problematic in the context of education, in that ascribing to an "in or out" view, we can completely miss opportunities of alternative possibilities, which Aoki calls "the landscape of this and that, and more" (p. 294) or the "landscape of multiplicity" (p. 297); in opening our mindset from a binary way of thinking, we shift from a limiting perspective to a landscape with many ways of doing and being. He speaks of the valorizing framework of the either/or binary and asks how it can lure individuals to be either "boosters" or "knockers" of technology (Aoki, 1993/2005, p. 294). My own confrontation with the limiting modernist binary of identity, reminds me of my Grade 8 students research participants' interactions within cloud-based spaces for collaborative work.

In reflecting on the problematic limits of binaries, I recall a student who recognized the experience of solely communicating through text through a chat box. The lack of visual cues, when compared to in-person or video communication, enabled the students to realize its effect on the social dynamics of their group. Their experiences in online spaces and in-person spaces helped their group open themselves to other ways of communication in their project:

> I think it's harder to do when you're on an online space, versus just being together, because when you're together it's easier to talk it out or find someone who can be a moderator and help talk it out. When you're online, it's hard to communicate more truthfully, because you could say anything or you could not say anything and they can't read your face. So they don't know if you're actually comfortable. I think that it's very important that everyone is comfortable.
>
> (Liu, 2016)

The observations of each space assisted this group in recognizing the limitations of each form of communication, which led this group of four boys to designing other ways of working together: they designed their own set of parameters for communicating and clarifying with each other.

These students were neither "boosters" nor "knockers" of technology (Aoki, 1993/2005, p. 294); sidestepping the limiting perspective of being for or against technology, these adolescents suggest a third option: A mixture and balance of both to generate understanding. The students' shift from miscommunication to mutual understanding is afforded by opening themselves to a blended practice and way of interacting.

By reflecting on my own teaching practice, I pay attention to my research participants' experiences in each side of the binary. In a wholly text-based space of communication, the boys were not able to fully express themselves and expressed a lack of visual cues. Thus, in my ISW session, I ensure that my students have multiple ways of communicating and expressing themselves to avoid misrepresentation and miscommunication, and to build a sense of community. During the COVID-19 pandemic, being physically present is not possible, thus I encourage other technologies which will enhance and open up possibilities of doing and being. Those who are artistic are given opportunities to communicate through drawing and speaking alongside their actions. Students who enjoy visual representations of themselves have the option to present a series of photos during initial class introductions. As I learn about my students' individual needs and preferences for ways of being and communicating, I open my seminar to online spaces, video-call moments, and email communications for questions, both within individual and group settings. By focusing on opening spaces and giving students access to a landscape of multiplicity, my students are able to shift their mindsets from working within the parameters of their own limited class settings and instead focus on the opening experiences they want to offer their own students.

I set foot from the pavilion and follow the circular path of the garden.

Distinguishing Instrumentalism from Praxis

As I round the curved path of the Nitobe Memorial Garden, the gravel beneath the soft soles of my shoes echo throughout the empty garden during my early morning walk. The clicking of the stones transports me back in time and I am sitting at my grandparents' kitchen table, feet unable to touch the ground, staring at the abacus in my grandfather's hand. The stained wood frame and rounded beads are evenly discoloured from use but unwarped, despite having survived the monsoon seasons of Thailand, the humidity of dense jungles in Vietnam, and the coastal sea air of Japan. My grandfather shakes the bead and hands me his claim to mathematical understanding from his university days in Shanghai. Recognizing my blank stare, my grandmother retrieves two jars from the pantry. She sorts black eyed beans into two piles for counting and pours grains of broken rice onto the vinyl table covering to explain fractions. Heads bowed, we three pour over familiar objects and save the abacus for a future lesson.

The memory of the abacus reminds me of how, at times, we can become so intent on the outcome, that we neglect to see who is in front of us. We prioritize efficiency, productivity, and possible results in our students that we can skip ahead and neglect to prioritize a relationship with our students, forget to build a relationship between the subject-matter and our students, or fail to recognize what our students already know and miss the opportunity to draw from their own lived experience.

In "The Dialectic of Mother Language and Second Language: A Curriculum Exploration" (1987/1991/2005), Aoki urges educators to look go beyond the surface application of a technological lifestyle. In examining a technicized approach to second language acquisition, he comments that when "language thus becomes a means to an end, a tool to permit the expression of preexisting thought" (p. 236) then "instrumentalized language is disembodied of the social and cultural crucible that alone engenders life within language" (p. 237). Aoki speaks to how language that is apart from its culture results in language and culture being alienated, "remaining in a nondialectical relationship, closed to the dynamic tension" between the two (p. 237). Culture is the connecting context and meaningful part of the lived experience of learning. Aoki reminds us:

> Each of us is born into a concrete language of our mother tongue. This mother language with which we are at home is the language belonging to a community—a language of sharing, a language of familiarity, a vernacular language of daily conversation, a language with a profound respect of the other as self.
>
> (Aoki, 1987/1991/2005, p. 239)

Aoki's words harken to my own memories of the abacus, unfamiliar and without meaning, and lead me to reflect on a conversation between two Grade 8 research participants, situated in a technology enhanced classroom. One student says:

> I find that a balance between actual physical communication while also using the help of online technology ... is the ideal way, personally ... Last year in my elementary school, our teacher was really technology centralized .... I never learned anything because he never regulated and never checked on us. He just wanted to see us on the computers at school on the website and that was all he asked for.
>
> (Liu, 2016)

Her classmate nods and responds:

> You can't just revolve learning or education around technology. There's a need for hands on work or physical communications like one-to-one communication. Emotions can also influence somebody's learning experience, but technology doesn't always include that within the experience that you may have. There should be a balanced view and value between technology and personal and physical communication.
>
> (Liu, 2016)

Both girls nod in unison. Their classmates' past experiences with a technology centric curriculum leads them to feel the limitations and loss of the physicality associated with being together. This very physicality of being, for this student, is connected to emotions and her experience of learning. For these two high school students, technology and in-person communication have existed on separate sides, and their emotional experience has been lacking or out of balance. In this example of curriculum implementation, the two students experience a limiting binary. The loss of the dialectic, the neglect of the social, and ignoring of culture all points to a lack of situational praxis (Aoki, 1983/2005) to create a connection and open the possibility between the two binaries.

The limiting perspective of binaries connects to Aoki's earlier chapter, "Curriculum Implementation as Instrumental Action and as Situational Praxis" (1983/2005), which illustrates a concern Aoki finds in curriculum implementation. It is a concern I recognize in my own research of educational technology. Aoki draws a clear distinction between "instrumentalism" and "praxis" (p. 122); the first is a frame of thinking which places emphasis on beings-as-things, while the second focuses on beings-as-human. An instrumental framework favours a specific purpose or goal, in which both implementation and beings are objectified, with an assumption of "beings-as-things oriented toward interest in control, efficiency and certainty" (p. 122). In comparison, a situational praxis framework focuses on "mutual understanding" (p. 122) and the goals of the individuals involved, rather than objective efficiency or certainty; this framework centres around the people involved, and competence is realized through "communicative action and reflection, and reality [...] is constituted or reconstituted within a community of actors" (p. 122). Aoki examined how curriculum is implemented over many waves of "technological thrusts" (Aoki, 1987/1999/2005, p. 151); this reflexive approach can be helpful for both educators and researchers and offers an opportunity to pause and reflect with each wave of technological innovation that enters the lives of our students and classrooms.

With this point of realization, I turn inwards and reflect on my own understanding of teaching with technology. When regarding current technologies and popular applications, we must ask ourselves whether our focus is placed on the technology or the individual. Does the technology elevate the person using it and encourage "mutual understanding" between a "community of actors," or are individuals forced to implement and ascribe to the constraints and set parameters of the programme, resulting in a measured "control," "certainty," and "efficiency" in using the technology (Aoki, 1983/2005 p. 122)? When designing workshops and seminars preparing graduate students to teach during the COVID-19 pandemic, reflections regarding instrumentalism, and the encouragement of meaningful connection with the assistance of technology are at the forefront of my mind. The four boys remind me how easy it is to be swept away with the transcendental lure of applications advertised as fun, engaging, and game based, to forget the underlying intentions of the application. To understand computer application, Aoki (1987/1999/2005) turns to Gadamer who explores the hermeneutic problem of application in *Truth and Method* (1960/1975). Aoki reveals:

> Computer technology, to be understood properly, must be understood at every moment, in every particular situation in a new and different way. Understood in this way, understanding is always application, and the meaning of computer technology and its application in a concrete curriculum situation are not two separate actions, but one process, one phenomenon, a fusion of horizons.
>
> (Aoki, 1987/1999/2005, p. 155)

As I draft the outline of my ISW session, Aoki's prompts guide me through the reflective process of implementation as situational praxis (1983/2005, p. 118). Am I helping my students achieve a deeper understanding of educational technology through the elevation of the social, even in a context such as the synchronous online classroom? Have I considered my underlying assumptions and the conditions which enable the use of the applications, I have selected, to engage in activities? Did I give my students opportunities to pause and reflect to critically reflect on their own transformative practices, the use of this technology, and technologically enabled teaching with their own students? Have I spoken candidly and openly regarding my own curriculum-as-plan and the actual situation of the curriculum-in-use which arose so naturally in this new hybrid context? Have I modelled the evaluation of my own implementation, for my students, with the demonstrated frameworks "to examine the quality of the activity of discovering underlying assumptions, interests, values, motives, perspectives, root metaphors, and implications for action to improve the human condition" (Aoki, 1983/2005, p. 119)?

In planning a workshop or seminar on the uses of technology for the synchronous classroom, I emphasize that I am showing these graduate students how to use technology for a specific intent, purpose, and context to build understanding; I am not merely showcasing a technology for the sake of an entertaining demonstration. The functions which enable students to chat in a side window during class time are fun but can be a meaningless distraction from the class and this depends on context. The situational praxis of this capability is to enable students who find it difficult to speak in front of thirty disembodied squares on a screen. Perhaps these students do not wish or cannot speak out loud. Perhaps they are physically or technologically not able to speak out loud due to un-updated personal devices, or faulty hardware. These are the instances where technology can assist in meaningful connections. As an educator, it is my responsibility to check these periodic contributions and bring them to the forefront of the class discussion and to model the enabling of the social in this new technological wave throughout the seminar.

The echo of the gravel and memory of the abacus fades away as I continue my walk in the Nitobe Memorial Garden.

Bridges of Lingering and Multiplicity

Climbing up the rocky steps in the Nitobe Memorial Garden, I see clouds of dust across a different dusty path in my memory. The steps are vaguely familiar. Prior to leaving for Japan, I spent hours on Google Maps street-view. I clicked on pathways, virtually traveling the same paths my father travelled to and from school in Kobe, Japan. I found the steep lane he trudged every day and the dusty hill he climbed behind the fence of the baseball field. The dust from the path that obscured his feet obscured mine too, now that I was finally in Kobe, physically retracing his steps after virtually floating over the same path. The distinct angles of my kneecaps, which everyone remarks I inherited from my father, pressed against the folds of my dirt laden dress and made it easy to scamper over smooth and jagged contours of embedded rock. The words of my grandmother's stories of my father returning home late, filthy from playing baseball with the other school children, combined with my father's memories of those hot sunny afternoons hurrying home down a steep lane. Their memories added layers of meaning to my own experience. I too, now climbed the same rocky path. Sweat beaded off my face with the effort of breathing the same humid air and walking the same hill my father once took to and from school. I quickly ascended the dusty path toward the old school yard.

This memory in the Nitobe Memorial Garden was an odd juxtaposition, as I experienced a memory from multiple points of view. Here I was living and experiencing a hybrid of experiences. I was reliving my father's story in my mind, replaying the digital images I had traced so many times before, and now finally walking the steps on my own—tracing hints of the familiar through the foreign, to generate a new meaning for myself and a new story within my own journey. These pieces of experience, both digital and physical, past and present, disrupted and joined, create a new experience full of personal meaning.

Aoki expands upon the limits of binaries through the creation of a bridge metaphor. In "Imaginaries of 'East and West': Slippery Curricular Signifiers in Education" (1996/2005), pp. 313–320), Aoki places each binary on either side of the structure, and proposes that we dwell on the bridge itself to imagine and experience a hybrid of the two binaries. This bridge is the embodiment of hybridization and a space of opening. Aoki (1996/2005, p. 319) quotes Ernesto Laclau:

> Hybridization does not necessarily mean decline through a loss of identity; it can also mean empowering existing identities through the opening of new possibilities. Only a conservative identity, closed on itself, could experience hybridization as a loss.
> (Laclau, 1995, p. 16)

Of this hybridization, Aoki reflects on the bridge and how it has become a third space, linking two separate spaces. He writes that "the tensioned space of both 'and/not-and' is a space of conjoining and disrupting, indeed, a generative space of possibilities, a space wherein in tensioned ambiguity newness emerges" (Aoki, 1996/2005, p. 318). In his shorter essay, "Bridges that Rim the Pacific" (1991/2005a), Aoki speaks explicitly of his personal connection with embodying and situating himself on bridges, as a child going back and forth between the East and West. He pauses on this metaphor and asks what the Japanese visionary, Dr. Inazō Nitobe, meant when he wished to serve as a bridge. To serve as a true bridge, one must become "more than a physical structure that connects two masses of land" for "it is a dwelling place for humans who, in their longing to be together, belong together" (Aoki, 1991/2005a, p. 438). Aoki speaks of a site we do not hurry past, traveling from point A to point B, nor is it a route for instrumentalism, such as commerce and trade. Aoki (1991/2005a) ends with an invitation for "educators to transcend instrumentalism and to understand what it means to dwell together humanly" (p. 439). Aoki invites all educators to recentre ourselves around situational praxis, to be of the moment and open spaces for curriculum-as-is, so that we might dwell together humanly and make meaningful connections.

These reflections of dwelling together humanely remind me of my research participants. I recall a 12-year-old boy gesturing to the row of computers, and he asks, "Why type in the thing when we could just talk to each other?" (Liu, 2016). After spending a month back and forth, online and in-person, this boy realizes that he does not need to rely on technology for his in-class group work. This boy's understanding of using this technology in this particular situation is reminiscent of Aoki's (1987/1999/2005) understanding of computer technology and thus, Gadamer's (1960/1975) hermeneutic approach to application: This boy attempts to understand this technology by understanding it "in every particular situation in a new and different way" (Aoki, 1987/1999/2005, p. 155), and the meaning of this computer technology and its application in a concrete situation is a singular process, not two separate actions. By lingering in both spaces, binaries of online and in-person, he understands the limits of each and recognizes how to mediate and bridge the two binaries to create a meaningful connection with his group members for this particular situation.

These reflections lead me to turn inward to the focus of my doctoral research, cyberbullying. The field of cyberbullying has been built upon the foundation of school bullying studies. Methods of measurement and tools have been taken from the field of school bullying and been applied to studying the phenomenon of cyberbullying (Espinoza & Juvonen, 2013, p. 117), which does not account for the difference in context. As a result, decades of application of traditional school bullying methods to cyberbullying, without considering the effect of the complexity and difference of online and digital contexts, has resulted in an inability for researchers to agree on a definition of cyberbullying (Smith, 2015). In adapting the tools used to measure traditional school bullying and then applying these same tools to cyberbullying, the uniqueness of the digital contexts in these incidents are not taken into consideration; thus, many studies have contrasting findings and concluded that there is still much to be understood about cyberbullying (Englander, 2019a). After reviewing two decades of cyberbullying research, Elizabeth Englander, a nationally recognized researcher in the field of psychology and expert in the area of bullying and cyberbullying from the US, surmised that "these approaches miss a critical element in assessing social interactions between children, namely, the context in which they occur" (p. 513). Together, Englander's (2019a) review of cyberbullying research and Aoki's (1987/1999/2005) approach toward understanding computer application can help us understand issues of a technological nature at a much deeper level. In understanding the complexity and nuance of computer technology, we cannot remain detached from the particular situation (Aoki, 1987/1999/2005), and similarly when understanding a problem that occurs in cyberspace, the context of an unkind online behaviour is even more important than the objective severity of a cruel act (Englander, 2019b)—the context of importance could refer to the frequency and repetition of an act or whether the individual was being targeted in multiple contexts at the same time. Englander (2019a) argues that without taking the broad social development of the adolescent or child into consideration, in conjunction with the online context, parents, teachers, and researchers may not have a comprehensive understanding of what cyberbullying entails or how to approach the issue. Aoki (1987/1999/2005) reminds us that to understand computer technology, "one must not seek to disregard oneself and one's particular hermeneutic situation. One must relate computer technology to this situation" and that "understanding computer technology will necessarily have to be restated in each new subject area situation" (p. 155). Both Englander and Aoki implore that context is the key to understanding.

The words of these Grade 8 research participants serve as reminders, that one does not rush across a bridge to get from point A to B. To serve as a human bridge, one must spend time and linger within a hybrid space to understand the limitations, create new ways of being, and form meaningful connections. By lingering in these in-between spaces of online and in-person contexts, and the third space—a combination of the two-this enables educators to recognize the problems of instrumentalizing technology. By practicing both in-person and online communication as this research participant shared, it is possible to create a new form of understanding through mutual points of connections: A third space, a place of lingering and meaning making, in the in-between to dwell together humanly.

Aokian Lingering through Contextual Walking

When situating myself in the context of the Nitobe Memorial Garden, I engage in an Aokian methodology by walking through multiple contexts to reflect on my relationship with technology in my personal lived experience, as a researcher, and as an educator/facilitator. This act of reflecting, lingering, and transformation through new realizations echo with relevancy through life memories, the words of past research participants, and reflections of what it means to teach with technology. By recalling Aoki's words on the limits of binaries, the importance of distinguishing instrumentalism from praxis, and lingering to become human bridges of hybridity and newness, it is possible to reconcile tensions which arise in one's lived experience. In my roles as a researcher, an educator, and facilitator, I recognize that those who experience an irreconcilable tension with technology in the classroom or their personal life still yearn for a thorough understanding of the context both of the situation, and its social implications or application.

Through this chapter, I habituate and embody a third space: I bridge the past and the present and reflect on the words of my research participants. Connections across experience and time—both before and after the COVID-19 pandemic started—help create a deeper and nuanced understanding of my own identity through the use of technology, the collaborative relationships my research participants develop with their selective use of technology, and the connections I foster in my technologically enhanced workshops and seminars during the COVID-19 pandemic. These bridges and links between research, teaching, and life experiences encourage me to reach out and step out into a place of ambiguous newness during this new lived reality.

The time spent online and in person is a hybrid lived experience. As Aoki reminds us, hybridization does not indicate a decline in identity or in the quality of the lived experience, as I have learned during this pandemic. Unable to be physically with my grandmother in the hospital COVID ward, I am indebted to technology, similarly to how Aoki's student, Carol Olson acknowledged her indebtedness to technology while sustained by a dialysis machine (Aoki, 1987/1999/2005, p. 157). I am indebted but not enslaved. The last moments shared with my grandmother on video call are no lesser than what it would have been in person. The culmination of these hybrid experiences enables me to dwell on the being-as-human and the "significance of that which is beyond the technological in the technological" (Aoki, 1987/1999/2005, p. 158). In the span of one pandemic and multiple waves, a wedding, four burials, and soon the news of a birth, have and will be shared through the use of technology and I am indebted.

Notes

1. The use of the word 'seat' and reflection on Chinese-Canadian identity is influenced by the exhibit, *A Seat at the Table: Chinese Immigration and British Columbia*, at the Museum of Vancouver and in Chinatown, co-curated by Denise Fong, Viviane Gosselin, and Henry Yu.
2. This research was funded through the SSHRC Joseph-Armand Bombardier Canada Graduate Scholarships Program and my Supervisor, Stephen Petrina's SSHRC Insight Grant. The research design was implemented in adherence to the guidelines and ethical grounds for research involving human subjects presented by The University of British Columbia Behavioural Research Ethics Board. Approval was granted under the certificate number H06-80670 by the Behavioural Research Ethics Board.

References

Aoki, T. T. (1979/2005). Reflections of a Japanese Canadian teacher experiencing ethnicity. In W. F. Pinar & R. L. Irwin (Eds.), *Curriculum in a new key: The collected works of Ted T. Aoki* (pp. 333–348). Lawrence Erlbaum.

Aoki, T. T. (1983/2005). Curriculum implementation as instrumental action and as situational praxis. In W. F. Pinar & R. L. Irwin (Eds.), *Curriculum in a new key: The collected works of Ted T. Aoki* (pp. 111–123). Lawrence Erlbaum.

Aoki, T. T. (1987/1991/2005). The dialectic of mother language and second language: A curriculum exploration. In W. F. Pinar & R. L. Irwin (Eds.), *Curriculum in a new key: The collected works of Ted T. Aoki* (pp. 235–245). Lawrence Erlbaum.

Aoki, T. T. (1987/1999/2005). Toward understanding "computer application." In W. F. Pinar & R.L. Irwin (Eds.), *Curriculum in a new key: The collected works of Ted T. Aoki* (pp. 151–158). Lawrence Erlbaum.

Aoki, T. T. (1991/2005a). Bridges that rim the pacific. In W. F. Pinar & R. L. Irwin (Eds.), *Curriculum in a new key: The collected works of Ted T. Aoki* (pp. 437–439). Lawrence Erlbaum.

Aoki, T. T. (1991/2005b). Taiko drums and sushi, perogies and sauerkraut: Mirroring a half-life in multicultural curriculum. In W. F. Pinar & R. L. Irwin (Eds.), *Curriculum in a new key: The collected works of Ted T. Aoki* (pp. 377–387). Lawrence Erlbaum.

Aoki, T. T. (1993/2005). Humiliating the Cartesian ego. In W. F. Pinar & R. L. Irwin (Eds.), *Curriculum in a new key: The collected works of Ted T. Aoki* (pp. 291–301). Lawrence Erlbaum.

Aoki, T. T. (1996/2005). Imaginaries of "East and West": Slippery curricular signifiers in education. In W. F. Pinar & R. L. Irwin (Eds.), *Curriculum in a new key: The collected works of Ted T. Aoki* (pp. 313–319). Lawrence Erlbaum.

Asselin, M., & Moayeri, M. (2010). Examining adolescent internet literacy practices: An exploration of research methods. *Journal of Theory and Practice in Education*, 6(2), 191–210

Bonanno, R. A., & Hymel, S. (2013). Cyber bullying and internalizing difficulties: Above and beyond the impact of traditional forms of bullying. *Journal of Youth and Adolescence*, 42(5), 685–697.

Bulger, M., & Davison, P. (2018). The promises, challenges, and futures of media literacy. *Journal of Media Literacy Education*, 10(1), 1–21.

Code, J. (2013). Agency and identity in social media. In *Digital identity and social media* (pp. 37–57). IGI Global.

Englander, E. (2019a). Back to the drawing board with cyberbullying. *JAMA Pediatrics*, 173(6), 513–514.

Englander, E. (2019b). Changes in digital bullying. Presented at: National school safety conference; February 27, 2019; Jacksonville, FL.

Espinoza, G., & Juvonen, J. (2013). Methods used in cyberbullying research. In S. Bauman, D. Cross, & J. Walker (Eds.), *Principles of cyberbullying research: Definitions, measures, and methodology* (pp. 112–124). Routledge

Fong, D., Gosselin, V., & Yu, H. (2020-2022). *A seat at the table: Chinese Immigration and British Columbia [exhibition]*. Vancouver, BC, Canada: Hon Hsing Building and The Museum of Vancouver.

Gadamer, H. (1960/1975). *Truth and method*. Seabury Press.

Laclau, E. (1995). Subject of politics, politics of the subject. *Differences: A Journal of Feminist Culture Studies*, 7(1) 146–164.

Liu, L. E. (2016). *Tweens, teens, and digital texts: designing affinity spaces to understand cyberbullying* [Unpublished master's thesis]. University of British Columbia. https://open.library.ubc.ca/collections/ubctheses/24/items/1.0320835

Petrina, S. (2020). Philosophy of technology for children and youth. In P. J. Williams, & D. Barlex (Eds.), *Pedagogy for technology education in secondary schools* (pp. 311–323). Springer

Smith, P. K. (2015). The nature of cyberbullying and what we can do about it. *Journal of Research in Special Educational Needs*, 15(3), 176–184.

8 Visualizing and Reconceptualizing Transformative Sustainability Learning through an Aokian Lens

Kshamta Hunter

Aoki believed in praxis—the intersection of theory and practice. Situational praxis, which asks for learner-centred, experiential, and integrative methods, is Aoki's approach to curriculum and implementation (Aoki, 1983/2005, p. 111). In the era of Anthropocene, urban migration, climate crisis, and pandemic, there is a need for a shift in the way we approach curriculum and adapt our pedagogies to navigate the complexities of the uncertain and changing world; Aoki's approach to situational praxis is key to the shifting needs of sustainability education and can provide the necessary changes in both teaching and learning. These approaches are key to sustainability teaching and learning. Aoki's perspective on curriculum-as-lived and curriculum-as-planned (Aoki, 1983/2005), bridging understanding (Aoki, 1984/2005), and leadership (Aoki, 1986/1991/2005) could offer a new understanding and an avenue for this shift.

According to United Nations, the estimated youth population in 2019 was 1.2 billion, growing, and focused especially in urban areas (United Nations, 2019). Over 7 million youth in Canada are between the ages of 15 and 29; they are the most diverse and socially engaged group and for the first time ever they made up the biggest voting bloc in a federal election in Canada (Statistics Canada, 2019). The World Economic Forum highlights the importance of education reform to enable our youth to be future-ready with the skills and competencies that are flexible, interdisciplinary, and relevant for tackling unprecedented challenges of our time (World Economic Forum, 2016). Osman and colleagues (2017) underscore the need for a 21st century transformative pedagogy to both foster awareness of the consequences of the global trends and offering opportunities for the key leadership competencies to flourish, in order to navigate the complex and wicked problems associated with an uncertain and changing world.

As a researcher and educator of Education for Sustainable Development (ESD), I consider Ted Aoki's ideas, concepts, and thoughts much ahead of his time and highly relevant to current understanding and challenges of sustainability learning and teaching and potentially transformative. To equip our youth with the competencies to tackle the uncertain challenges faced by the world today, we need a transformative perspective and Aoki's work

DOI: 10.4324/9781003037248-14

has the capability to facilitate new models of understanding. While reflecting on Aoki's work and situating my own research within his paradigm, I revisited my own sustainability curriculum, specifically the leadership programme for post-secondary students and my attempt at making meaning of and connections between concepts. The main goal of the programme is to increase awareness and action on sustainability and climate related issues. As a programme manager, I design and implement the sustainability curriculum, facilitate discussions and workshops on various sustainability related topics, as well as offer guidance and mentorship to a multi-disciplinary and multi-year university students on their experiential group projects.

Although I knew that this work is important and making a difference, I did not know how to create meaning within my own pedagogical framework, which is situated in traditional models of teaching and learning that may (intentionally or unintentionally) propagate systemic and social inequalities and tendencies. In this process, I realized that the experience I was offering or wanting to strive for was missing its intended goal; this was primarily due to missed opportunities of integrating lived experiences and personal characteristics. Unless students could make tangible and direct links at a personal level, the *changes* would not be sustainable. Applying knowledge through skills to seek a goal in the absence of values is meaningless, and that took a while for me to realize in the midst of running and facilitating a robust programme. In this meaning-making process, I borrow from Carl Rogers (1980) on person-centred therapy:

> It is that the individual has within himself or herself vast resources for self-understanding, for altering his or her self-concept, attitudes and self-directed behavior—and that these resources can be tapped if only a definable climate of facilitative psychological attitudes can be provided.
> (p. 115–117)

I believe these conditions could be facilitated through an integrative and supportive curriculum as well.

After deep reflection, I was able to make that connection and thus able to facilitate more relevant and effective dialogue and targeted conversations. The result was the offering of more discussions on the exploration of personal values and lived experiences, and how students might link to their goals and the work they would like to do within sustainability. In the latter portion of this chapter, I discuss competencies and how they encompass knowledge, skills, perspectives, and values. I have witnessed the effectiveness of the competencies framework in sustainability education, and I believe it is worth exploring how Aoki can build understanding within this framework and sustain a transformative change within students. For effective and sustained social praxis, I needed to make connections between knowledge, skills, and values with personal goals and career directives for post-secondary students. How do I make these connections for myself but more importantly for the students?

Aoki's critical perspective on curriculum offers a means to integrate and make connections. In employing individual or person-centred experiential learning opportunities through a competencies framework with an Aokian lens, these processes could offer opportunities of growth and self-determined learning for students to make their own path to change.

In this chapter, Aoki's bridge metaphor serves as a helpful focal point when creating connections between sustainability learning and leadership and Aoki's perspectives on curriculum and praxis. These connections led to a transformative process of cultivating competencies model that has been instrumental in my own work, as it helps me visualize the interplay of numerous complicated elements and put into perspective the centrality of values in this process. I should emphasize the circularity of this process, in that my praxis has informed this conceptual model and I hope to learn and built upon this model to further inform my praxis. I primarily use Aoki's bridge metaphor to visualize and make connections of understanding. As Aoki (1984/2005) suggests, these bridges lure us into pausing, reflecting, and making connections. At the same time, I realize there are many parallels between sustainability learning elements and Aoki's thoughts and ideas on curriculum, which I have attempted to identify and describe to a certain extent; however, I acknowledge that this chapter does not deeply analyze the parallels between sustainability learning and Aoki's perspectives, which could be another chapter in itself. The focus of this chapter is to visualize the connections between sustainability concepts and primary aspects using Aoki's paradigm of situational praxis for transformative learning.

Before I introduce the model, it is important for me to acknowledge and clarify my understanding and translation of Aoki's concepts. It is also important to highlight that these are early attempts at adopting Aoki's lens to the work I do in sustainability education; therefore, my understanding and application of his perspectives into my own sustainability praxis may be different from other curriculum scholars. It is my understanding that in Aoki's view curriculum-as-lived is important; however, curriculum-as-plan is equally significant. I believe that majority of teachers or facilitators would agree to having a plan or set of goals that they would like to achieve before going into the class. How they "implement" this plan or how this plan unfolds can be somewhat of a contentious issue. Although it is extremely important to not let this plan dictate the lived experiences in the classroom, to be flexible and negotiable to student needs, in my translation of Aoki's thoughts on curriculum, he does not negate the importance of curriculum-as-plan (Aoki, 1993/2005, p. 202) or to have a set of learning objectives or a design; what he questions is the inflexibility in changing that design or the instrumental application of that design. In my work within sustainability education, I need to be able to go into my class with a set of learning objectives or goals or an idea. Moreover, given the global and local developments, knowing my students' interests is vital; I need to have prior knowledge and understanding of those needs in the global and local context. But I also need to be able to alter my plan for each student depending on their interests and needs. The competencies discussed in this chapter are a set of outcomes proposed after much research with students and what students are *asking* for (Osman et al., 2017; Wiek et al., 2011). *How* we cultivate these competencies is flexible and altered by person-centred perspectives in the classroom. I also believe that as *teachers* we are facilitators of learning, not to say that as facilitators we do not need a plan or objectives or have our own throughs or perspective on a topic. In fact, these perspectives become ever more important in this context. I believe both education and sustainability are inherently value laden and it is imperative that these values are shared in an open, evidence-based, and cooperative process. How students learn and what prior knowledge and lived experiences they integrate into their own translation of knowledge is unique for each student, how knowledge and skills are facilitated through person-centred experiential learning is important. According to Aoki, "in the framework of 'praxis' (practical action), reality is constituted by the intersubjective actions of beings-as-humans, oriented toward cognitive interests in mutual understanding, and also the practical interest in securing authentically the always precarious intersubjectivity" (Aoki, 1984/2005, p. 132). "Becoming aware that personal praxis involves social praxis" (Aoki, 1984/2005, p. 135) is significant in this context.

In this chapter, I use Aoki's perspectives and bridge metaphor to visualize and explore connections to transformative sustainability learning. This alternate perspective offers a practical framework that harmonizes the core elements of sustainability learning and leadership to support social praxis. I start by offering readers contextual background of sustainability learning and leadership, then focus on key sustainability leadership competencies development as practical action and agency and end by demonstrating how Aoki's bridge may offer us a new perspective on cultivating competencies to support transformative learning. This conceptualization is a personal approach to how the sustainability relevant elements could be interlinked and connected to accomplish personal and social praxis. I offer this conceptualization here in hopes that it may also be useful to others in developing their own praxis in their own fields of study.

Sustainability Learning and Leadership

Sustainability is an interdisciplinary global issue that needs critical and comprehensive understanding and integrative approaches. In this sense, sustainability encompasses environmental, economic, and social aspects of our lives. In my work, I consider social elements of sustainability, including equity, ethics, justice, and diversity as essential and fundamental for deep understanding and awareness of overall sustainability issues we see in our communities. As such, Education for Sustainable Development (ESD) integrates both a holistic and transformative activity that integrates elements of personal and experiential reflection (UNESCO, 2015).

Sustainability learning and leadership seek to build upon four primary aspects: (1) knowledge of current global and local issues that might be relevant to one's practice and influence action. This includes knowledge of human cultures and the physical and natural world; (2) skills associated with leadership and development, such as communication, conflict management, problem-solving etc., these are also considered intellectual and practical skills; (3) perspectives that are based in interdisciplinary understanding and interpretations, also considered integrative learning; and (4) values that connect one's assumptions and opinions to their work and interactions as well as understanding of other's values, beliefs and frames of reference, could be considered as personal and social responsibility. Values are the inner standards that individuals or groups hold for themselves (Bloom et al., 1971; Carter, 1985; Chalkley, 2006; Gonzalez, 2015; Osman et al., 2017).

Skills, knowledge, values, and perspectives are needed for life and work in an evolving world with ever-changing challenges (Osman et al., 2017). The four key aspects are interconnected. Values and attitudes are integral to receiving and translating knowledge and understanding of concepts and issues, which in turn are fundamental to opportunities for skills development and consequently sharing of values and perspectives through relevant means. Values and perspectives also influence behaviour and vice versa (see Figure 1.1 in Transparencies for introduction to psychology, 2004). These four key aspects are highly connected to and enhance sustainability learning in students to be a positive role model and agents of change (Barth et al., 2007), specifically translating the values in the context of social sustainability, which includes conversations on equity and justice. The development of these key aspects is crucial to the practice of leadership and engaging students towards personal behaviour changes or community-based projects (Shriberg & Harris, 2012).

Social scientists and numerous agencies recognize that agency (Bandura, 2006; Mayr, 2011) is at the core of education and building resilience while preparing the next generation for the social, economic, and environmental changes (Environment and Climate Change Canada, 2007; Osman et al., 2017, United Nations, 2015). Agency is "what a person is free to do and achieve in pursuit of whatever goals or values he or she regards as important" (Sen, 1985, p. 203). Agency is vital in sustainability education as "agency implies a sense of responsibility to participate in the world and, in so doing, to influence people, events and circumstances for the better" (OECD, 2018, p. 5). It is through programmes that support Education for Sustainable Development, where agency could be promoted through the development of competencies like critical thinking, imagining future scenarios and collaborative decision making (Rychen & Tiana, 2004). It is critical to understand agency in the context of curriculum and pedagogy and building upon and cultivating the necessary knowledge, skills, values, and attitudes (de Haan, 2006; Rieckmann, 2012; Wiek et al., 2011) associated with sustainability (Osman et al., 2017). I want to emphasize the role of values and individual value exploration within the concept of agency and therefore sustainability education. The proposed model discussed later in the chapter builds upon this.

Transformative Learning and Competencies

Individual attributes are fundamental to investigating any social process or phenomena, including sustainability education. Transformative learning aims to challenge and potentially change individual's beliefs, attitudes, and behaviors through critical reflection and discourse (Mezirow, 1998). "Self-awareness" is vital for helping students reach their full potential (Rosen, 2014, p. 59). Transformative learning challenges the learners' values and beliefs through "a disturbing and unsettling process" (Butler, 1996, p. 275). Mezirow (1990) defined transformative learning as "the process of learning through critical self-reflection, which results in the reformulation of a meaning perspective to allow a more inclusive, discriminating, and integrative understanding of one's experience, [and] acting on these insights" (p. xvi). He goes on to describe transformational learning as "a process by which we transform our frames of reference to make them more inclusive, open, emotionally capable of change, and reflective so that they may generate beliefs and options that will prove more true or justified to guide action" (Mezirow, 2000, pp. 7–8). In this context, the educator's role is to challenge assumptions and encourage accepting and integrating other worldviews. The concept of *meaning perspective* is foundational to transformative learning, which refers to the "structure of assumptions within which new experience is assimilated and transformed by one's past experience during the process of interpretation" (Mezirow, 1990, p. 2). Mezirow (1978) defines *perspective transformation* as "a structural change in the way we see ourselves and our relationships" towards meaning perspectives which are "more inclusive, discriminating and integrative of experience" (p. 186). This aligns well with Aoki's thoughts on "'praxis' and emancipatory actions, [where] actors and speakers are oriented toward 'de-naturalizing' that which common sense declares to be human nature; they explore and condemn the commonsensical dismissal of alternative realities" (Aoki, 1984/2005, p. 133).

Competencies are the amalgamation, aggregation, and interplay of knowledge, skills, values, and perspectives, including ethics, emotions, as well as social and behavioural components (Lozano, et al., 2017; Rychen & Tiana, 2004). They include "cognitive, affective, volitional (with deliberate intention), and motivational elements" (Rieckmann, 2012, p. 5). Competencies can be learned and acquired with *affective* learning processes. The OECD (2018) frames the concept of competency as "more than just the acquisition of knowledge and skills; it involves the mobilization of knowledge, skills, attitudes and values to meet complex demands. Future-ready students will need both broad and specialized knowledge" (OECD, 2018, p. 5). Aoki (1984/2005) captures the essence of competence by noting the Latin root meaning of the word *competere* meaning to be able "to seek together or to be able to venture forth together" (p. 130). Recognizing that developing competence requires interplay of discourse and interaction, Aoki also explores the notion of competence as praxis or practical action that may lead to transformational change in the context of sustainability. It is important to note that change is not necessarily a behaviour change or an action, in the sustainability context the change could be perspective transformations that may result in broader societal impact. I will re-visit the aspect of transformation in sustainability education later in this chapter.

Competencies-based education, in literature and in practice, has several understandings. For example, competency development and learning could result in an externally identified goal-oriented process, which may or may not explore or incorporate lived experiences, culture and personal or individual reasons of behaviour or societal change (Rychen & Salganik, 2003). There is an inherent absence of human agency in the process of competence development as instrumental action. Aoki critiques the instrumentalization approach of competencies and compares the consequences of competence as instrumental-action and competence as practical-action (Aoki, 1984/2005, pp. 133–134). Although, competencies are described as "internal mental structures in the sense of abilities, dispositions, or resources embedded in the individual" (Rychen & Salganik, 2003, p. 44), Aoki questions the process through which these are embedded and practiced within curriculum and pedagogy that may achieve thoughtful personal and ultimately social praxis. I hope to present a model that emphasizes the role of values in building the key competencies.

In the context of sustainability education, competencies-based learning shares characteristics of Indigenous ways of learning and knowing by emphasizing self-awareness and lived-experiences through value exploration and interconnections to appreciate the complexities of both human and non-human realities (Toulouse, 2016). If realized and facilitated appropriately, the competencies approach could be a highly efficient approach to exploring and mitigating sustainability issues, as well as encouraging innovative actions through thoughtful practical skills, knowledge mobilization and meaningful engagement with relevant societal issues. There are proposed competencies that offer academic programmes in higher education a reference point to build their learning pathways (de Haan, 2010; Osman et al., 2017; Rieckmann, 2012; Wiek, et al., 2011). For example, Wiek and colleagues' (2011) model proposes building upon five key competencies: systems-thinking competence, anticipatory competence, normative competence, strategic competence, and interpersonal competence.

Research shows the importance of providing opportunity and trust to students to develop their intellectual capabilities and participation in the sustainable development of their communities while learning critical hands-on career skills and gaining experience (Brunetti et al., 2003). Tilbury (2004) describes *affective* learning outcomes as the core components for sustainability education, described as critical reflection, values clarification, and participative action. Burns (2011) and Sterling (2001) urge that if educators are to effectively encourage personal and social praxis, a transition must be made from transmissive teaching models to transformative, transgressive learning processes. I believe, these perspectives are well aligned with Aoki's thoughts on curriculum, situational praxis and practical action (Aoki, 1983/2005).

A more comprehensive approach that involves heuristic value exploration is needed to support learning in the 21st century (Schleicher, 2019). The competencies approach needs to be able to recognize that social structures strongly determine the degree to which individuals can mobilize their abilities, skills, and knowledge to develop agency. Individuals need to be supported to be a contributing member of society in ways that honour personal motivations. Hence, the pedagogical approach utilized cannot be a value-free approach. There needs to be a balance between learning relevant skills and understanding of deep societal issues that need sustainable solutions, while also keeping in mind that competence development without values and agency is inadequate.

The competencies approach, with its own challenges and pitfalls, can offer viable models for sustainability education if operationalized effectively to support practical action. To date, there are no agreed upon models that offer a good framework in sustainability education to cultivate the competencies in youth, for example to "cope with failure and to move forward in the face of adversity" (OECD, 2018, p. 2). Although there is agreement on the four aspects that need to be explored in any sustainability-related education, research lacks to present or offer a relevant and functional model that captures the essence of sustainability learning while offering a practical framework for facilitators. In the next section, I attempt to capture the relationship between these aspects and integrate them using Aoki's bridge.

Transformative Sustainability Learning on Aoki's Bridge: A Conceptual Model

Aoki's comparison of competence as instrumental and practical action (Aoki, 1984/2005, p. 133) is helpful in realizing some of the downfalls and dangers of instrumentalism, especially in the sustainability context and within the competencies-based learning. A transformational change requires active engagement and leadership of students, which in turn requires educators to offer students opportunities for contemplation and cultivation of skills for success. The notion of transgressive learning (Lotz-Sisitka et al., 2015) goes even further and challenges the status quo to prepare learners for "disruptive" thinking and encourages co-creation of new knowledge. The transformative transgressive learning is considered critical in addressing the uncertain adaptive challenges by encouraging sustainability as social praxis.

Aoki's understanding of curriculum implementation has offered a means to better translate and conceptualize sustainability learning and its core aspects into a practical yet relevant framework (Aoki 1996/2005). Aoki's bridge metaphor is a space to linger and reflect on our values, make connections and accommodate new information into our existing framework. In some sense, the bridge is our existing human condition and social realities that we are all facing. We are all on this bridge of transition in human social existence during climate catastrophes, pandemic, and social inequities. Just as Aoki's bridge lures us to linger and pause, our environmental and social realities are an invitation, and an opportunity, for us to consider the alternate possibilities. Perhaps this bridge could help us pivot our realities through reflection on our individual but also social values.

In attempting to offer a rendition of Aoki's bridge (see Figure 8.1), I have visualized a sustainability model to support transformative integrative learning and I am proposing a model to achieve situational praxis through the competencies approach.

In the proposed model, *Knowledge* encapsulates *disciplinary knowledge*, which captures discipline-specific content but also the capacity to make connection across disciplines; *epistemic knowledge*, which involves knowledge *about* specific disciplines (i.e. how to think like a historian or a scientist), which

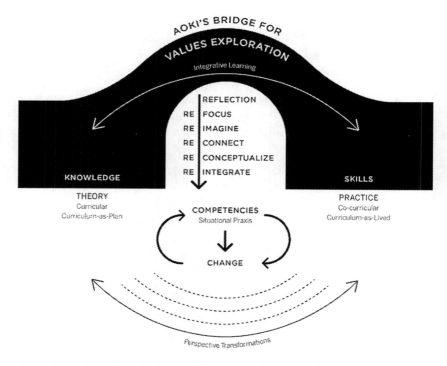

Figure 8.1 Aoki's Bridge for Values Exploration offers a Transformative Sustainability Learning Model and a Competence Development Approach | Image: Natalie Hawryshkewich.

furthers disciplinary knowledge; and *procedural knowledge* is the understanding of the process, of how things are made or done (OECD, 2018).

In order to apply the knowledge to uncertain and evolving situations, students need to develop key analytical skills. *Skills* such as *cognitive and meta-cognitive skills*, which include critical and creative thinking; *social and emotional skills*, such as empathy and collaboration; and *practical or physical skills*, e.g. project management and communication skills (OECD, 2018).

The knowledge and skills will be mediated and translated through *Aoki's Bridge for Values Exploration*. Values such as trust, kindness, respect for diversity, and virtue. These values can be at personal, societal, and global levels, and arise from, or may differ, depending on various cultural and contextual backgrounds. However, there are some key human values that are consistent across cultures and cannot be compromised with respect to sustainable development, such as respect for life and human dignity and respect for the environment (OECD, 2018). These common human values offer teachers and facilitator a shared starting point for discussions and conversations to unfold.

Aoki's bridge *lures* to *reflect, re-focus, re-imagine, re-connect, re-conceptualize,* and *re-integrate*. Since development of competencies cannot be done in isolation, lingering on Aoki's bridge to reflect on individual values is important; interaction and discourse is an essential part of cultivating competencies, specifically in the sustainability context, which requires community-engaged *integrative learning* approaches. Aoki (1984/2005) reconceptualized competence as "communicative action and reflection" that "reality is constituted as a community of actors and speakers" through "venturing forth" together (p. 133). To co-dwell in the hyphen through reflection, anticipation, and discourse builds upon the idea of co-agency—"the interactive, mutually supportive relationships that helps learners to progress toward their valued goals. In this context, everyone should be considered a learner, not only students but also teachers, school managers, parents and communities" (OECD, 2018, p. 4). This act of reflecting on personal goals enables learners, more specifically students in sustainability education, an opportunity for transformation.

This bridge acts as a *third space* (Bhabha, 1990), where students are given the opportunity to explore, pause, and reflect to make connections and translate their understandings and interpretations of knowledge and skills towards cultivating their *competencies*. Every student creates their own connections through their own lived-experiences, realities, and perspectives, so the connections that are made are unique and relevant at the individual level. This is also a space for *situational praxis* for instructors, teachers and facilitators as well as a space for bridging the gap between curriculum-as-plan and curriculum-as-lived (Pinar, 2005). As facilitators of learning, we are also equal participants in the process of learning and, therefore, need to make the space for exploration of values and making connections. This understanding of *facilitator* is different from facilitators of pre-programmed learning packages or blindly *implementing* a competency-based prescriptive curriculum, and adds to Aoki's understanding of competence as practical action or praxis by proposing a Competence Development Approach, which suggests acting and reflecting upon the world, becoming aware of one's own practice, seeking moments of conscious, becoming aware of one's history, making connection between personal and social praxis, and becoming aware of the contextual influences on one's praxis (Aoki, 1984/2005, pp. 133–134). Without having the time to pause and reflect on these values to make tangible connections could lead to superfluous engagement and actions.

Another aspect of this model is the connection between *competencies* development and *change*, which is a two-way connection; taking an action for social change utilizing competencies in turn further develops the competencies. Furthermore, the ripple effect of the *change*, as in the water under Aoki's bridge, further strengthens the connections between knowledge (theory) and skills (practice) by proliferating and influencing change in the community through interactions between actors. *Perspective transformation*s could also occur through enactment of the competencies towards social change. However, it is important to note that perspective transformations, as identified by Mezirow (1978), typically require consistent action and knowledge mobilization for a period of time. This cycle of learning-action-reflection is depicted by the ripples in the water under Aoki's bridge.

While bringing the proposed model to life, facilitating conversations and offering opportunities to students to bridge their lived experiences, knowledge and skills into competencies, as a facilitator I am transformed in the process myself through each interaction and *dialectical relationship* with individuals and in groups going through the process of learning and questioning concepts and processes or values exploration perhaps leading to perspective transformation. These interactions are what I consider to be truly transformational for both the teacher (facilitator) and the student, where we both become aware of own personal praxis that involves social praxis.

Model in Action

Although I have incorporated various aspects and forms of this model into my practice, a complete immersion into my practice is a methodical and gradual process. I am in the process of developing ways to integrate this conceptual model into practice. In my own sustainability leadership programme, I scaffold this model through in-depth conversation about values and how students may connect and influence behaviours and action while contemplating the role of knowledge and development of skills in the process. As an example, I offer an exercise that I facilitate within the leadership programme with post-secondary students. The exercise is called *Head, Heart,* and *Hustle* (an adapted version of the exercise from Ashoka Changemakers Canada, 2020); it offers focused space for students to reflect on each of the three key areas of their being. In this exercise, students start by reflecting back on their personal values, which they have previously done in the programme by focusing on some key aspect of values. Students reflect on where these values come from, how are they visualized or appear in their daily lives, how are they impacted and influenced, and whether they change. Then through a series of reflective prompts, students are encouraged to reflect on the heart, head, and hustle aspects of their lives. *"Heart" encompasses the issues, ideas, and peoples that move you. These are things that you are connected to, things that make your heart beat faster, whether because you find then deeply compelling, infuriating, or thrilling. "Head" is your unique gifts; the skills, abilities, knowledge, connections, and everything else you bring to the table. This includes the insights you have as a result of your experiences, your access to communities that others may have difficulty connecting to and so on. "Hustle" is what happens when you align your heart and your head, doing work that draws from both of these spheres. This refers to those times in which you are really moving. You are in the zone, losing track of time, doing the work you would do for free (even when you get paid for it). Why? Because you are driven by something extraordinary: your personal purpose.* Through this reflective exercise, students are encouraged to identify their personal hustles and connect them to the community project that they would like to work on, which is another major experiential aspect of the programme. Through on-going communicative action and reflection, students constitute reality as a community of actors and speakers (Aoki, 1984/2005, p. 133) and in the process, students increase their understanding of personal and social praxis. Students have reported having a profound "personal experience" to the extent of perspectives transformations. They appreciate the safe space and permission that this model offers them to be vulnerable to the certain failures they will face as well as the intersectional and nuanced nature of the process of exploring their personal values and their connection to how they perceive social change.

In this sense, leadership is seen as a process, where students explore their own identity. Aoki's views leadership and identity (1987/2004) as two intertwined concepts that require to be explored in relationship to the other. In a process similar to that in my programme, Aoki reflects on his own identity when tasked to explore the concept of leadership (1987/2004, pp. 349–355). In my own practice, the question posed to the students is in regard to how they perceive their own identity in the face of existential crisis due to climate change that is primarily a result of human activities; hence, the era is termed the Anthropocene. Here, I urge them to compare and contrast the duality of their identity in the current social existence versus a *different* world. Aoki's note of Heidegger's *Identity and Difference* is critical and pertinent in this context, in which he "points to how the traditional notion of 'identity' tends to truncate the situational context of our lives, leaving the possible danger of reducing our life reality to an abstracted totality of its own, pretending to wholeness" (Aoki, 1987/2005, p. 354). The *seduction* of the current life to forget the possibilities of "alternate realities" (*fuller life*) is overpowering. Could we complimentarily dwell in a space where we could visualize or imagine a world of possibilities where there is social and environmental equity? Can they visualize a world with no climate crisis or social inequity?

What does that look like? And what do we need to do to get there? Through reflective practice and discussions, students explore the notion of identity in the context of leadership, while revisiting the values that influence their life decisions. While it may be hard for students to grapple with the current situation and visualize a possibility of an ideal world, the notions of agency and identity are critical to reflect on.

By no means do I claim that this process indeed transforms every student. However, I do believe that it starts a conversation, a discussion and a process that may lead to realizations and possible transformations.

Conclusion

Cultivating competencies requires situational praxis through experiential and integrative learning approaches, which are essential for sustainability learning, leadership, critical thinking, and action. Aoki challenges the dichotomized view of theory and practice and encourages us to integrate theory thoughtfully while reflecting upon our practice. Aoki's bridge offers "a generative space of tensionality allowing new things to emerge" (Lee, 2017, p. 19) and meaning perspectives to flourish. By inhabiting the space in-between theory and practice, knowledge and skills, or curricular and co-curricular experiences one engages in an immersive and transformative experience. Aoki's bridge engages us to discern the lines of movement from values exploration to competencies through reflection, from competencies to change through situational praxis, and between knowledge and skills through integrative learning; ultimately leading to perspective transformation towards social change. Aoki's bridge helps us visualize and reconsider the four key sustainability learning aspects into a working framework for application. This is relevant in co-curricular settings and programmes and necessary to integrate at the curricular level.

Beyond the conceptual framework, Aoki's perspectives offer new avenues of exploration for sustainability education, including re-imagining of education in the Anthropocene. Aoki offers us pathways to explore a more holistic approach to education amidst our drastically changing world of uncertainties, pandemics, climate crisis and inequity. Perhaps if we integrate Aoki's thoughts and perspectives into our curriculum and pedagogy, we may be able to achieve a more holistic approach and re-imagine education for the new era.

References

Aoki, T. T. (1983/2005). Curriculum implementation as instrumental action and as situational praxis. In W. F. Pinar & R. L. Irwin (Eds.), *Curriculum in a new key: The collected works of Ted. T. Aoki* (pp. 111–123). Lawrence Erlbaum.

Aoki, T. T. (1984/2005). Competence in teaching as instrumental and practical action: A critical analysis. In W. F. Pinar & R. L. Irwin (Eds.), *Curriculum in a new key: The collected works of Ted. T. Aoki* (pp. 125–135). Lawrence Erlbaum.

Aoki, T. T. (1986/1991/2005). Teaching as in-dwelling between two curriculum worlds. In W. F. Pinar & R. L. Irwin (Eds.), *Curriculum in a new key: The collected works of Ted. T. Aoki* (pp. 159–165). Lawrence Erlbaum.

Aoki, T. T. (1987/2005). Revisiting the notions of leadership and identity. In W. F. Pinar & R. L. Irwin (Eds.), *Curriculum in a new key: The collected works of Ted. T. Aoki* (pp. 349–355). Lawrence Erlbaum.

Aoki, T. T. (1993/2005). Legitimating lived curriculum: Toward a curricular landscape of multiplicity. In W. F. Pinar & R. L. Irwin (Eds.), *Curriculum in a new key: The collected works of Ted. T. Aoki* (pp. 199–215). Lawrence Erlbaum.

Aoki, T. T. (1996/2005). Imaginaries of "East and West": Slippery curricular signifiers in education. In W. F. Pinar & R. L. Irwin (Eds.), *Curriculum in a new key: The collected works of Ted. T. Aoki* (pp. 313–319). Lawrence Erlbaum.

Ashoka Changemakers Canada (2020). *Ashoka changemakers*. Ashoka Canada. https://www.ashoka.org/en-ca/program/ashoka-changemakers

Bandura, A. (2006). Toward a psychology of human agency. *Perspectives on Psychological Science, 1*(2), 164–180.

Barth, M., Godemann, J., Rieckmann, M., & Stoltenberg, U. (2007). Developing key competencies for sustainable development in higher education. *International Journal of Sustainability in Higher Education, 8*(4), 416–430.

Bhabha, H. (1990). The third space. In J. Rutherford (Ed.) *Identity: Community, culture, difference*. Lawrence & Wishart.

Bloom, B. S., Hastings, J. T., & Madaus, G. F. (1971). *Handbook on formative and summative evaluation of student learning*. McGraw-Hill.

Brunetti, A. J., Petrell, R. J., & Sawada, B. (2003). SEEDing sustainability: Team project-based learning enhances awareness of sustainability at the University of British Columbia, Canada. *International Journal of Sustainability in Higher Education, 4*(3), 210–217.

Burns, H. (2011). Teaching for transformation: (Re)designing sustainability courses based on ecological principles. *Journal of Sustainability Education, 2*, 24.

Butler, J. (1996). Professional development: Practice as text, reflection as process, and self as locus. *Australian Journal of Education, 4*(3), 265-283.

Carter, R. (1985). A taxonomy of objectives for professional education. *Studies in Higher Education (Dorchester-on-Thames), 10*(2), 135–149.

Chalkley, B. (2006). Education for sustainable development: Continuation. *Journal of Geography in Higher Education, 30*(2), 235–236.

de Haan, G. (2006). The BLK '21' programme in Germany: A 'gestaltungskompetenz'-based model for education for sustainable development. *Environmental Education Research, 12*(1), 19–32.

Environment and Climate Change Canada (2007). *Core competencies*. Government of Canada. http://www.ec.gc.ca/default.asp?lang=En&n=B69A8571-1&xml=B69A8571-E14C-43A8-A90E-268B2B5BA4A9

Gonzalez, J. M. (2015). *Transformative education for sustainability leadership: Identifying and addressing the challenges of mobilizing change*. PhD Dissertation. University of British Columbia.

Lee, Y. L. (2017). Lingering on Aoki's bridge: Reconceptualizing Ted Aoki as curricular technotheologian. *Journal of Curriculum Theorizing, 31*(3), 18–30

Lotz-Sisitka, H., Wals, A. E., Kronlid, D., & McGarry, D. (2015). Transformative, transgressive social learning: Rethinking higher education pedagogy in times of systemic global dysfunction. *Current Opinion in Environmental Sustainability, 16*, 73–80.

Lozano, R., Merrill, M., Sammalisto, K., Ceulemans, K., & Lozano, F. J. (2017). Connecting competences and pedagogical approaches for sustainable development in higher education: A literature review and framework proposal. *Sustainability*, *9*(10), 1889.
Mayr, E. (2011). *Understanding human agency*. Oxford University Press.
Mezirow, J. (1978). Perspective transformation. *Adult Education*, *28*(2), 100–110
Mezirow, J. (1990). *Fostering critical reflection in adulthood: A guide to transformative and emancipatory learning*. Jossey-Bass.
Mezirow, J. (1998). On critical reflection. *Adult Education Quarterly*, *48*(3), 185–198.
Mezirow, J. (2000). *Learning as transformation*. Jossey-Bass.
OECD (2018). *The Future of Education and Skills: Education 2030*. https://www.oecd.org/education/2030-project/
Osman, A., Ladhani, S., Findlater, E., & McKay, V. (2017). *Curriculum framework for the sustainable development goals*. Commonwealth Secretariat. https://www.thecommonwealth-educationhub.net/wp-content/uploads/2017/01/Curriculum_Framework_for_SDGs_July_2017.pdf
Pinar, W. F. (2005). "A lingering note": An introduction to the collected works of Ted T. Aoki. In W. F. Pinar & R. L. Irwin (Eds.), *Curriculum in a new key: The collected works of Ted. T. Aoki* (pp. 1–85). Lawrence Erlbaum.
Rieckmann, M. (2012). Future-oriented higher education: Which key competencies should be fostered through university teaching and learning? *Futures*, *44*(2), 127–135.
Rogers, C. R. (1980). *Way of being*. Houghton Mifflin.
Rosen, C. C. H. (2014). Encouraging transformational learning and reflective practice with 2nd year IT students using a skills inventory. In G. Motta & B. Wu (Eds.), *Software engineering education for a global e-service economy: Start of the art, trends and developments* (pp. 59–64). Springer International Publishing.
Rychen, D. S., & Salganik, L. H. (Eds.). (2003). *Key competencies for a successful life and a well-functioning society*. Hogrefe & Huber Publishers.
Rychen, D. S., & Tiana, A. (2004). *Developing key competencies in education: Some lessons from international and national experience*. Unesco International Bureau of Education.
Schleicher, A. (2019). *The case for 21st-century learning*. https://www.oecd.org/general/thecasefor21st-centurylearning.htm
Sen, A. (1985). Well-being, agency and freedom: The Dewey lectures 1984. *The Journal of Philosophy*, *82*(4), 169–221.
Shriberg, M., & Harris, K. (2012). Building sustainability change management and leadership skills in students: Lessons learned from "sustainability and the campus" at the university of Michigan. *Journal of Environmental Studies and Sciences*, *2*(2), 154–164.
Statistics Canada (2019). Retrieved from https://www150.statcan.gc.ca/n1/pub/11-631-x/11-631-x2019003-eng.htm
Sterling, S. (2001). *Sustainable education: Re-visioning learning and change*. Green Books.
Tilbury, D. (2004). Environmental education for sustainability: A force for change in higher education. In P. B. Corcoran & A. E. J. Walds (Eds.), *Higher education and the challenge of sustainability: Problematics, promise and practice* (pp. 97–112). Springer.

Toulouse, P. (2016). *What matters in Indigenous education: Implementing a vision committed to holism, diversity and engagement.* Measuring What Matters, People for Education.

Transparencies for introduction to psychology (2004). Allyn & Bacon - Pearson Education.

UNESCO (2015). *UN decade of ESD.* https://en.unesco.org/themes/education-sustainable-development/what-is-esd/un-decade-of-esd

United Nations (2015). *Transforming our world: The agenda 2030 for sustainable development.* Retrieved from https://www.un.org/ga/search/view_doc.asp?symbol=A/RES/70/1&Lang=E

United Nations (2019). *Ten key messages.* https://www.un.org/development/desa/youth/wp-content/uploads/sites/21/2019/08/WYP2019_10-Key-Messages_GZ_8AUG19.pdf

Wiek, A., Withycombe, L., & Redman, C. L. (2011). Key competencies in sustainability: A reference framework for academic program development. *Sustainability Science, 6*(2), 203–218.

World Economic Forum (2016). *The future of jobs: Employment, skills and workforce strategy for the fourth industrial revolution.* http://www3.weforum.org/docs/WEF_Future_of_Jobs.pdf

9 Listen to What the Situation Is Asking
Aoki and Music Education

Margaret O'Sullivan

A conversation begins as Aoki says, "walk with me" (Aoki, 1979/2005, p. 345). A new space is created, a co-dwelling out of time. A many-layered interaction unfolds, as I repeatedly encounter my world afresh in relation with his words and his thinking.

Since encountering the curriculum theorizing of Ted Tetsuo Aoki (Pinar & Irwin, 2005), I find myself repeatedly asking, "what would Ted say?" and searching within his words for *a new key*.[1] Curricular choices informed by locality and difference appear radical in a music education world in love with normative paradigms for what counts as music education, and what gets valued in music curriculum development. Aoki advises that "mindfulness allows the listening to what it is that the situation is asking" (Aoki, 1987/1999/2005, p. 155). Scholarship on music education has largely been infused with theoretical underpinnings of *behaviourism* (Ecker, 1970; Madsen, 1999; Miksza, 2007), *aestheticism* (Arnstine, 1966; Beardsley, 1966; Fossum, 2017; Madeja, 1970; Reimer, 1972; Reimer 1991), and, more recently, *pragmatism* through a lens of experience (Elliott, 1995; Elliott, 2005; Määttänen, 2000; Schmidt, 2010; Vogt, 2003).[2] The influence of *narrative* is reflected in the emergence of arts-infused scholarship that troubles positivist foundational orientations within music education scholarship (Gouzouasis, 2019; Gouzouasis & Lee, 2002; Gouzouasis et al., 2014). Replete with modernism's certainties (Elliott, 2001; Johansen, 2007), music education scholarship is dominated by studies of institutional, school-based, largely North American music education systems in the classroom and in the band room. The situations under study in positivist research models often depend on understandings of human development as linear and biologically determined, underpinned by behaviourism. Knowledges gained from such situations are offered as replicable models in a "what works" (Regelski, 2002) curricular orientation. The universal applicability of findings from such studies beyond the specified situations of music education from which they are derived remains largely untroubled. Such music education scholarship stands on its certainties, to reproduce the values of institutional curriculum beyond the institution to tacitly frame diverse situations of music learning.

DOI: 10.4324/9781003037248-15

In this chapter, I consider the situations of music education that do not fit the fixed imaginary fed by behaviourist, aestheticist, positivist, and post-positivist music education scholarship. Dwelling[3] in curiosity about what happens and what is valued outside of the institutional context, I aim to trouble and unsettle normative music education paradigms that tacitly shape music education experiences in non-institutional settings. To do so, I engage with two Aokian theoretical explorations: Aoki's enriching analysis of the concept of application (Aoki, 1987/1999/2005, pp. 151–158); and his conceptualization of community (Aoki, 1995/2005, pp. 303–312). Approximating a currere (Pinar, 1975/1991) as a means of connecting events in my working life with my study of music education curriculum, I relate two stories from my experience in education settings that exist outside of the institutional mainframe of schooling and the music conservatoire. Dwelling in/on Aoki's deconstruction of concepts of application and community, I pull on entangled threads of a theory-practice orientation in my own music education, and attempt to unravel those threads to better understand the influential role of dominant (theory-practice) paradigms in my work as an instigator of arts and music education programmes (Aoki 1996/2005). Through this inquiry, I hope to contribute enriched understandings of quality in the music of what happens in the unruly lived reality of learning in community, through a mindful listening to what the situation is asking.

Story Note 1: Re/Viewing

In January 1994, freshly graduated from my music degree followed by an arts administration graduate diploma,[4] I was appointed the first Education Officer for a multi-arts venue in Galway, a city with a lively festive scene in the west of Ireland. I was fortunate to be involved in imagining my new role after taking up this appointment. I set about equipping myself with "a new lexicon" (Aoki, 1991/2005, p. 248) by listening to and talking with artists of all disciplines. A performance-oriented paradigm was common to university music education in Ireland at that time, in combination with music history, analysis, and musicology. This curriculum had shaped my intellectual growth in material ways, that largely negated the subjective encounter in favour of a performative athleticism prized in institutional contexts of music education. The training for my new job included a week-long residency at the Irish Museum of Modern Art (IMMA). Under the mentorship of founding members of IMMA's education department, I gained an expansive introduction to museum-based visual arts education and unlimited access to the documented records of every programme since its launch in 1991.

Influenced by immersive exposure to exhibitions and associated educative actions, I returned to Galway nurturing ideas for how an arts venue could begin to foster social engagement through its artistic programming. While the term "community arts" had been in general use in Ireland and the UK since the 1970s (Matarasso, 2013), a "social turn" (Bishop, 2005) in the

1990s brought the concepts of dialogic, relational, and collaborative processes of art-making in the visual arts into focus (Hand, 2013; Kester, 2005), with an emphasis on social engagement. Such dreaming provoked multiple possibilities for what and for whom an education programme might be in a multi-arts facility in a particular place and time, inadvertently bringing me into tension with the management's more instrumentalized vision for arts education as audience development. This latter objective was accompanied by concrete measurables and indicators, to be determined by attendance numbers in the absence of other means of gathering "evidence" of the success of the new arts education programme. While the Director's ambition for the venue was inspiring and generative (he had, after all, been the instigator of my trip to IMMA), the ambiguity and uncertainty characteristic of socially engaged arts practice presented a challenge to the more quantitative concepts of success that were then valued by the organization. We gradually found common ground through programming opportunities that merged definitive outputs with actions that allowed space for the unknowable potentialities of artist-led socially engaged practice. We transformed an old disused shop into a workshop and exhibition space for the women of a local Traveller education project.[5] A weekly storytelling session with youth and elders facilitated intergenerational encounters, culminating in an exhibition and theatre performance.[6] The children's stream of our annual literature festival expanded to incorporate writers-in-residence, youth poetry events, book-making workshops.[7] Collaborations with artists, arts organizations, and communities vivified the arts centre connecting with the local cultural life of the city.

Encountering Aokian concepts of curriculum-as-plan and curriculum-as-lived (Aoki, 1986/1991/2005, pp. 159–165), I feel afresh the scorch of frustrations and humiliations mingled with the remembered joy of encounters and events. Was I dwelling in tensionality between two horizons of curriculum-as-audience development (corporate marketing agenda) and curriculum-as generative experiential situation (with implied creative unpredictability)? In a fusion of horizons that will be recognized by most arts managers, I somehow navigated between the language of objectives-implementation-evaluation (i.e., funding applications and reporting) and the lived experience of human engagement in situated encounters (i.e. events, workshops, and spaces) that emerged. Artists, public groups, and individuals were open to engagement in new modes of experiencing the arts centre as concept and as space. In the years that have passed, I can revisit those memories with a fresh appreciation for the challenges that pushed me to learn and work to seek out the possibilities within the situation, by listening to what the situation was asking.

In all of these tensions, where was "I"? Dwelling in the "zone of between" (Aoki, 1986/1991/2005, p. 161), in a role that is open to interpretation, can be a stressful, difficult space. In tension with the specificity and abstraction of a job description was a seamless curriculum of art-making and living, the teachings of artists and participants, the pedagogies of what happens in and between events. Aoki's reconceptualization of humiliation (Aoki, 1993/2005a, p. 299) beyond the human-centred discourse of the ego is a balm, although no mere formula, as it emphasizes the human-ness in my endeavours to learn how to open the venue to multiple communities. Re-viewing that time with fresh lenses I am newly aware of how I facilitated opportunities for the organization to act as host to those who were considered "diverse" amongst the audience for the arts at that time, and in so doing, allowed the institution to celebrate its diversity, while not really changing the epistemological foundation of the organization itself. Ahmed (2012) crystallizes the dilemma of inclusion in her observation that "to be welcomed is to be positioned as the one who is not at home" (p. 43). To conceptualize community as difference contrasts with diversity discourse that obscures difference within community and between communities. Aoki's space-between "where the otherness of others cannot be buried" (Aoki, 1995/2005, p. 308), enables ideas of equality, equity, and justice to be examined for the "semblance of equivalence" (p. 314) they provide. Objections from senior staff members inevitably arose when encountering bodies that did not traditionally belong—participants smoking in the workshop on their tea breaks; noisy attendees unschooled in the normative behaviour and etiquette of arts events and spaces—these were gaps that I was ill-equipped to bridge. Hospitality instincts kicked in as I sought to emphasize the centre as a place of welcome without realising how unspoken codes that perpetuate exclusion are often reinforced in such contexts. Guests were welcomed into a space that afforded them a "semblance of equivalence" while continuing to configure their "otherness" in that situation. Later, as I moved from a multi-arts education context to more focused music education settings, I continued to pull these threads of heightened awareness of community and socially engaged arts dynamics through my work.

Engaging with Aokian conceptualizations of community (Aoki, 1995/2005, pp. 303–312) and application (Aoki, 1987/1999/2005, pp. 151–158) provokes me to articulate ideas of Community Music Education (CME) that appear radical in a world that continues to enshrine ways of knowing in music education through positivist lenses that are tacitly informed by traditionally privileged forms of music-making. Aoki considers instrumental, anthropological, and hermeneutic understandings of computer technology (pp. 151–158) to reveal possibilities of understanding application in the tension between the language of technology (or any given phenomenon) and the language of the particularities of a situation (p. 155). The specificity of a situation is salient in how the idea of a standard that travels across situations in time and space can result in the application of quality standards that are operable and relevant to one situation being unfit for application in another situation, given the multiple subjectivities in situations that cannot be known. In this way, normative perspectives travel across situations in time and space to influence and shape experiences of music learning within different streams of music education. Forms of music education that are widely understood as an alternative or "other" are in reality the more prevalent forms of music education that happen in the world, for example, contemporary popular, folk, and traditional musics that carry their own pedagogies and epistemologies. Thus, a false binary is constructed between so-called mainstream and non-mainstream. Non-mainstream music learning takes place outside of institutions (and is therefore unofficial) encompassing a vast delta of musical ways of being in our world, constantly being replenished, changing, drying up, taking on new streams, always flowing from generation to generation. In the fixed certainties of official music education curricula, the application of terms of reference for determining quality in music education frames music learning and making in terms of *that which can be known*, or in Aokian terms, "the correct" (Aoki, 1987/1999/2005, p. 153), after Heidegger's "uncannily correct but not yet true" (Aoki, 1987/1999/2005, p. 153; Heidegger, 1977, p. 6). By focusing on the correct, music education may obscure the not yet known. By defining and determining quality within the terms of reference of what can be known, music education discourse fails to realise the full potentiality within and between learning, innovation, and mastery that may reveal essences of what it is to *be in music*.

A new form of music education is emerging in Ireland, and more specifically in Cork, a hybrid form that builds on concepts of community education (Allen & Martin, 1992, pp. 29–30) and offers a space "where the otherness of others cannot be buried" (Aoki, 1995/2005, p. 308). Community Music Education (CME) combines the ethos of community education in which community is considered "primarily as an evaluative, and only secondarily a descriptive, concept" (Allen & Martin, 1992, pp. 29–30) with an ethos of community music.[8] Community education emerged as a movement in vocational education in Ireland in the 1960s, as a responsive and adaptive process that fosters concern for community and repudiates fixed and pre-determined externally designed frameworks and goals. In using community education as a platform or space for music learning and making, notions of practical application based on instrumentalized procedural concepts of music education are countered by the non-static, adaptive ethos of community education that refuses the correct in favour of the possible. The CME "situation" is asking for an attuned listening to the spaces within and between where the essence of *being in music* may be encountered. In CME, I listen to teenage rappers producing and performing words and sounds that both re/sound and re/make their inner and outer worlds, connecting with each other and "others" to stand out in flow—in their inter/est.[9] Children choosing to play complex Irish traditional music engage in modes of learning that are slow and deliberate that require deep practice and connection, mindfully keeping old and new ways in community. The CME situation allows attunement to a young trumpeter seeking out a live improvisatory solo for the first time, chasing notes, phrases, rhythms, and silence in a fusion of instrument, breath, body, mind, and spirit that signals a becoming as a musician. These unpredictable and unknowable events of encounter with self in music are made possible in the space(s) between planned programme and lived experience, in the space of *opportunities offered* rather than pre-set goals and outputs measured. Teachers and learners come together to enliven the curriculum-as-lived, revealing vast potentialities beyond dry, concrete notions of quality represented in the language of implementation and application.

In CME's diversity of provision, the event of subjective encounter with music is valued, and an emphasis on community is privileged. This offering is a radical act. Normative frameworks are also influential in determining what counts as music education. Emphasizing opportunities over goals, focusing on process over output, on creative freedom and autonomy for both teacher and learner—these acts resist established frameworks for music education curriculum in which pre-determined goals with universally measurable outputs, as in the globalized grade exam systems, are so often the determining factor in the music education experience.[10] Curriculum informed by locality and difference is a bridging of worlds with offerings of generative CME opportunities.

Story Note 2: Re/Sounding

Almost 20 years on from my first role in arts education, I found myself facilitating a new entity as it came into being in 2011: a working group of musicians, musician educators, and community educators towards the formation of a local not-for-profit music education partnership (LMEP) in Ireland. Composed of multiple community music groups, the LMEP exists to provide music education opportunities for children and young people towards a goal of lifelong music-making. Whilst the provision of local music education services may not immediately suggest the radicality of the hip hop studio or the improvisatory jazz solo, the partnership's explicit mission is to create opportunities that address inequities in access. The group generated the CME approach as the best means of providing active music learning, diverse music-making, and performance activities according to locality and difference.

As part of an open call for funding,[11] we resisted defining our proposed approach as a fixed model, in preference for an adaptive approach based on evolving local needs. Decision-making and delivery processes are shared and devolved to multiple partners with local community knowledges and musical heritages. In response to the quality proviso on which our funding depended, and partially arising from the expressed concerns of members both within and outside of our partnership (based on often tacit perceptions of low musical quality in the community approach to delivery) the partnership decided to create a Quality Team (QT), composed of music education practitioners from different music traditions and genres. Provision of advice and guidance on programme development and oversight of programme delivery were to be the panel's designated roles in consultation with LMEP music groups. The rapid pace of implementation and roll-out of programme both compromised and negated the functionality of the QT, as there was little space for it to provide advice and guidance on programme development and delivery. This is an example of how externally designed policy imperatives often interfere in the situation they are designed to enhance.

From the beginning, I was both fascinated and troubled by the discourse in meetings with this team of deeply passionate musicians and music educators. Around the long boardroom table, I documented as many different understandings of quality as there were musician identities in the room.[12] Attitudes towards dimensions of music learning were largely derived from musicians' own trajectories and experiences.[13] For example, although the introduction of group music learning was a key principle of the LMEP, responses to this dimension differed amongst members of the QT and musician team. All those around the table had experienced the standardized practice of individual tuition in their own learning, with some engagement in ensembles, including orchestras, pop groups, Irish traditional music groups and sessions, brass and reed concert bands, choirs, and so on. Most of the QT members agreed that group *music-making* can benefit musicians at all stages of learning, but responses were more divided when considering group *learning*. Positive aspects such as peer learning, peer influence, and social engagement were almost unanimously trumped by the importance of technical advancement by individual learners. In this way, the normative experience of institutionalized models of music learning shaped the imaginary of those tasked with the role of quality support, negating the potential for generating new understandings of quality in diverse contexts. Thus, limitations that are tacitly imposed on non-normative or non-mainstream music learning experiences, such as the use of adaptive instruments and technologies for children with disabilities, contemporary song writing, rap, and music production, can be traced back to these fixed imaginaries of what constitutes a music education. The difference within community that is so easily obscured in diversity discourse was glaring through the cracks, as often contradictory beliefs were held by people schooled in fighting their corner, accustomed to doing battle for meagre resources while acting in solidarity together within the identity of community musician. In order to access funding, a community partnership that is explicitly designed to be adaptive and responsive to local situation and need may be required to present a singularity of purpose and unity of process that risks masking the difference within. In resonance with Ahmed's provocation of the euphemism of community in diversity discourse, as "an appearance that is a disappearance" (Ahmed et al., 2006, p. 30; Ahmed, 2012), differences within community and between communities are flattened and erased in the language of application.

What is the situation asking? While it would be easy to consider how this situation acts as an "exemplar" of notional hierarchical arrangements of theory and practice, and the "unhappy marriage" within which both are forever locked (Pinar, 2004, p. 3), it is also fruitful to resist perpetuating binaries of theory and practice, curriculum-as-planned and curriculum-as-lived (Aoki, 1986/1991/2005, pp. 159–163). Aoki dismantles dualistic tendencies in discourses around theory and practice (Aoki, 1986/1991/2005, pp. 159–165; Aoki, 2000/2005), suggesting that such hierarchical binaries are created by both practice-oriented and theoretically oriented discourses that reveal little beyond the value systems informing those positionalities. This echoes how the discourse of quality undertaken in the QT revealed differing positionalities of the members of the partnership. While often reflective of the musical heritages around the table, this revealing of positionalities was also indicative of unexamined concepts as a basis for strongly held positions received either as part of the musician's trajectory or in acts of resistance to an individual's negative experience.

Walking with Aoki, I linger with patterns in my working life in which the processes of negotiation and compromise between worlds—traditional and contemporary, so-called art music and folk music, institutional and de-colonial/de-institutional—weigh more heavily on artists and teachers than on the institutions and corporations that demand such processes. I draw parallels between his theoretical untangling of notions of implementation and application (Aoki, 1987/1999/2005, pp. 151–158) with received ideas of quality and merit that travel mindlessly across situations of music education, as means to understanding in a new and different way according to every particular situation. Aoki's suggestion of a space-in-between that allows for a non-hierarchical and non-linear relationship between theory and practice (Aoki, 1987/1999/2005), a "double vision" (Chambers, 2003, p. 40) keeps traditional and new curricular discourses in view. Expanding on this double vision to invoke other senses, I turn to music and the hearing sense, to a doubled mindful listening that has the potential to liberate CME of its baggage as eternally marginalized "other."

A Closing and an Opening

Attuned and repeated listening to what the situation is asking has the potential to reveal a breadth of understandings concealed within situations of music learning and making. In the Irish sean-nós song tradition[14] the song is often sung with two eyes closed—the singer has tread this road so often that seeing is felt, in dwelling, in body. The singer is sung by the song—the song is part of the singer. Dwelling within and between concepts of application and community, I tread and re-tread well-worn pathways in memory and experience even as I continue to grow through ever new situations that demand new understandings, like the singer of the traditional song for whom each new singing contains both old and new knowing. To dwell is to be *in situ*, in place and in time, in community, to listen for the stories a situation may tell when mindfully attended to. The situation, this present moment, is asking for attuned, mindful, repeated listening. What *would* Ted say? Perhaps his call resounds in ever new keys, towards an opening?

Notes

1. Taken from the title of the collection of writings by Ted T. Aoki, *Curriculum in a New Key*, published in 2005, edited by William F. Pinar and Rita L. Irwin.
2. Based on a review of literature on concepts of quality in music education from 1966 to 2018 in the following publications; *Journal of Aesthetic Education (1966–1996)*, *Journal of Research in Music Education (1970–2018)*, *Philosophy of Music Education Review (1990–2018)*, and *Action, Criticism, Theory in Music Education (1991–2018)*. (Unpublished at time of writing.)
3. I use the word "dwelling" throughout the text, in a deliberate echoing of Aoki's precise yet evocative use of the word—dwelling within, indwelling—to evoke an active presence or way of being in the zone or space between concepts, ideas, and spaces. This active presence is central to his exploration of the space between curriculum-as-planned and curriculum-as-lived, Aoki invites a dwelling with Miss O in her experience of teaching in the zone of between (Aoki, 1986/1991/2005, pp. 159–165).
4. In the early 1990s, the Irish arts sector was transitioning from voluntary and community organising to professionalization and institutionalization. I attended as a member of the first cohort of students in an NUIG graduate programme for the cultural management sector.
5. Irish Travellers/Mincéirí are a recognized ethnic minority in Ireland. One of Ireland's most marginalized groups, they experience entrenched inequities in access to education, healthcare, and culturally appropriate secure housing. They have rich and distinct traditions of language, music, sports, and crafts, and a proud history of cultural and political activism.
6. The Telling Our Stories project.
7. Cúirt International Festival of Literature.
8. Disagreement on a definition of community music underpins much of the research in that area (See Schippers & Kors (Eds.) (2002). *ISME Community Music Activity Commission 2002 Proceedings*). The question of the necessity for a definition was once again revisited in the introduction to the 2018 Oxford Handbook on Community Music (Bartleet & Higgins, 2018). In relation to music education intersections with community music, a significant debate centres on how and whether the teaching and learning that occurs in community music contexts constitutes music education. Koopmans (2007) asserts that durable musical growth can occur in community music contexts, in response to Mullen's (2002) ISME conference paper which argues that the defining characteristic of community music is exploration rather than teaching. In contrast I propose that CME relies on concepts of teaching beyond didactic, teacher-centred notions that have skewed the argument heretofore.
9. "Interest comes from "inter/esse" (esse - to be), being in the "inter." So "to be interested" is to be in the intertextual spaces of inter-faces, the places where "betweens" and "ands" reside, the spaces where "and" is no mere conjoining word but, more so, a place of difference, where something different can happen or be created, where whatever is created comes through as a voice that grows in the middle" (Aoki, 1993/2005b, p. 282).
10. ABRSM, Trinity College London, and Royal College of Music are three of the major exam systems that are globally franchised and are employed as indicators of universal standards of quality.
11. Music Generation Ireland operates on a public-private partnership basis, stimulated by philanthropic donations from U2, the Ireland Funds (a diaspora foundation) and the Irish government with matched funding raised by locally based Music Education Partnerships.

12 Based on ethnographic interviews and qualitative survey conducted for my Master's in Research (O'Sullivan, 2015) at UCC, National University of Ireland, Cork.
13 A Likert-type survey of responses to 26 statements of quality derived from discourse amongst the QT and musician teams formed part of the data for the study.
14 Sean-nós (lit. "old style") song is a distinctive song tradition in Ireland in the Irish language (Gaeilge) and in Scotland (in Gaelic). As an unbroken tradition, it is both an old and a contemporary artistic practice at the same time (Mac Con Iomaire, 2004/2011, p. 627). Sean-nós songs were historically orally transmitted (both passively and actively) through the generations in communities and families, performed unaccompanied, and are often highly ornamented with many regional stylistic, thematic, and form variations. They are now also learned from recordings, archival collections, broadcasts, and transmitted in performance and education settings.

References

Ahmed, S. (2012). *On being included: Racism and diversity in institutional life*. Duke University Press.

Ahmed, S., Hunter, S., Kilic, S., Swan, E., & Turner, L. (2006). *Race, diversity, and leadership in the learning and skills sector*. (Unpublished Report). Available at http://www.gold.ac.uk/media/finaldiversityreport.pdf

Allen, G., & Martin, I. (1992). *Education and community: The politics of practice*. Cassells.

Arnstine, D. (1966). Shaping the emotions: The sources of standards for aesthetic education. *Journal of Aesthetic Education*, 1(1), 45–69.

Aoki, T. T. (1979/2005). Reflections of a Japanese Canadian teacher experiencing ethnicity. In W. F. Pinar & R. L. Irwin (Eds.), *Curriculum in a new key: The collected works of Ted T. Aoki* (pp. 333–348). Lawrence Erlbaum.

Aoki, T. T. (1986/1991/2005). Teaching as indwelling between two curriculum worlds. In W. F. Pinar & R. L. Irwin (Eds.), *Curriculum in a new key: The collected works of Ted T. Aoki* (pp. 159–165). Lawrence Erlbaum.

Aoki, T. T. (1987/1999/2005). Toward understanding "computer application." In W. F. Pinar & R. L. Irwin (Eds.), *Curriculum in a new key: The collected works of Ted T. Aoki* (pp. 151–158). Lawrence Erlbaum.

Aoki, T. T. (1991/2005). Five curriculum memos and a note for the next half-century. In W. F. Pinar & R. L. Irwin (Eds.), *Curriculum in a new key: The collected works of Ted T. Aoki* (pp. 247–261). Lawrence Erlbaum.

Aoki, T. T. (1993/2005a). Humiliating the Cartesian ego. In W. F. Pinar & R. L. Irwin (Eds.), *Curriculum in a new key: The collected works of Ted T. Aoki* (pp. 291–301). Lawrence Erlbaum.

Aoki, T. T. (1993/2005b).The child-centered curriculum: Where is social pedocentricism?. In W. F. Pinar & R. L. Irwin (Eds.), *Curriculum in a new key: The collected works of Ted T. Aoki* (pp. 279-289). Lawrence Erlbaum.

Aoki, T. T. (1995/2005). In the midst of doubled imaginaries: The Pacific community as diversity and as difference. In W. F. Pinar & R. L. Irwin (Eds.), *Curriculum in a new key: The collected works of Ted T. Aoki* (pp. 303–312). Lawrence Erlbaum.

Aoki, T. T. (1996/2005). Narrative and narration in curricular spaces. In W. F. Pinar & R. L. Irwin (Eds.), *Curriculum in a new key: The collected works of Ted T. Aoki* (pp. 403–411). Lawrence Erlbaum.

Aoki, T. T. (2000/2005). Language, culture, and curriculum.... In W. F. Pinar & R. L. Irwin (Eds.), *Curriculum in a new key: The collected works of Ted T. Aoki* (pp. 321–329). Lawrence Erlbaum.

Beardsley, M. (1966). The aesthetic problem of justification. *Journal of Aesthetic Education, 1*(2), 29–39.

Bishop, C. (2005). The social turn: Collaboration and its discontents. *Artforum, 44*(6), 178–183.

Chambers, C. (2003). "As Canadian as possible under the circumstances": A view of contemporary curriculum discourses in Canada. In W. F. Pinar (Ed.), *International handbook of curriculum research* (pp. 221–252). Lawrence Erlbaum.

Ecker, D. (1970). Thinking in different categories: The problem of alternative conceptions of aesthetic education. *Journal of Aesthetic Education, 4*(2), 21–36.

Elliott, D. J. (1995). *Music matters: A new philosophy of music education*. Oxford University Press.

Elliott, D. J. (2001). Modernity, postmodernity and music education philosophy. *Research Studies in Music Education, 17*(1), 32–41.

Elliott, D. J. (Ed.) (2005). *Praxial music education: Reflections and dialogues*. Oxford University Press.

Fossum, H. (2017). From relevance rationality to multi-stratified authenticity in music teacher education: Ethical and aesthetical frameworks revisited. *Philosophy of Music Education Review, 25*(1), 46–66.

Gouzouasis, P. (2019). What are ABER and CAP? *Action, criticism, and theory for music education, 18*(2), 1–24.

Gouzouasis, P., Bakan, D., Ryu, J. Y., Ballam, H., Murphy, D., Ihnatovych, D. ... Yanko, M. (2014). Where do teachers and learners stand in music education research? A multi-voiced call for a new ethos of music education research. *International Journal of Education & the Arts, 15*(15), 1–23.

Gouzouasis, P., & Lee, K. V. (2002). Do you hear what I hear? Musicians composing the truth. *Teacher Education Quarterly, 29*(4), 125–141.

Hand, B. (2013, July 21). *A struggle at the roots of the mind: service and solidarity in dialogical, relational and collaborative perspectives within contemporary art*. https://imma.ie/magazine/a-struggle-at-the-roots-of-the-mind-service-and-solidarity-in-dialogical-relational-and-collaborative-perspectives-within-contemporary-art/

Heidegger, M. (1977). *The question concerning technology, and other essays*. (W. Lovitt, Trans.). Garland Publishing.

Kester, G. (2005). Conversation pieces: The role of dialogue in socially-engaged art. In Z. Kucor & S. Leung (Eds.), *Theory in contemporary art since 1985* (pp. 76–88). Blackwell.

Koopman, C. (2007). Community music as music education: On the educational potential of community music. *International Journal of Music Education, 25*(2), 151–163.

Määttänen, P. (2000). Aesthetic experience: A problem in praxialism—on the notion of aesthetic experience. *Action, Criticism, Theory, 1*(1), 1–9.

Mac Con Iomaire, L. (2004/2011). Song in Irish: Sean-nós. In F. Vallely (Ed.), *The companion to Irish traditional music* (2nd ed., pp. 627–628). Cork University Press.

Madeja, S. S. (1970). Guest editorial: On the third domain. Curriculum development in aesthetic education. *Journal of Aesthetic Education, 4*(2), 5–8.

Madsen, C. K. (1999). Research in music behavior. *The Journal of Aesthetic Education, 33*(4), 77–92.

Matarasso, F. (2013). "All in this together": The depoliticisation of community art in Britain, 1970–2011. In E. van Erven (Ed.), *Community, art, power: Essays from ICAF 2011*. Wijktheater.

Miksza, P. (2007). Effective practice: An investigation of observed practice behaviors, self-reported practice habits, and the performance achievement of high school wind players. *Journal of Research in Music Education, 55*(4), 359–375.

Mullen, P. (2002). We don't teach we explore: Aspects of community music delivery. In H. Schippers & N. Kors (Eds.), *Proceedings of the 2002 ISME commission on community music activity*. Rotterdam. http://www.cdime-network.com

O'Sullivan, M. (2015). *Deconstructing the conceptualisation of quality in music education: A reflexive study of Music Generation Cork City musicians*. [Unpublished master's thesis]. University College Cork, National University of Ireland.

Pinar, W. F. (1975/1991). Currere: Toward reconceptualization. In W. F. Pinar (Ed.), *Curriculum theorizing: The reconceptualists* (pp. 396–424). McCutchan Publishing Corporation.

Pinar, W. F. (2004). *What is curriculum theory?* Lawrence Erlbaum.

Pinar. W.F. & Irwin R.L. (Eds.). (2005). *Curriculum in a new key: The collected works of Ted T. Aokii*. Lawrence Erlbaum.

Regelski, T. A. (2002). Musical values and the value of music education. *Philosophy of Music Education Review, 10*(1), 49–55.

Reimer, B. (1972). Putting aesthetic education to work. *The Journal of Aesthetic Education, 6*(3), 99–108.

Reimer, B. (1991). Essential and nonessential characteristics of aesthetic education. *The Journal of Aesthetic Education, 25*(3), 193–214.

Schippers, H., & Kors, N. (Eds.). (2002). *Proceedings of the 2002 ISME commission on community music activity*. http://www.cdime-network.com

Schmidt, M. (2010). Learning from teaching experience: Dewey's theory and preservice teachers' learning. *Journal of Research in Music Education, 58*(2), 131–146.

Vogt, J. (2003). Philosophy—music education—curriculum: Some casual remarks on some basic concepts. *Action, Criticism, Theory, 2*(1), 1–25.

Interlude
The Inspirited Curriculum

Peter P. Grimmett

It is one thing to be fired by existing traditions; it is most remarkable when one person courageously bursts forth with a new one. The significance of tradition is echoed in George Grant's[1] words: "A tradition is a channel of memory through which fierce and unrequited longings surge, longings which define and shape a life" (as cited in Ignatieff, 2009, p. 153). When I first studied under Ted Aoki in the mid-1970s at the University of Alberta and then The University of British Columbia, the tradition of curriculum was under attack and needed to be re-conceptualized. It needed someone who could embrace and embody the words of Victor Hugo: that *nothing is more powerful than an idea whose time has come*. Dr. Aoki was that person in Canada. With tremendous fortitude, he introduced the nascent re-conceptualist tradition framed around the phenomenological, critical, and post-structural perspectives on curriculum theory; but it was a struggle of gargantuan enormity. Emerging curriculum theory in Canada was imprisoned at that time by a "single vision and Newton's sleep"[2] like a caged bird: It was attacked within the university, characterized as "dubious and unreliable"[3] by other traditions of educational research and non-education disciplinary research (what I'm calling the free birds), it was attacked by policy makers (particularly neoliberalist ones) who saw it as redundant and irrelevant; and yet a small group of researchers led by Ted Aoki sang a curriculum song in a new key, they sang about the freedom from Cartesian rationalism and instrumentalism. Just as in Maya Angelou's (1983) poem *I know why The Caged Bird Sings*, that small bunch of Aokian curriculum scholars sang loudly of things unknown, foreshadowing the release that accompanies non-instrumentalist ways of thinking in teaching and learning; for, before Aoki, curriculum studies in Canada was like a caged bird. It was Aoki who enabled those of us in that small group to sing about the worth of making *curriculum and pedagogy trump the politics of instrumentalism* both within our universities and in society in general.

In 1965, George Grant (2000) publishes *Lament of a Nation*, where he argued that Canada had gone from colony to nation and back to colony; from imperial subservience to Britain to imperial subservience to the USA. Grant spoke to a teach-in of 5,000 students at the University of Toronto in Dylan Thomas-esque style, *We should rage against the dying of the Canadian light*,

DOI: 10.4324/9781003037248-16

but we should be under no illusions that it is dying (Ignatieff, 2009, p. 146). As educators, we need to continue to rage against the dying of the Aokian Canadian light in curriculum studies. We need to take up and enact Aoki's notion of inspiriting the curriculum.

The Aokian Inspirited Curriculum

What is it about inspirited curriculum that means so much and helps us pedagogically in our efforts to promote study? Let me illustrate. I was walking the other day and a golden leaf came drifting into my face. I picked it up to examine the details of its splendor, and was in awe of the magnificent work of nature, which, having made it, then throws it blissfully away. In a similar way, an inspirited curriculum affords teachers the consummate privilege of indulging in many august possibilities for invoking study, which we then throw away, as it were, to our students as an offering of sacrificial pedagogy that then returns to us in the gift of delightful professional fulfilment. Inspirited curriculum is like that, giving back to students the best that they have given to us, and in promoting study with and for them, we find that we delight in educational work together. As teachers, then, our role is to pilot ourselves and our students toward engagement with the world through channels of rhapsodic pedagogy that bring love, joy, and beauty, even laughter, to the lives we contact in this imperfect world.

To do so, we follow the example of Ted Aoki and his impassioned heart for curriculum and pedagogy. Inspirited curriculum is related to the wonderful insight that the material world is now forever infused with the breath of life, perfumed with spirituality. A *crust of bread can be sacred; and all water can become wine.*[4] The inspirited curriculum is the instructional *crust of bread* that ignites a form of pedagogy that turns the commonplace *water* of everyday teaching into the *wine* of joyous study and learning.

Artistic genius, and our delight in what it produces, is an example of the profligate overflow of the world's grace and goodness, given without limit or condition to those who see things through spiritual eyes. Avoiding distractions, creating new and better material out of mistakes, balancing self-demand and self-esteem, are all qualities that unite an educational and spiritual life. And Aokian scholars and teachers set out to do this through the care and thoughtful instruction they offer each day.

Notes

1 My first tenure-track appointment in 1980 was at Dalhousie University where I had the privilege of the late George Grant as a colleague.
2 This line comes from William Blake's (1802) poem *With happiness stretched...* — a poem in which Blake expressed his disaffection with the impact of Newton's universalizing materialist frame on Western culture.
3 Publicly stated by a well-known structural functionalist scholar when Dr. Aoki was recruited from the University of Alberta in 1976 to be the Director of the Centre for Curriculum and Instruction at The University of British Columbia.

4 The symbols of bread and wine, although predominantly identified today with the Christian Eucharist, go back to Abram and his interaction with Melchizedek, the king of Salem (later called Jerusalem) and High Priest, who offered Abram bread and wine while blessing him. It subsequently represented the manna and quail that the Israelites ate in the desert, celebrated in the Jewish Passover before Jesus used it as a sign of his sacrifice for all the descendants of Abram, i.e., Jews, Muslims, and Christians. They are symbols of life in a barren wasteland.

References

Angelou, M. (1983). Caged bird. *Shaker, why don't you sing?* Random House Inc. https://www.poetryfoundation.org/poems/48989/caged-bird

Blake, W. (1802). Poem: With happiness stretched .... In Keynes, G., *The letters of William Blake* (3rd edition revised, No. 40). Oxford University Press.

Grant, G. M. (2000). *Lament for a nation: The defeat of Canadian nationalism.* McGill-Queen's University Press.

Ignatieff, M. (2009). *True patriot love: Four generations in search of Canada.* Penguin.

Part 4
Curriculum Theorizing
Introduction

Nicole Y. S. Lee

This part on curriculum theorizing includes chapters by Bruce Moghtader, Yu-Ling Lee, and Patricia Liu Baergen and Karen Meyer that reverberate with the triadic strengths of pedagogy, theory, and scholarship in Aoki's work (Pinar, 2005, p. xv). Stirred by Aoki's (1985/1991/2005) call to tackle the "taken-for-granted understandings of … curriculum practices" (p. 233), the authors attend to core paradigmatic considerations surrounding the question: What is teaching? Writing from sociological, anthropological, historical, philosophical, and theological genealogies of scholarship, the authors meet at the intersection of concern regarding the ontological being-ness of teachers. They follow the Aokian (1992/2005) shift from centring the "whatness" of teaching as modes-of-doing, to the "isness" of teaching as modes-of-being (pp. 190–191).

The authors approach the ontological question of pedagogical being-ness praxically, embracing the both-and of theory and practice "as twin moments of the same reality" (Aoki, 1983/2005, p. 120). On this topic, Aoki (1983/2005) advises that, "[r]ather than seeing theory as leading into practice, we need now more than ever to see it as a reflective moment in praxis" (p. 120), and that "knowing arises not from inward speculation but from intentional engagement with, and experience of, lived reality" (p. 120). Moghtader, Lee, and Liu Baergen and Meyer further disrupt the value-laden bifurcation of ideas—like teaching and learning, curriculum-as-plan and curriculum-as-lived—that come into play where they are situated: in the Scholarship of Teaching and Learning, teacher education, and curriculum scholarship, respectively. They call for an inspirited curriculum. Each writer draws insights from their engagements with distinct educational communities, where "situation meaning … [is] cocreate[d], guided as they are by their personal and group intentionalities" (Aoki, 1983/2005, p. 121). In their situated contexts, the authors grapple with the challenges inherent in considering not only what teaching is, but also what it means to teach and what it is to learn to become teachers.

Read together, the chapters in this part resist instrumentalization and reveal yearnings for situational aliveness that foregrounds "beings-as-human" rather than "beings-as-things" (Aoki, 1983/2005, p. 122). The authors question "the almost oppressive technological ethos that prevails and enframes [educators]" (Aoki, 1985/1991/2005, p. 233). They complicate the instrumentalization of teachers where teaching performance is measured based on outcomes of student learning, oppose the de-intellectualization of teacher education, and push against the economy-driven, producer-consumer rationale of curriculum implementation, application, and competency. The chapters propose a moment of pause for readers to consider the worldview, paradigm, orientation, root interests, assumptions, and approaches—hidden or otherwise—underlying their own educational experiences, the pedagogical spaces in which they may inhabit, and their understandings of education (see Figure P.4).

The positions from which the authors argue are politically-charged, particularly in the face of education's neoliberalization, which has intensely shaped and regulated the practices of teachers and educators based on market-oriented values. One of the implications of this pervasive climate is the undermining of a humanist view of what it means to be human, which emphasizes the value and agency of human beings. Recognizing the concern behind instrumental action as a kind of control over individual thinking and action, the authors invite readers to open spaces for multiplicities, tensions,

Figure P.4 Nitobe Memorial Garden Sato-Zakura Tree | Photo: Simon Wong.

and dilemmas where the human agency and self-governance to discern the pedagogic good of a situation can thrive.

The following guiding questions offer openings to think with the authors in this part.

Chapter 10: Thinking Creatively with Ted T. Aoki about Scholarship of Teaching and Learning—Bruce Moghtader

1. Through what frames do we evaluate teaching and learning practices?
2. How do interdisciplinary and multi-disciplinary conversations that recognize individual context, history, and place strengthen theory and practice?
3. What values and assumptions are embedded in the systems of which one is part?

Chapter 11: Lingering Notes: Sounds of Learning in Teacher Education—Yu-Ling Lee

1. How might one attune to the interwoven pedagogical lines of movement in educational contexts?
2. How might one live heartfully in the praxis of theory and practice?
3. How might students teach teachers about the beingness of education?

Chapter 12: Contemplating the Relation between Theory and Practice through Three Aoki Inspirited Themes—Patricia Liu Baergan and Karen Meyer

1. How might educators understand our everyday practice within the tensions and dilemmas between systematic demands and individual needs?
2. How can a dialectic mode of *and* conjoin theory *and* practice, curriculum-as-plan *and* curriculum-as-lived, and scholarly *and* pedagogical practices?
3. How might binary thinking be disrupted through double vision?

References

Aoki, T. T. (1983/2005). Curriculum implementation as instrumental action and as situational praxis. In W. F. Pinar & R. L. Irwin (Eds.), *Curriculum in a new key: The collected works of Ted T. Aoki* (pp. 111–123). Lawrence Erlbaum.

Aoki, T. T. (1985/1991/2005). Signs of vitality in curriculum scholarship. In W. F. Pinar & R. L. Irwin (Eds.), *Curriculum in a new key: The collected works of Ted T. Aoki* (pp. 229–233). Lawrence Erlbaum.

Aoki, T. T. (1992/2005). Layered voices of teaching: The uncannily correct and the elusively true. In W. F. Pinar & R. L. Irwin (Eds.), *Curriculum in a new key: The collected works of Ted T. Aoki* (pp. 187–197). Lawrence Erlbaum.

Pinar, W. F. (2005). Foreword. In W. F. Pinar & R. L. Irwin (Eds.), *Curriculum in a new key: The collected works of Ted T. Aoki* (pp. xv–xvii). Lawrence Erlbaum.

10 Thinking Creatively with Ted T. Aoki about Scholarship of Teaching and Learning

Bruce Moghtader

Introduction

According to Pinar (2005) one of "Aoki's key contributions is his traversal for the theory-practice divide. He traverses it, as he might say, by dwelling within the space between the two" (p. 2). Aoki's dwelling in the space between theory and practice continues to contribute to deliberations on the valuing and evaluating of teaching, as he creatively nurtured the pedagogical space for being. As a curriculum scholar, teacher, and researcher, Aoki provoked thinking by complicating certain assumptions about teaching. His demonstrated understanding of theory and practice continues to be generative in educational inquiries, particularly as his works remain under-developed in higher education. I plan to show that Aoki's attention to the relationship between theory and practice strengthens the disciplinary and interdisciplinary considerations pertaining to Scholarship of Teaching and Learning (SoTL).

SoTL is often defined as the systematic study of teaching practices and lived experiences in higher education (Hubball & Clarke, 2010; Webb & Welsh, 2019). Hubball and Gold (2007) introduced the Scholarship of Curriculum Practice (SoCP) as a distinct and complementary field within SoTL to argue for "methodological rigor" in public dissemination of scholarship of teaching. Hubball et al. (2013) suggested that SoCP, "internalizes theory and practice through a systematic, rigorous, and cyclical process of inquiry" (p. 45). The authors found that theoretical and methodological considerations of curriculum are important in transforming limited conceptions of SoTL, which at times is narrowly conceptualized as applying research on classrooms. They posed that such considerations render substantive contribution to educational leadership, programme-level reform, curriculum renewal initiatives, and implementation processes in higher education (Hubball et al., 2013, p. 50). In this context, Aoki's scholarship assists with examining whether an inquiry of teaching ought to be intrinsically linked to learning. I suggest he offers practitioners and researchers with the possibility that teaching may inform teaching.

From his early works onwards, Aoki (1978/1980/2005) devoted particular attention to educational research asking for "a critical awareness that conventional research has not only a limiting effect but also to some degree a

DOI: 10.4324/9781003037248-18

distorting effect on new possibilities" (p. 94). He encouraged educators "to seek out new orientations that allow us to free ourselves of the tunnel vision effect of mono-dimensionality" (p. 94). His inquiries connected curriculum to teaching as experiences irreducible to observational metrics, behavioural checklists, standardized tests, and planned curricula. As the first section demonstrates, Aoki reconceptualized teaching as more than a mere doing of acts. I will explore, in the second section, how the initial aims of SoTL in its institutional context may benefit from Aoki's (inter)disciplinary considerations of history and context in teaching. By addressing issues of interest and knowledge in evaluation paradigms, Aoki moved curriculum development as a series of implementation of steps towards a deeper understanding of human relationships in education. Aoki's (1977) consideration of evaluation paradigms, discussed in the third part of the chapter, allowed him to explore scholarly research in education as a pragmatic endeavour reliant on perspective-taking. Aoki's grasp of underlying theories demystifies methodological assumptions and enhances scholarly practices.

Ted Aoki as a Teacher

Education and educating are human activities to serve humanity; however, in theory and practice, there exist misconceptions in which humans are taken as means to certain ends. One example for this was the "ends-means scheme" explained by Ralph Tyler (1965) in *Basic Principles of Curriculum and Instruction* orders the work of teachers as mere doing steps: (1) determine purposes; (2) identify learning experiences; (3) organize those experiences; and (4) evaluate achievements. The four steps when taken as doctrine, cast students as objects that learn and teachers as instruments that produce learning (Aoki, 1978/1980/2005; Burns, 2018; Pinar, 2005, 2006). The rationale for such principles, if any, aligns education with business and industrial procedures to increase efficiency as the goal of teaching (Aoki, 1978/1980/2005). Aoki's concern was the diminishing of human agency to think and act in the processes of education.

Today, the instrumentalization of teachers continues to be centred on securing learning. Such a movement emphasizes the credibility of econometrics that often value mathematical models and managerial procedures, which serve to limit humans' capacity to make decisions and act. The categorizing and mainstreaming of the doing of teaching has transformed teaching one-sidedly with the over-reliance on technology, techniques, and skills. While teaching strategies that make content accessible, students engaged, and communications enhanced are important, they remain as part of developing professional *judgement* that require thought and skills beyond the mere ends of producing learning. What is a *skill?* According to Max van Manen (1996), "Etymologically *skill* means 'to have understanding,' (p. 208) and pedagogical skills comes from perceptiveness through practice of teaching coupled by thoughtful reflection. van Manen elaborates: "Pedagogical perceptiveness relies in part on a tacit, intuitive knowledge that the teacher may learn from personal experience, or through apprenticeship with a more experienced teacher" (van Manen, 1996, p. 208). Learning from a more experienced teacher has been part of teacher education programmes (Clarke & Elfert, 2015) and recently has been cultivated in higher education professional development in teaching whereby new faculty members collaborate, observe, and converse with more experienced faculty members (Stang & Strubbe, 2017). Institutive knowledge, to some degree, comes from having time to think, study, reflect, and relate to one's lived experience, as well as recognizing that it is *knowing* rather than knowledge by a right of access that makes an experienced educator experienced.

In the acknowledgements of his book, *The Tact of Teaching: The Meaning of Pedagogical Thoughtfulness*, van Manen (1996) offered a hint to an exemplar: "A memorable teacher, Ted Aoki, who possesses the teacherly tact of 'letting learn'" (p. viii). Aoki lived to be an experienced teacher and scholar, re-conceptualizing skills and acts by encouraging different ways of understanding. Aoki's reflections on pedagogy are particularly relevant in the present culture of higher education, where instructors are often pressed to publish and tasked with "managing" increased enrolment in their classrooms, while also engaging in efforts to promote learning instead of becoming skilful teachers. The act of improving learning rather than lingering on teacherly acts reduces the scholarship of teaching to a scholarship on learning. Such a misconception has come from misconstruing higher education as both consumption and investment, and so equating students with consumers and teachers with service-providers. Integrating higher education as part of a market has relentlessly focused on the production and consumption of information and facts instead of valuing intelligence, critical thinking, and liberal arts (Nussbaum, 2010). Teaching is a service (a contribution) to humanity, but a service unlike any other, for it guides people to become certain beings.

Aoki suggests that "pedagogical perceptiveness" is not a linear hardwiring of knowledge; knowledge that measures teaching by improving learning outcomes redirects thoughtfulness to ends-means schemes and often neglects how teaching is received and experienced. The scholarship of teaching is no stranger to thoughtful reflection on practice. Aoki's erudition of teaching offers a background for deliberating on what "scholarship" may *be*, not what it must *do*. His clarity in discerning the historical associations that reduce teaching to depersonalized functions, channelled by devices, underscores the role of thought and theory in understanding scholarly inquiries *of* and *to* educational activities.

Scholarship of Teaching and Pedagogical Thoughtfulness

When Boyer (1990) initiated the field of scholarship of teaching, he too addressed the narrow visions in the intellectual climate and noted the overemphasis on discipline specific research that had distracted attention from teaching in higher academic institutions. Boyer's (1990) attention to the role of teaching as a scholarly discipline was centred on the goals of: (1) moving beyond traditional disciplinary boundaries; (2) providing faculty with opportunities to reflect on practices of teaching; and (3) engaging faculty in interdisciplinary and multi-disciplinary conversations with others. Here, Boyer (1990) was describing an integrative study into teaching itself. He acknowledged that teaching was a service with social and civic function that required professional activity and rigor in research activities with theoretical and practical underpinnings. He explained that the goals of SoTL were in light of growing bureaucratization of higher education and so he considered teaching required "serious scholarship" (p. 22).

Boyer (1990) invited faculty to assess and reflect on the values directing their teaching and also examine the institutional determinants that entangled teaching with putting students through a system. He recognized that every discipline has a set of values and teaching was no exception. He encouraged inquiries to go beyond instrumental and procedural acts of teaching, to reflect, converse, and study philosophies and practices that direct one's professional judgment in teaching. The articulated aims of scholar teachers indicated an inquiry towards the processes of meaning-making and inquiring where and how meaning and understanding of teaching practices come about. As Simmons and Poole (2016) have stressed, "Boyer introduced the notion of the Scholarship of Teaching, suggesting that teaching that contributed to others' enlightenment was, in and of itself, scholarly work" and "should be seen as equivalent to … disciplinary research. Over the years," they continued, "*learning* was added to make explicit the focus on student learning" (p. 13). Learning, when judged by student outcomes and reduced to administering teaching acts, does little for teaching to become a scholarship.

Not far from Boyer's position, Aoki (1985/1991/2005) recognized that the narrow measures to produce learning has made "many feel that life in education just cannot go on without the word 'learning.' In fact, teaching is often seen as the flip side of 'learning'" (p. 230). Was Aoki right that for many "to understand teaching is to understand learning" (p. 230)? An inquiry of teaching, beginning with the assumption of securing learning, can arguably (and paradoxically) inform and reform the concept of "learning." Boyer's advocacy for interdisciplinary and multi-disciplinary conversations, can be participatory, transformative, and as well as subversive. It can shake the overdominance of learning. Such a process involves learning to unlearn teaching as means for learning. Inquiries of teaching beyond a set of classroom techniques may consider the role of place and time and/or examine the regime of truth about certain techniques to unearth their loaded values and assumptions.

Similarly, Boyer (1990) was intentional in not binding teaching to learning as a "plan" for the scholarship he envisioned. Perhaps Boyer recognized the contradiction in the term "scholarship." The etymology of the word "scholar" refers to someone who learns (Wilensky, 2017). As a practice, it dates back to curiosity and concern with authenticity of the teachings of the ancient texts and philosophies. Such studies informed and contributed to early Christian learning but also to modern science and political constitutions. Wilensky (2017) showed the transition from antiquity's philosophical schools, where "learning acts" became "in the service of faith" (p. 33), were intertwined with study, self-reflection, contemplation, and service. These ideals were transformed by the economic rationality that subjected teaching to industrial ideals of speed and profit.

A scholar is someone who learns, and so the scholarship of teaching for some time avoided the doubling down on learning. The case for the disciplinary autonomy of the scholarship of teaching may be hindered when it is tightly bound to production of learning and outcomes. The scholarship of teaching without its narrow association to learning, Boyer thought, could become a mode of engagement in interdisciplinary and multi-disciplinary conversations, as one of the goals of SoTL. Boyer's (1990) lamentation of the "restricted view of scholarship" designed by "hierarchy of functions" (p. 15), argued that the scholarship of teaching can enable one to look outside and around the hierarchies. He cited anthropologists and cultural scholars such as Clifford J. Geertz and Edward Said to establish a stand against the limited scope prescribed to teaching. Boyer's (1990) attention to the cross-discipline scholarly trends shook the norms instituted by 19th century masculine, Eurocentric, depoliticized, and elitists approaches, and conceived teaching as connected to "intellectual questions and to pressing human problems" (p. 21). The call for an interdisciplinary approach to teaching broke away from conventional practices of production of learning to scholarship of teaching.

The shift from medieval scholarship grew gradually by changes in science and technology and by reliance on the material philosophies of Descartes and Bacon. The former approach knowledge mechanically and the later propose a utilitarian value to advancement of learning. Referencing, "I think: Therefore, I am?" of the Cartesian view, Aoki (1993/2005) wrote: "Many of us have been schooled to teach that way" (p. 294), the way in which perhaps teaching and learning are situated in two realms of "Cartesian either/or" (p. 293). Aoki (1993/2005) was addressing the dividing gap in theory/practice as well as teaching/learning that supports the expansion of science and technology in personal and social imaginaries, whereby "even the notion of 'education' has become instrumentalized" (p. 295). Aoki suggested the gap continues to close on Cartesian precepts when teachers surrender their agency in favour of controlling students' learning. This, Aoki diagnosed, grew from "contemporary 'intoxication' with technology and science" (Pinar, 2019, pp. 142–143). There ought to remain an in-between space left unmediated for dynamism, improvisation, and agency so humans, as thoughtful beings, can practice, redeem, deliberate, and attend to their relations.

The Cartesian either/or concerns pedagogical situations conceptualized as mere doings: "Indeed, teachers are more than they do; They belong to that which is beyond their doing; they are the teaching" (Aoki & Aoki,

1990, p. 16). Aoki (1992/2005) added: "What seems to be concealed and hence unseen and unheard is an understanding of thinking that might be understood as thoughtfulness" (p. 196). In this sense, thoughtfulness is "an embodied doing and being—thought and soul embodied in oneness of the lived moment" (Aoki, 1992/2005, p. 196).

Teaching and inquiry are interconnected in lived experiences. Human beings, conscious of their limitations towards what is left unseen and unheard, have the capacity to go beyond taking generalizations and data at face value—the Latin root of the word *data* suggests "something given." However, the interrogation, interpretation, and collection activities of the 18th century scholars transformed particularities to evidence and useful facts (Poovey, 1998). The reference here is to the growing literature on strategies defined as *evidence-based* practice. Such evidence has defined *practice* and *evidence* by certain values and evaluations rooted in Western philosophies of Descartes and Bacon, informing habits and norms of a scholarship oriented to maximizing outcomes and increasing efficiency as priorities for learning engagement. Evidence-based teaching is derived from culture, thoughts, relations, and human particularities that are often left outside or on the margins when teaching is tailored to instrumental ends.

Aoki (1981/2005) promotes curiosity so learning for knowledge's sake may foster authentic conversation about teaching. His reflections take instructors and students beyond classrooms and into society and history, so teaching and learning becomes concerned with human life. There may be logical conclusions as to why teaching needs improving, why certain learning is a necessity and to why inquiring into their conditions is important, but these are not resolved by pre-conceived notions devoid of context. Aoki (1981/2005) encouraged enquiring into how human development and relations are becoming ever more determined by the demands of economic development and technologies that accompany it. In broadening methodological understandings of educational research, his scholarship considered *interest* and knowledge.

Educational Researcher: Theory and Practice in SoTL

According to Hubball and Clarke (2010), SoTL is a "distinctive form of practice-based research" that "provides unique opportunities for faculty members to reflect on and initiate positive changes to their teaching" and develop appreciation of complexities in teaching and learning (p. 1). Aoki (1991/2005b) spoke of education research as processes to gain such appreciation of experiences, and to "understand and reunderstand more deeply the insistently enduring question for us who profess to be educators—the questioning of what it means to be truly pedagogic" (p. 389). His expansive capacity and his care were evident in his gestures to listen and relisten to "the sound of pedagogy emerging from the earthy silence" (Aoki, 1991/2005b, p. 389). Such a listening perhaps is too poetic for some, who find research to proceed methodically based on the Cartesian manner of human/machine and, in Baconian terms, to discover, order, and prescribe living processes as isolated events and things. Instead, concerned with the "ways of knowing," Aoki (1987/2005, p. 365) pragmatically examined human interests.

Aoki began in evaluating the intents of those who inquire and interpret and added complexity to scholarly undertakings. He saw that "in educational research the availability of a research tool often determines the nature of the research done and how research is understood" (Aoki, 1991/2005a, p. 168). Methods adopted to examine the nature, domains, and processes not only impose a framework but also become the prism through which understanding and valuing pedagogical phenomenon is made possible. Initially, Aoki (1978/1980/2005) identified three inquiry orientations: Empirical analytic, situational interpretive, and critical (p. 100). Some years later he returned to these frameworks and added a fourth approach: Critical-hermeneutic evaluation. More than guidelines for scholarly research, Aoki demonstrated the necessity of relistening, re-examining, and revising theoretical research approaches. His clarification on methodological orientations expanded the horizons of conducting research in SoTL.

In the first approach, Aoki (1986/2005) had discovered that empirical analytic research often accommodates the "end-means orientation." Such a research framework entertains a set of "concerns" (p. 140) that include measurements of efficiency, goals, objectives, effectiveness, organizational goals, congruency between and among intended outcomes, and instructional materials. Such managerial concerns often become the ends in themselves in understanding teaching and learning. Aoki pointed out that the "end-means evaluation" approach has gained its credibility by assuming "the status of consensual validity of legitimated educator 'scholars.' Such legitimated authenticity led many evaluators to regard this evaluation orientation as *the* orientation" (p. 141). He added that ends-mean orientation is "deeply rooted [in an] interest ... [for] *control*" and those subscribing to the "ends-means views are technologically oriented" (p. 141). When teaching is an instrument for learning, learning is reducible to predefined performances and achieved by manipulation applied on people and/or their environment. In the *ends-means* research framework, control and manipulations are often enveloped in humanistic logics, maximizing utility, and introducing new optimization metrics to teaching and learning. Aoki suggested the need for expanding understanding about facts and generalizations in the end-means research designs.

In the second evaluation approach, the *situational interpretive* the scholar-teacher is guided by an interest to understand meaning-making processes as well as the structure of communications and relations among persons (Aoki, 1986/2005). And so, the scholar is oriented to "human experience as socially lived" (Aoki, 1986/2005, p. 142) with an *awareness* that social actors make meaning in situations and are not partial in the construction of understanding. Unlike the first approach, where the notions of environment and observation seemingly present themselves devoid of value, culture, and history, the second approach considers values, context, and interpretation in processes. Aoki (1991/2005a) referred to the situational interpretive approach as the emic evaluation orientation, clarifying what is at stake is "subjective understanding" (p. 176) as insiders to a reality aim to better understand the *quality* of pedagogical experiences and processes, views, perspectives, interactions, and relations that accompany them in micro cultures such as classrooms. The interpretive approach offers a methodological tool to counter "the standardized way in which people recognize correctness and incorrectness based on the strict outsiders' objective format that dominates the view of knowing stressed in ends-means evaluation" (Aoki, 1991/2005a, p. 177). Attention is directed to understanding settings by case studies that acknowledge conceptions and constructions at play and expose how actors are impacted as a result. The aims of such a research is to "describe" realities.

The third approach, "critical evaluation" is oriented to understanding "underlying perspectives" in programmes and procedures that are "typically taken-for-granted and therefore, hidden from view" (Aoki, 1986/2005, p. 145). The questions of values and valuing are central to education. If there is a dominance of certain values, be it efficiency, accessibility, sustainability, and saving time and money, how do these values inform teaching and direct performativity? Furthermore, critical evaluations examine how certain regularities are taken for granted to direct institutional expectations, metrics, decisions, and behaviours. The framework unearths interests, assumptions, and intentions in a place and time. It aims to increase awareness and transform habits in practices by scholarly study and reflection. Aoki (1991/2005a) added that critical reflections are not applied solely on situations, events, and facts but also to the evaluators as part of the practices they examine. As he explained, "Critical reflection leads to an understanding of what is beyond the actor's ordinary view by making the familiar unfamiliar, by making the invisible visible" (p. 174). The element of scholarly aim to think and rethink teaching-learning, classroom spaces, or the "evidence" in the evidence-based practices is generative of creative actions—beginning by attending, listening and relistening. The framework supports transformation, since the inquiry expands to see for oneself whether "Truth" is a reducible stand-alone fact, and whether evidence in literature is applicable in one's context and experience as a teacher.

The fourth orientation is the "critical-hermeneutic evaluation" (Aoki, 1991/2005a, p. 179). Aoki suggested that such an approach is not simply the coming together of the situational interpretive and critical framework, for any combination of two methodologies will render each with different tools and sets of assumptions. He found: "The interests in the nature and quality of the beingness of human beings are" to support understanding of "the quality of ontological meanings in the lived experiences of students, teachers, administrators, and parents" (Aoki, 1991/2005a, p. 179). He integrated what is often held distant in research: The inquiry into lived experiences to go beyond the lexical and representational in studying theories and practices. The inquiry of lived experiences is to advance the quality of being human. Contrasting this framework with the "ends-means evaluation," Aoki (1991/2005a) noted the evaluator "must enter deeply into intersubjective conversation with the people in the evaluation situation" (p. 180). Such conversations require one to go beyond "the informational level as simply exchanges of messages," requiring human presence. In the "Age of Technology and the Age of Information," Aoki noted, such an inquiry helps recognition of beings who not only make meaning but live as "beings that they are" (pp. 180–181). Such recognition of beings finds humans, students and teachers, and as ends to themselves.

Aoki is in search of deepening the existential themes of teaching and learning. Such an evaluation begins in the realm of language and representation as an entry to understanding the practices that makes us think and act as we do. Aoki (1991/2005a) added "the world of lived experience is considered as the ground for the four evaluation orientations" (p. 168). Each orientation framework enables standing in relation to scholarship as Aoki contextualized learning about teaching:

> It has been said that an educator's understanding of his [or her] task as educator is most clearly demonstrated by his [or her] method of evaluation. If that be so, the evaluation approaches we used disclose our understanding of possible ways of understanding what it means to be an educator and what it means to be educated.
>
> (Aoki, 1986/2005, p. 149)

In this manner, each methodological approach carries interests with ever-widening circles of significance in how we live, think, and act as embodied beings.

Conclusion

Similar to Boyer, Aoki (1986/2005) gauges effort in evaluation to realize the importance of "philosophical anthropology" (p. 137). However, Aoki (1978/1980/2005) enabled a re-centring of the human in-relation into the task of curriculum thought (teacher-centred, student-centred, disciplined-centred, technology-centred, and society-centred, etc.). Finding each research framework and their centres as insufficient to grasp the scope and context of teaching, Aoki (1978/1980/2005)

> center[ed] curriculum thought on a broader frame, that of '[hu]man/world/relationships,' for it permits probing of the deeper meaning of what it is for persons (teachers and students) to be human, to become more human, and to act humanly in educational situations.
>
> (p. 95)

Such integrative search and practice may not instantly lead to instrumental changes, but it may help to cultivate pedagogical perceptiveness and nurture SoTL as a reiterative scholarly process.

Scholarly inquiries in teaching are deeply associated with theories and practices that are historical and cultural. Aoki's dwelling of the space between theory and practice offers a way of living one's teaching, in the in-between spaces where scholars become intimate and compassionate towards the contexts and persons they learn with and from. Here, engagement is pivotal and an outside position of an evaluator lacks perceptiveness into experience of teaching and learning. Aoki (2003/2005) suggested that teaching is learning to live with one's self and the other, surpassing the dualities and recognizing it is in being in-between and being in relation that self and other enact themselves as such. And so, Aoki (1987/2005) wrote of ways of knowing to invoke a "deep sense of humility" and orienting teaching to "the grace by which educator and educated are allowed to dwell in the present that embraces past experiences" and remain "open to possibilities yet to be" (p. 365). This orientation to experience, perhaps, contributes to a better understanding of why we think and live as such. It also offers a prospect for interdisciplinary approaches to SoTL with recognition of context, history, and place.

Acknowledgement

The author would like to thank Paulina Semenec for her comments and editorial assistance. He is grateful to the editors for their support in making this chapter possible.

References

Aoki, T. T. (1977). Theoretic dimensions of curriculum: Reflections from a micro-perspective. *Canadian Journal of Education/Revue Canadienne De L'éducation*, 2(1), 49–56.

Aoki, T. T. (1978/1980/2005). Toward curriculum inquiry in a new key. In W. F. Pinar & R. L. Irwin (Eds.), *Curriculum in a new key: The collected works of Ted T. Aoki* (pp. 89–110). Lawrence Erlbaum.

Aoki, T. T. (1993/2005). Humiliating the Cartesian ego. In W. F. Pinar & R. L. Irwin (Eds.), *Curriculum in a new key: The collected works of Ted T. Aoki* (pp. 291–301). Lawrence Erlbaum.

Aoki, T. T. (1987/2005). Inspiriting the curriculum. In W. F. Pinar & R.L. Irwin (Eds.), *Curriculum in a new key: The collected works of Ted T. Aoki* (pp. 357–365). Lawrence Erlbaum.

Aoki, T. T. (1981/2005). Toward understanding curriculum: Talk through reciprocity of perspectives. In W. F. Pinar & R. L. Irwin (Eds.), *Curriculum in a new key: The collected works of Ted T. Aoki* (pp. 219–228). Lawrence Erlbaum.

Aoki, T. T. (1985/1991/2005). Signs of vitality in curriculum scholarship. In W. F. Pinar & R. L. Irwin (Eds.), *Curriculum in a new key: The collected works of Ted T. Aoki* (pp. 229–233). Lawrence Erlbaum.

Aoki, T. T. (1986/2005). Interests, knowledge and evaluation: Alternative approaches to curriculum evaluation. In W. F. Pinar & R. L. Irwin (Eds.), *Curriculum in a new key: The collected works of Ted T. Aoki* (pp. 137–150). Lawrence Erlbaum.

Aoki, T. T. (1991/2005a). Layered understandings of orientations in social studies program evaluation. In W. F. Pinar & R. L. Irwin (Eds.), *Curriculum in a new key: The collected works of Ted T. Aoki* (pp. 167–186). Lawrence Erlbaum.

Aoki, T. T. (1991/2005b). The sound of pedagogy in the silence of the morning calm. In W. F. Pinar & R. L. Irwin (Eds.), *Curriculum in a new key: The collected works of Ted T. Aoki* (pp. 389–401). Lawrence Erlbaum.

Aoki, T. T. (1992/2005). Layered voices of teaching: The uncannily correct and the elusively true, In W. F. Pinar & R. L. Irwin (Eds.), *Curriculum in a new key: The collected works of Ted T. Aoki* (pp. 187–197). Lawrence Erlbaum.

Aoki, T. T. (2003/2005). Locating living pedagogy in teacher "research": Five metonymic moments. In W. F. Pinar & R. L. Irwin (Eds.), *Curriculum in a new key: The collected works of Ted T. Aoki* (pp. 425–432). Lawrence Erlbaum.

Aoki, J., & Aoki, T. T. (1990). Silent voices of teaching. *Voices of teaching. Monograph #1*. The British Columbia Teachers' Federation. 14–17.

Boyer, E. L. (1990). *Scholarship reconsidered: Priorities of the professoriate*. Princeton University Press.

Burns, J. P. (2018). The past in the present: The historic reach of the "Tyler rationale." In *Power, curriculum, and embodiment. Curriculum studies worldwide* (pp. 65–93). Palgrave Macmillan.

Clarke, A., & Elfert, M. (2015). Surprising that anyone would want to be a cooperating teacher. *Education Canada, 56*(2), 1–5. https://www.edcan.ca/articles/surprising-that-anyone-would-want-to-be-a-cooperating-teacher/

Hubball, H. T., & Clarke, A. (2010). Diverse methodological approaches and considerations for SoTL in higher education. *The Canadian Journal for the Scholarship of Teaching and Learning, 1*(1), 1–11.

Hubball, H. T., & Gold, N. (2007). The scholarship of curriculum practice and undergraduate program reform: Integrating theory into practice. *New Directions for Teaching and Learning, 112*, 5–14.

Hubball, H. T., Pearson, M. L., & Clarke, A. (2013). SoTL inquiry in broader curricular and institutional contexts: Theoretical underpinnings and emerging trends. *Teaching & Learning Inquiry: The ISSOTL Journal, 1*(1), 41–57.

Nussbaum, M. (2010). *Not for profit: Why democracy needs the humanities*. Princeton University Press.

Pinar, W. F. (2005). "A lingering note": An introduction to the collected works of Ted T. Aoki. In W. F. Pinar & R. L. Irwin (Eds.), *Curriculum in a new key: The collected works of Ted T. Aoki* (pp. 1–85). Lawrence Erlbaum.

Pinar, W. F. (2006). *The synoptic text today and other essays: Curriculum development after the reconceptualization*. Peter Lang.

Pinar, W. F. (2019). *What is curriculum theory?* Lawrence Erlbaum.

Poovey, M. (1998). *The history of the modern fact: Problems of sciences of wealth and society*. University of Chicago Press.

Simmons, N., & Poole, G. (2016). The history of SoTL in Canada: Answering calls for action. *New Directions for Teaching and Learning, 146*, 13–22.

Stang, J., & Strubbe, L. (2017). Paired teaching for faculty professional development in teaching. *Discussions on university science teaching: Proceedings of the Western Conference on science education*, *1*(1), 1–11. https://ojs.lib.uwo.ca/index.php/wcsedust/article/download/3780/3003

Tyler, R. W. (1965). *Basic principles of curriculum and instruction*. University of Chicago Press.

van Manen, M. (1996). *The tact of teaching: The meaning of pedagogical thoughtfulness*. The Althouse Press.

Webb, A., & Welsh, A. J. (2019). Phenomenology as a methodology for scholarship of teaching and learning research. *Teaching & Learning Inquiry*, *7*(1), 168–181.

Wilensky, J. (2017). *The intellectual properties of learning: A prehistory from Saint Jerome to John Locke*. The University of Chicago Press.

11 Lingering Notes
Sounds of Learning in Teacher Education

Yu-Ling Lee

In this chapter, I follow Ted Aoki by lingering in the space of curriculum and pedagogy, finding pause, and dwelling in the sounds of teaching and learning in teacher education. Aoki lingers in the space between curriculum-as-plan and curriculum-as-lived (Aoki, 1986/2004). Teacher education can offer a space for teacher candidates to linger as they mature, ready, and shape themselves for their vocation as teachers.

Teacher education remains a complicated conversation (Pinar, 2004) with varied programming issues, economic challenges, and socio-political concerns. Globally, teacher education has emphasized reform with policies that can be seen as excessively promoting professional practice while concomitantly de-intellectualizing teacher education (Clarke & Phelan, 2017). Barrow (1990) has evaluated teacher education programmes and found they favoured materialistic and technocratic values above all else. Pinar (1989) continues this criticism and states that a fitting response is "a curricular reconceptualization of teacher education" (p. 9). In Kincheloe's (1993) reconceptualization project, he proposes a "postformal expansion of inquiry-oriented teacher education" (p. 197). This entails a kind of teacher education that serves the excluded and the oppressed, dedicated to an ethos of emancipatory change. Phelan (2015) reconceptualises the possibilities in this transformation and proposes that "teacher education must be primarily concerned with the teacher's subjectivity" (p. 4), which is often impeded by bureaucratic practices and policies. Such subjectivity is necessary so that teacher candidates discern their own agency and responsibility in pedagogy. In the Canadian context, Phelan et al. (2020) propose cultivating responsiveness as a Canadian reframing of teacher education. They suggest that such responsiveness entails themes of academic erudition, civic particularity, and ethical engagement. Within this context, we encounter Ted Aoki.

Much like Aoki, I am hoping to share the sounds of learning from my own educational journey as a Chinese-Canadian, a former doctoral student, and now an assistant professor in education. My personal voice, is joined by the chorus of my students, these teacher candidates who I am privileged to journey alongside. As Aoki has drawn from Kierkegaard about the auditory sense as being the most spiritual (cf. Aoki, 1991/2005a, p. 372), he is decentring

DOI: 10.4324/9781003037248-19

our visual sense as the primary means of establishing educational identities. Following Aoki's move to the *sonare*, I draw on Aoki's call for us to be "more fully sonorous beings" (Aoki, 1991/2005a, p. 373). This call requires that we linger on the stories and complexities of teachers, students, and their pedagogical beingness.

In the following sections, I weave together my experience as a student and teacher, thinking and theorizing new curricular lines of movement, with a reflection on pedagogical being. Aoki's ideas of multiplicity (Aoki, 1992/2005a), bridging (Aoki, 1996/2005), curriculum-as-lived (Aoki, 1986/1991/2005), technology (Aoki, 1987/1999/2005), and inspirited curriculum (Aoki, 1987/2005) were all theorizations that imprinted on me. These sections encompass three Aokian motifs that I find especially resonance with the lived experience within teacher education.

Thinking and Theorizing

During my tenure as an education student, one of Aoki's citations of Heidegger remained at the forefront of my mind. Toward the end of an article exploring the landscape of curriculum theory, Aoki recalled Heidegger's statement that "the most thought-provoking thing about our thought-provoking times is that we are not yet thinking" (Aoki, 1993/2005a, p. 298). At times, this prioritization of thinking was not true for my own development as a student. Instead, gleaning educative tips and tricks for better instruction and classroom design was at the forefront of my mind. Theories about education were left to boring classes about the philosophy of education and my desire was for immediacy in learning the so-called practical aspects of classroom teaching.

This debate between the primacy of theory versus practice seems quite consistent with the storied history in education (Biesta et al., 2014). I see the tension between theory and practice continuing today in many university education programmes where theory and practice are compartmentalized and divided between specific courses and programmes. Some courses such as classroom management seem intended on developing skills, while an educational philosophy course may focus entirely on theory. Yet, as I continued my path in academia into doctoral studies, I began to understand that this split between theory and practice is an artificial divide in education. As a doctoral student, I encountered William Pinar's (2004) work, in which he pointed out that educative thinking and curriculum theorizing is a "commitment to the intellectual character of our professional labour" (p. 9). As I continued reading Aoki, I began to understand the potential of how and why educational theory is important for myself and for all. A deeper understanding of theory allowed me to glean new understanding of curriculum, deconstruct my learning biases, and draw insights into my own subjectivity. This thinking and theorizing was an important process of my studies. It continues to be a restorative and life-giving process for me as an emerging assistant professor.

Now, at my university, I am trying to pass on these Aokian lessons of curricular thinking to my students. I am part of a small and intimate school of education with some faculty serving in the professorial and others in the professional year programme (PYP). Such a programme design allows teacher candidates to concurrently study in educational courses throughout their undergraduate, while the professional year is reserved for intensive subject specialization and professional practice. At times, it seems that both parts of our programme position the undergraduate courses as theoretical while the PYP focuses on professional development. Our students, much like my former self, are learning to be teachers. For some of them, they use the theological language of calling (Aoki, 1991/2005b, cf. Palmer, 1998/2007) to describe their purpose for being an education student. Theology, in this sense, follows a historical religious tradition which "includes discussions of morality, ethics, values, hermeneutics, cosmology, and religious beliefs" (Pinar et al., 2008, p. 606). Despite this ontological-theological framework, some students continue to decry my emphasis on theorizing and would rather focus on the development of teaching skills. Perhaps, as I also have a similar theological framework of my own educational calling, I continue to venture into educational complexities, especially in this space in-between theology, theory, and practice.

It is here that I find great appreciation for what Aoki would describe as the difference between curriculum-as-planned and curriculum-as-lived (Aoki, 1986/1991/2005). Aoki's conception of curriculum-as-planned, and curriculum-as-lived, was a "bridge" between the bifurcation of theoretical and applied knowledge in the very nature of university coursework. Aoki (1987/2005) questioned the trajectory of theory to practice within education. He gave an example of having previously taught at a Hutterite school whereby he used a primer entitled *We Think and Do*. Aoki explains that as a novice teacher, he used the primer as a vehicle for teaching reading, but by reducing language into mere reading skills. This emphasis on pragmatics in education is indicative of a "technological ethos" (p. 358) that overemphasized "doing," which can be derivative of a mechanical view of education. Pinar (2005) highlights the risk of the technological ethos, that "this binary means that university coursework is sometimes viewed as 'theory,' which is then to be 'applied' in school settings" (Pinar, 2005, p. 62). For Aoki, both theory and application are important human concerns.

Inspired by Aoki, my goal in serving these students and preparing them as teacher candidates, is one that accounts for their lived encounter between themselves, theory, and practice of education. This stands in sharp contrast to many in the teacher education landscape that are overemphasizing the pragmatics and programming of their skill-based programmes. I echo what Riecken (2014) observes about teacher education programmes and the reification of planning as the central component of teacher preparation. Riecken notes that there are "educational liturgies of planning—lesson planning, term planning, unit planning, practicum planning, individual educational planning—all contribute to a kind of curriculum-planning idolatry" (p. 23). The curricular planning and the course design pragmatics has seemingly invented its own religiousness. This "pedagogical orthodoxy" (Riecken, 2014, p. 23) is limited to a technical model of education where teacher candidates are subservient to the liturgies of planning. Missing, then, are the lived encounters that are crucial for a robust and abundant teacher education programme (Jardine et al., 2006). For me, an aim for my participation in this fruitful teacher education programme is to encourage the lived encounter with theory, question the "linearized form of 'from theory into practice'" and suggest "other possibilities for understanding theorizing and practicing, as well as the relationship between 'theory and practice'" (Aoki, 1987/2005, p. 358). In this way, one nourishing possibility beyond this linearity is towards multiplicity found in generative curricular inquiries.

Curricular Lines of Movement

Through Aoki, we see there is much to explore beyond the linear trajectory of theory to practice within education. Instead, Aoki sees a multiplicity which "grows as lines of movement" (Aoki, 1992/2005a, p. 269) in-between curriculum-as-plan and curriculum-as-lived. For teacher education, life in the classroom is not found solely by emphasizing the student, or teacher, or the subject of study. Such a noun-orientedness, with all its good intentions, results in different ideologies such as the claims of student-centred versus teacher-centred education. Rather, this multiplicity requires educators to "learn to speak a noncentered language" (Aoki, 1993/2005b, p. 282) without erasing the unique educative subjectivities. Teacher education is lived in-between the spaces among all. In my own development as a teacher, I have been wrestling with different ways of expressing this language of in-between within teacher education. Much like Phelan (2015), I turn to curriculum theorizing to re-vitalize teacher education through various curricular lines of movement, including my teacher identity, the question of curricular origins, and Aoki's (1986/1991/2005) bridge between curriculum-as-plan and curriculum-as-lived.

I first begin one curricular flight by exploring my teacher identity. Clarke (2009) describes the substance of teacher identity as addressing forms of subjectivity and its involvement with cognitive and affective aspects of our being. As such, I move into my own subjectivity, both cognitively and affectively, to discern my particular curricular line of movement within teacher education. Beginning with my experience as a Chinese-Canadian, I found it mirrors Aoki's de-nouned identity as a Japanese-Canadian. As a Japanese-Canadian, he spoke about producing a new language which is neither Japanese nor English, but grows within the "uniquely Japanese Canadian lines of movement" (Aoki, 1992/2005a, p. 270). My own Chinese-Canadian language, is a mix of Chinese ideas and words, inter-spoken with casual English. In many ways, this is a hybrid way of speaking, a new space in-between my

Chinese and Canadian heritage. Just as I found this language of de-nouned cultural identity from Aoki, I bring the same questioning and reflecting on my de-nouned teacher identity, resulted in wanting to discern my particular historicity as a teacher. I understand that my teacher identity is situated in a "historical discourse that is embodied in culturally established ways of thinking, speaking, and acting on educational issues" (Phelan & McLaughlin, 1995, p. 166). This desire for understanding my historicity motivated the exploration of curricular origins. In one project which began with my doctoral supervising professor, Stephen Petrina, we pressed into the question of curricular origins and discerned four etymological signifiers of curriculum (Lee & Petrina, 2018):

1. A carriage, chariot, conveyance, or vehicle and attendant parts, arenas, circuses, crowds, and infrastructure (e.g. *curriculum artis* and *currus igneus*).
2. The run or race, autobiography, career and works, experience, journey, or life (e.g. *curriculum vitae* and *currere*).
3. The sphere or extension of the mind (e.g. *curriculum mentis*).
4. A course of study (e.g. *cursus studiorum*).

Curriculum as a course of study has been examined by many scholars (Connelly et al., 2008). Pinar has helpfully elaborated on the notion of *currere* (Pinar, 1976/2014). My own interests were in discerning other historical tracings of curriculum through *curriculum mentis* and *currus igneus*. *Curriculum mentis* "manifested as the noosphere, defined as the infrastructure of the mind and mindhacks, draws metaphysics into history" (Lee & Petrina, 2018, p. 16). My interest continued in the exploration of *curriculum artis* and *currus igneus*, concretizing in the curricular encounter via architectural materiality (Lee, 2019). For me, participation in architecture is a lived encounter, which Huebner (1975) would describe as the fullness of educational activity. This lived encounter resulted in exploring three architectural objects with curricular significance: the roman circus, the cathedral, and the bridge. In all three cases, I situate this "spatial turn in curriculum" (Lee, 2019, p. 53) as a middle way, or in-between third space in conceptualizing curriculum as technotheological curricular spaces. All four etymological signifiers of curriculum elaborate into distinct curricular lines of movement that are significant for teacher education.

Other curricular flights (Reynolds & Webber, 2004) in this complicated conversation involve lingering with Aoki on a "bridge" in-between technology and theology within his educational discourse (Lee, 2017a). In his theorizing, especially bridging curriculum-as-plan and curriculum-as-lived, I found that Aoki addressed the challenges of technicized curricular implementation with possibilities from the ontological and theological (Pinar, 2005, p. 13). In this way, I reconceptualized Aoki as a curricular techno-theologian who taught me how to live and teach in a technological world with wonder and awe.

In another curricular line of movement (Lee, 2017b), I followed Huebner and his concern for temporality as a way to live historically and humbly educate one another. Huebner, like Aoki, offered a critique about the inauthentic ways of educating and living. My study of Huebner, transformed into a temporal tracing of the theological and phenomenological connections between Augustine, Heidegger, and Huebner. This particular trajectory became an act of discerning authentic learning via theological-phenomenological traditions, and more specifically, theorizing a temporal understanding of teacher education which advocates for ontological potentialities of both teachers and students. A prioritization of temporality in teacher education is an invitation to live historically. The practice of *currere*, the autobiographical reflection on educational experiences, allows the teacher candidate to address temporality. Authentic temporality in teacher education speaks to the unfolding biography of the teacher candidate with the unfolding history of the teacher, the education programme, and the wider society (Huebner, 1967/2008).

Along with my own theorizing in this in-between space, I continue to follow Aoki who proffered other lines of movement in curriculum. One of his suggestions is that an in-between curriculum should have a "language of humility, as the curriculum has to await the invitation of the teacher and students in the classroom" (Aoki, 1993/2005a, p. 299). This posture considers the many possibilities of the lived curricula, while also having concerns for the mechanics of curriculum planning. There is a complexity and multiplicity within this in-between way. This idea of multiple directionality, with possibilities and newness emerging, is what Aoki describes as "a fertile place" (Aoki, 1993/2005a, p. 299). Indeed, along with my students, I hope we all find vitality and discover more lived encounters with various curricular trajectories in this fertile place.

Pedagogical Being

During Aoki's tenure as teacher and professor, the term "competence" and its mechanistic framework was a driving force in education (Aoki, 1984/2005, p. 125). He noted that competence-based testing and competence-based teacher education were ideas that became mainstream metaphors for teaching and schooling. Through those ideas, the prioritization of business and economic factors became a powerful ideology in education. One can see how this ideology has not changed, per se, but rather the term competence has been replaced with any number of newer metaphors: learner-centredness, STEM learning, etc. I do not think Aoki would dismiss these movements and ideas as damaging to education. Instead, I believe Aoki wanted to redirect education towards more meaningful questions by probing deeply into what is meant to teach. Aoki (1983/2005) quotes Aristotle in describing the pedagogical act as a "holistic activity of the total person—head, heart, and lifestyle, all as one" (p. 116). Through this exploration of holistic pedagogy, Aoki turned to phenomenological scholars such as Karol Wojtyla who later became Pope

John Paul II. In his reading of Wojtyla's *The Acting Person*, Aoki discerned that a worthy life is not "circumstances conditioned and encapsulated by [their] social milieu," but rather, one of "self-disclosure and self-governance [by fashioning] a personal and social life worth living" (Aoki, 1984/2005, p. 130). For Aoki, this turn in his own curricular understanding reveals the distinction between an instrumentalist view of education and one of true practice. Or, rephrased by Aoki (1983/2005), pedagogically we are discerning "actions of beings as-things and beings-as-human" (Aoki, 1983/2005, p. 122). In this way, Aoki's great educational question is about the beingness of a teacher.

In this question of being, Aoki responds by pointing to his favourite teacher exemplar of Miss O (Aoki, 1993/2005c, p. 207). Aoki showcases Miss O as a teacher who is grappling with the multiplicity of teaching. She may wonder, how can she best teach the mandated curriculum? How can she teach students who have learning challenges? What are expectations from the school, parents, and community? Perhaps more profoundly, who *is* Miss O as a teacher? Aoki descriptively represents Miss O as a teacher who indwelled dialectically, lived in tensionality, and demonstrated the meaningfulness of teaching. Aoki describes the ideal of teaching this way:

> Within this tensionality, guided by a sense of the pedagogic good, we are called on as teachers to be alert to the possibilities of our pedagogic touch, pedagogic tact, pedagogic attunement—those subtle features about being teachers that we know, but are not yet in our lexicon, for we have tended to be seduced by the seemingly lofty and prosaic talk in the language of conceptual abstractions. We must recognize the flight from the meaningful and turn back again to an understanding of our own being as teachers. It is here, I feel, that teachers can contribute to fresh curriculum understandings.
> (Aoki, 1986/1991/2005, p. 164)

Aoki is articulating the "lived world of teachers and students" (Aoki, 1992/2005b, p. 197), the place of pedagogical attunement to ourselves and to one another. For me, the example of Miss O demonstrates that "an educated person, first and foremost, understands that one's ways of knowing, thinking and doing flow from who one is" (Aoki, 1987/2005, p. 365). She is attuned to the "aliveness of the situation" (Aoki, 1986/1991/2005, p. 162) of her own beingness, her students, and her classroom. This aliveness speaks to teacher education as a place of abundance whereby teachers may live together with students. In my context, this aliveness is experienced in my particular teacher education programme. Within the locality of the classroom, students and teachers take up a posture of reflection, being truly themselves with one another, in order to find life in each another. Like Miss O, I am seeking to understand my students in their own beingness, listening to their voices, and attending to them with an ethic of care. In these ways, I am trying to articulate and dwell in what Aoki describes as *praxis* within the beingness of a teacher.

Aoki adopts Freire's (1970/2005) sense of praxis as "reflection and action upon the world in order to transform it" (p. 51). In teacher education, Aoki (1983/2005) articulates a situational praxis whereby "living in pedagogy is to engage wholeheartedly in a teaching life" that has "implications for knowing the self as an engaged historical and teaching being" (Lewko, 2014, p. 168). Aoki's centring on Freire's praxis (Freire, 1970/2005), advocates for teacher education that is "constantly remade in the praxis" for "in order to *be*, it must *become* (p. 84). The question of beingness for a teacher, a teacher candidate, or teacher education programme, is one of praxis. Teaching praxis is no mere realization of theory situated appropriately for the classroom. Rather, as students and teachers, we are living heartfully by meditatively reflecting on our interwoven pedagogical lines of movement.

In my own educational journey guided by Aoki, he kindly points me to continually know and be known by my students as beings-as-humans. While this is foreign in academic culture, it compels me to speak about my inner self and have the courage to truly be known by my students. The fragile safety found in scholarly programming and the pedagogical abstraction is lifted such that relational trust is given and received. Much like Palmer (1998/2017), "as I teach, I project the condition of my soul onto my students, my subject, and our way of being together" (pp. 2–3). There is a beautiful risk in this way of teaching as I strive for self-reflection, being sensitive in my pedagogic attunement to the lived encounters with others in my teacher education programme. The other important educative elements, such as the classroom, educational theory, and curriculum conversations, all help shape this pedagogical life lived together. This whole discovery process of praxis and attunement to pedagogical being, is where I feel alive as an educator.

A Lingering Note

Having spent time as both student and teacher, I meditate on Aoki's (1992/2005b) question: "what is the voice of teaching that this story speaks?" (p. 195). I want to linger on a particular instance of my teaching voice as revealed during my first year as assistant professor. At that time, I was tasked with teaching a fourth-year course about critical issues in education. This course emphasized the analysis of cultural, social, legal, and ethical dimensions of education connecting with broader society. As I happily found myself in this new job, I wanted to over-prepare for the course by reading and processing all the relevant materials. I read the textbook, the optional readings and references, and made detailed notes about how I would engage these texts. Adopting my predecessor's syllabus, I further prepared by revising the course design and assignments, while adapting and personalizing all lesson plans. Indeed, I was being conscientious by preparing the curriculum-as-plan and wanted to promote a lived encounter with the texts and with theorizing. As I began to teach my newfound students, I began to shift from curriculum-as-plan to curriculum-as-lived. The formal curriculum remained necessary; however, what I found nourishing were the lived encounters with these students, my fellow educators. As we analyzed and interpreted educational issues, we began sharing our inner selves, together. Throughout the semester, the students revealed more about themselves which contributed to the greater whole of the class. At times we had intense discussions, resulting in different curricular and pedagogical trajectories as evidenced by what the students shared in their assignments. We laughed and cried as several students shared challenges from their personal lives amidst being teacher candidates. Remarkably, many students ably supported one another and formed a resilient cohort.

I particularly treasured the fleeting moments with the students: discussing teacher ethics while walking in-between classes, sharing personably over coffee, and receiving handwritten notes of encouragement under my door. These students were teaching me about the pedagogical beingness of education. Their stories, as sonorous beings, gave voice to my continued experience of teacher education. Why are these particular pedagogical stories important to myself, or to Aoki? "Could it be that that which is remarkable is the indwelling presence of the shimmering being of teaching that is open to those whose listening is attuned aright?" (Aoki, 1992/2005b, p. 195). I think Aoki is guiding us, students and teachers alike, to the important questions, pedagogically attuned, to the sounds of teaching and learning in teacher education.

References

Aoki, T. T. (1983/2005). Curriculum implementation as instrumental action and as situational praxis. In W. F. Pinar & R. L. Irwin (Eds.), *Curriculum in a new key: The collected works of Ted T. Aoki* (pp. 111–123). Lawrence Erlbaum.

Aoki, T. T. (1984/2005). Competence in teaching as instrumental and practical action: A critical analysis. In W. F. Pinar & R. L. Irwin (Eds.), *Curriculum in a new key: The collected works of Ted T. Aoki* (pp. 125–135). Lawrence Erlbaum.

Aoki, T. T. (1986/1991/2005). Teaching as in-dwelling between two curriculum worlds. In W. F. Pinar & R. L. Irwin (Eds.), *Curriculum in a new key: The collected works of Ted T. Aoki* (pp. 159–165). Lawrence Erlbaum.

Aoki, T. T. (1987/1999/2005). Toward understanding "computer application." In W. F. Pinar & R.L. Irwin (Eds.), *Curriculum in a new key: The collected works of Ted T. Aoki* (pp. 151–158). Lawrence Erlbaum.

Aoki, T. T. (1987/2005). Inspiriting the curriculum. In W. F. Pinar & R.L. Irwin (Eds.), *Curriculum in a new key: The collected works of Ted T. Aoki* (pp. 357–365). Lawrence Erlbaum.

Aoki, T. T. (1991/2005a). Sonare and videre: A story, three echoes, and a lingering note. In W. F. Pinar & R. L. Irwin (Eds.), *Curriculum in a new key: The collected works of Ted T. Aoki* (pp. 367–376). Lawrence Erlbaum.

Aoki, T. T. (1991/2005b). The sound of pedagogy in the silence of the morning calm. In W. F. Pinar & R. L. Irwin (Eds.), *Curriculum in a new key: The collected works of Ted T. Aoki* (pp. 389–401). Lawrence Erlbaum.

Aoki, T. T. (1992/2005a). In the midst of slippery theme-words: Living as designers of Japanese Canadian curriculum. In W. F. Pinar & R. L. Irwin (Eds.), *Curriculum in a new key: The collected works of Ted T. Aoki* (pp. 263–277). Lawrence Erlbaum.

Aoki, T. T. (1992/2005b). Layered voices of teaching: The uncannily correct and the elusively true. In W. F. Pinar & R. L. Irwin (Eds.), *Curriculum in a new key: The collected works of Ted T. Aoki* (pp. 187–197). Lawrence Erlbaum.

Aoki, T. T. (1993/2005a). Humiliating the Cartesian ego. In W. F. Pinar & R. L. Irwin (Eds.), *Curriculum in a new key: The collected works of Ted T. Aoki* (pp. 291–301). Lawrence Erlbaum.

Aoki, T. T. (1993/2005b). The child-centered curriculum: Where is the social in pedocentricism? In W. F. Pinar & R. L. Irwin (Eds.), *Curriculum in a new key: The collected works of Ted T. Aoki* (pp. 279–289). Lawrence Erlbaum.

Aoki, T. T. (1993/2005c). Legitimating lived curriculum: Toward a curricular landscape of multiplicity. In W. F. Pinar & R. L. Irwin (Eds.), *Curriculum in a new key: The collected works of Ted T. Aoki* (pp. 199–215). Lawrence Erlbaum.

Aoki, T. T. (1996/2005). Imaginaries of "East and West": Slippery curricular signifiers in education. In W. F. Pinar & R. L. Irwin (Eds.), *Curriculum in a new key: The collected works of Ted T. Aoki* (pp. 313–319). Lawrence Erlbaum.

Barrow, R. (1990). *Understanding skills: Thinking, feeling, and caring*. The Althouse Press.

Biesta, G., Allan, J., & Edwards, R. (Eds.). (2014). *Making a difference in theory: The theory question in education and education question in theory*. Routledge.

Clarke, M. (2009). The ethico-politics of teacher identity. *Educational Philosophy and Theory*, 41(2), 185–200.

Clarke, M., & Phelan, A. (2017). *Teacher education and the political: The power of negative thinking*. Routledge.

Connelly, F. M., He, M. F., & Phillion, J. (Eds.). (2008). *The SAGE handbook of curriculum and instruction*. Sage.

Freire, P. (1970/2005). *Pedagogy of the oppressed* (*30th anniversary* ed.). Continuum.

Huebner, D. (1967/2008). Curriculum as concern for man's temporality. In V. Hillis, & W. F. Pinar (Eds.), *The lure of the transcendent: Collected essays by Dwayne E. Huebner* (pp. 131–142). Routledge.

Huebner, D. (1975). Curricular language and classroom meanings. In W. F. Pinar (Ed.), *Curriculum theorizing: The reconceptualists* (pp. 217–237). McCutchan.

Jardine, D., Friesen, S., & Clifford, P. (2006). *Curriculum in abundance*. Lawrence Erlbaum.

Kincheloe, J. (1993). *Toward a critical politics of teacher thinking: Mapping the postmodern*. Bergin & Garvey.

Lee, Y. (2017a). Lingering on Aoki's bridge: Reconceptualizing Ted Aoki as curricular techno-theologian. *Journal of Curriculum Theorizing*, 31(3), 18–30.

Lee, Y. (2017b). Discerning a temporal philosophy of education: Understanding the gap between past and future through Augustine, Heidegger, and Huebner. *Philosophy of education 2016* (pp. 242–249). Philosophy of Education Society.

Lee, Y. (2019). Technotheological curricular spaces: Encountering the circus, cathedral, and bridge. In T. Strong-Wilson, C. Ehret, D. Lewkowich, & S. Chang-Kredl (Eds.), *Provoking curriculum encounters across educational experience* (pp. 42–56). Routledge.

Lee, Y., & Petrina, S. (2018). Hacking minds: Curriculum mentis, noosphere, internet, matrix, web. In B. Smith, N. Ng-A-Fook, L. Radford, & S. S. Pratt (Eds.), *Hacking education in a digital age: Teacher education, curriculum, and literacies* (pp. 15–35). Information Age Publishing.

Lewko, C. P. (2014). Lived experiences of loss: Living perceptibly as a teacher in new familiarities. In W. Hurren, & E. Hasebe-Ludt (Eds.), *Contemplating curriculum* (pp. 166–171). Routledge.

Palmer, P. (1998/2017). *The courage to teach: Exploring the inner landscape of a teacher's life*. Jossey-Bass.

Phelan, A. (2015). *Curriculum theorizing and teacher education: Complicating conjunctions*. Routledge.

Phelan, A. M., & McLaughlin, H. J. (1995). Educational discourses, the nature of the child, and the practice of new teachers. *Journal of Teacher Education, 46*(3), 165–174.

Phelan, A. M., Pinar, W. F., Ng-A-Fook, N., & Kane, R. (2020). *Reconceptualizing teacher education: A Canadian contribution to a global challenge*. University of Ottawa Press.

Pinar, W. F. (1989). A reconceptualization of teacher education. *Journal of Teacher Education, 40*(1), 9–12.

Pinar, W. F. (1976/2014). Preface. In W. F. Pinar & M. Grumet (Eds.), *Toward a poor curriculum* (3rd ed., pp. xiii–xvii). Educator's International Press.

Pinar, W. F. (2004). *What is curriculum theory?* Lawrence Erlbaum.

Pinar, W. F. (2005). "A lingering note": An introduction to the collected works of Ted T. Aoki. In W. F. Pinar & R. L. Irwin (Eds.), *Curriculum in a new key: The collected works of Ted T. Aoki* (pp. 1–85). Lawrence Erlbaum.

Pinar, W. F., Reynolds, W. M., Slattery, P., & Taubman, P. M. (2008). *Understanding curriculum*. Peter Lang.

Reynolds, W. M., & Webber, J. A. (2004). *Expanding curriculum theory: Dis/positions and lines of flight*. Routledge.

Riecken, T. (2014). As neither/both teds: Theodore reflects upon Tetsuo. In W. Hurren, & E. Hasebe-Ludt (Eds.), *Contemplating curriculum* (pp. 22–25). Routledge.

12 Contemplating the Relation between Theory and Practice through Three Aoki Inspirited Themes

Patricia Liu Baergen and Karen Meyer

I[1] took this picture during my first visit to the Nitobe Memorial Garden—a poetic place to dwell on a late summer day (Figure 12.1). I found this Japanese garden tucked away, quietly, in the corner of campus at The University of British Columbia. Once inside its perimeter of bamboo fencing, my path came across an authentic teahouse and surrounding roji. The small roji garden invites visitors to pause their presence and attention before entering the teahouse. Roji 露地 literally means "dewy ground," on the pebble way to the Chashitsu 茶室, teahouse. While I sat on the bench there in the roji, the sun shone through cracks between the tall bamboo and spread its gentle warmth over me.

Basking in sunlight, I breathed in an ephemeral scent of tea, sweet, and mellow. In exhale, I spent a reflective moment appreciating the garden's natural allure, its simplicity. Little did I know, this place would later become a site of contemplation that speaks dearly to my heart.

I soon left the rhythm of my breath. My mind wandered away from that roji waiting bench, connecting to a memory. I revisited a fundraising concert for Japanese Tsunami victims I attended a few years ago in Ottawa. Two Canadian born artists organized this special concert, my *Chanoyu Omotesenke sensei* 茶の湯表千家先生 (teacher for an ancient Japanese practice in the Way of Tea from the School of Omotesenke) and her friend, a *shakuhachi sensei* 尺八先生 (an ancient Japanese bamboo flute master). Both have lived and learned these ancient skills in Japan for years.

I vividly recalled that hot summer evening, sitting cross-legged on the floor waiting for music to commence. When the arcane sound of shakuhachi soloed in ancient notes, my body felt the coolness of autumn nights where I once strolled along the streets of Kyoto and walked slowly through a moon-lit Japanese temple.

That feeling broke as the shakuhachi sensei asked the audience to close our eyes for her next composition. I followed her instruction. In a meditative state, I heard an unfamiliar sound joining into the play of traditional shakuhachi music. I could not resist opening my eyes. I saw an accordion player had joined in the play. These two instruments in concert challenged me visually, sonically, and conceptually. A box-shaped, free-reed, instrument originating from Europe was playing with the shakuhachi, an ancient bamboo flute traditionally played by Japanese monks in Zen meditation.

DOI: 10.4324/9781003037248-20

Figure 12.1 Nitobe Memorial Garden | Photo: Patricia Liu Baergen.

Again, I noticed the wandering of my thoughts. I closed my eyes once more and followed the rhythm of my breath. I gradually attuned to the play; I was pulled into the unfamiliar accent of the accordion that generated tension—the unexpected syncopations between consonance and dissonance. Through the provocation of this tensionality, I began to hear the nuanced melody of music. Eyes still closed, now, I could *see* the voices of the two instruments dancing, like a pair of butterflies between flowers, in a space anew.

* * *

The opening photo of the Nitobe Memorial Garden features one of its bridges. This traditional Japanese garden celebrates the memorial of Inazō Nitobe (1862–1933), a Japanese scholar who sought to "become a bridge across the Pacific" to provoke intercultural understanding. The above narrative portrays East and West in one space: A Japanese garden on a Western campus and a musical performance between Zen and folk with the shakuhachi and accordion. When we escape thinking differences as disparate worlds and allow them to unfold their existential essence, we see a new space that stands apart and between estranged spaces, disrupting dualism, while opening gateways of ambiguity and unpredictability.

Likewise, in education, we often see this unpredictability and ambiguity as causing tensions and dilemmas *between* the systematic demand and the individual needs in the classroom. How might we, as educators, understand our everyday practice within such tensions and dilemmas? Ted Tetsuo Aoki, a Canadian curriculum scholar, took us to such sites of tensionality, where he saw dualistic thinking, like sun and moon, day and night. More so, he brought us squarely into the disparate worlds of thought between theory and practice.

In this chapter, we engage three Aoki inspired themes to contemplate the complicated relation between theory and practice (Pinar & Irwin, 2005): Disrupting binary thinking, curriculum-as-lived, and the unplanned curriculum. We offer our situated voices, suggesting Aoki positioned himself concurrently in both scholarly and pedagogical practices, subscribing to a non-linear relationship between theory and practice. For Aoki, every moment of practice is saturated in/with theory.[2]

Disrupting Binary Thinking by Dwelling on a Bridge

Aoki remained a strong critic of the binary between East and West as well as the division between theory and practice. In education, he reminded us time and again about the danger of pushing theory aside to our periphery vision or trying to understand and define "theory" by looking at "theory" itself. At the same time, he pointed out the danger of understanding and defining "practice" by looking only at "practice" itself. In doing so, he argued we ultimately reflect a positivist worldview wherein theory is defined by theory; practice is defined by practice (Aoki, 1985/1991/2005).

As a way forward, Aoki (1979/2005) proposed we conjoin theory and practice into a "thought-style" he described as a "dialectic mode" of *and* (p. 346). Such thinking attunes us to an ambivalent place and invites us to create the im/possibilities towards meaning-making in a space anew. How do we imagine a "dialectic mode" of *and* in conjoining theory *and* practice? Aoki imagined dwelling on a bridge as a metaphor. For him, a bridge is not merely a thing that connects two places, here and there, but an extension of place—a space in-between. That is, from an instrumentalist point of view, a bridge serves as a tool to connect two sites, a means to an end. However, "from a value-laden, culturally-bounded ontological point of view, the bridge becomes a locality of gathering" (Liu Baergen, 2020, p. 69) that engages a conversation between two worlds. Such a "conversation entails two ways of knowing and becomes a 'trans-epistemological process' that is 'not a bridge'" (Aoki, 1981/2005 in Liu Baergen, 2020, p. 69). Thus, conjoining theory and practice as dwelling on the bridge means to "see" with "double vision." Seeing, for Aoki, "does not only mean perceiving with the bodily eyes, nor does it mean the mere non-sensory perception" (Liu Baergen, 2020, p. 46). Rather, it is dwelling between theory and practice, which moves beyond a single way of seeing and knowing: A tactful phenomenological gesture on Aoki's part to unfold a trans-epistemological process.

To continue such unfolding in contemplating the East and West binary, Aoki became inspired by the two root metaphors of Sakura and Rose in Inazō Nitobe's (2002) book, *Bushido: The Soul of Japan*. He encouraged us, to "see" the Western symbol of Rose and the Japanese symbol of Sakura with "double vision," as a dialectic mode: "Two ways of seeing, two ways of knowing, two ways of living" (Liu Baergen, 2020, p. 45). By keeping the two flowers simultaneously in view, he revealed the "power of double vision or learning to see life within the fullness of a double or even multiple vision"[3] (Liu Baergen, 2020, p. 46). More so, to expand this trans-epistemological process in his contemplation of East and West, Aoki "theorized" the notion of ethnicity through the meaning-making of the dialectic mode of two ways seeing and knowing from his own live(d) experience as a Japanese-Canadian curriculum scholar.

In pedagogical moments, he tactfully teased out the binaries of East/West and theory/practice, sound and resound in Inazō Nitobe's words: It is my wish to serve as a bridge over the Pacific Ocean. Resisting the binaries of dualism, Aoki lingers, dwells and contemplates bridges that rim the Pacific, East and West. For Aoki, "there is no elevating moment towards a comprehensive, rational absolute in understanding theory" (Liu Baergen, 2020, p. 122). Rather the lived ground of practice calls for "theorizing as poetic dwelling" (Liu Baergen, 2020, p. 123) and an unfolding of an existential essence.

Imagine standing on that bridge. A gathering exists—lived practice *and* theorizing as poetic dwelling, situated, and pedagogical. With double vision, how might we *see* such a gathering existing in the wor(l)d of curriculum? Here is where Aoki turned to next—curriculum-as-lived.

Escaping Generalized Abstraction by Returning to the Lived Ground of Curriculum

Aoki (1987/1999/2005) was critical about the issue of theory and practice in the curriculum world where application has become a word "caught up within a theory/practice nexus where practice is thought to be applied theory, a secondary notion deriving its meaning from the primacy of theory" (p. 154). To him, such linear thinking placed teaching as an application under the umbrella of instrumentalism. He pointed out that instrumentalism embeds much of the education system, wherein teachers and educators feel an unconscious pressure to produce. As such, successful and useful teaching and learning experiences mean relentless translations of theories into applications in practice. He saw the role of teaching manifesting itself as technical in nature—attending to the producing. Thus for him, education becomes removed from life. Pedagogical moments become the unrecognizable "things" for many.

Drawing from critical theory and phenomenology, Aoki deeply questioned the concepts of application and expertise, particularly from this instrumentalist point of view. In contrast, he took up the idea of praxis from a phenomenological position. Back in 1980, Aoki presented his paper, "Understanding Situational Meanings of Curriculum In-service Acts: Implementing, Consulting, In servicing," at a Canadian Summer Institute and again in 1983 at an American Education Conference. Aoki elaborated:

> What I have attempted in this paper is to portray implementation employing the distinction between "instrumentalism" and "praxis," that is, between instrumental action and situational praxis, between actions of

beings-as-things and being-as-human, signifying two frames of reference in which the reality of implementation activity can be constituted.

(1983/2005, p. 122)

Aoki pointed out a continuing practice in Canada of curriculum implementation: A group of experts in a field (educators, professors, etc.) develop curriculum in a particular subject. These curriculum producers then travel to various school districts offering their product to groups of teachers—the consumers. In this way, he explained that the term "implementation," in the traditional field of curriculum, takes root in an instrumental understanding. Furthermore in education, the producer-consumer model of teachers' competency then becomes evaluated on how teachers implement *the* curriculum. He believed this scientific, technological framework reduces human competence to instrumental action.

Aoki further pushed against the instrumentalism. In his 1984 paper, "Competence in Teaching an Instrumental and Practical Action: A Critical Analysis," he proposed the term "competence" has been reduced to techniques and skills (Aoki, 1984/2005, p. 125), an instrumental "know-how-to-do" view. Aoki (1983/2005) earlier implied that instrumentalism pervades our culture to the point of becoming a crisis in Western reasoning (p. 113). This claim coincides with the thinking of critical theorists Jurgen Habermas and phenomenologist Edmund Husserl. Aoki further elaborated an apparent contradiction between the position committed to improving personal and situational life with that committed to technological progress. As such, teachers and students in the classroom have become inebriated with the technical power of science and technology and business management techniques.

This linear, instrumentalist view of curriculum implementation and teaching competency "strips" the "humanness" of teachers' and students' being and reduces them to a "being-as-thing, a technical being devoid of [their] own subjectivity" (Aoki, 1983/2005, p. 115). Aoki was clear that accepting instrumental implementation or competence as the only way is not the way to go. In its place, he offered an alternative: A situational praxis, "grounded in human experiences within the classroom situation" (Aoki, 1983/2005, p. 116).

Again, concerning praxis, Aoki first pointed to the ancient Aristotle's notion of theoria and praxis; he stipulated that the dichotomy of theory and practice resides in Aristotle's "preference to theoria over praxis" (Aoki, 1983/2005, p. 119). Here, theory exists as the first order of intellectual knowing, while practice exists as the second order of applying the knowledge. He believed such a position had haunted the contemporary field of education. Furthermore, he acknowledged the Aristotelian concept of praxis, aligned with practice (an ethical life within a political context) needed to be restored in a "contemporary sense" (Aoki, 1983/2005, p. 119).

For a more current view on praxis, Aoki cited Paulo Freire, a Brazilian educator and advocate of critical theory. According to Freire "praxis is reflection (thought) and action (practice) upon the world in order to transform it" (as cited in Aoki, 1983/2005, p. 119). Aoki affirmed this position by following phenomenology and Karol Wojtyla's (1979) approach to praxis as "both dealing with the personal and communal venturing of man as he experiences life through action and reflection on his experiences" (as cited in Aoki, 1983/2005, p. 120). For Aoki, understanding praxis situationally requires "an estrangement from the dichotomized view of 'theory and practice' and embracing of that which sees them as twin moments of the same reality" (Aoki, 1983/2005, p. 120).

Aoki thoughtfully placed a critical theory lens and a phenomenological understanding of lifeworld to disturb the binary between theory and practice. He suggested that "rather than seeing theory as leading into practice, we need now more than ever to see it as a reflective moment in praxis" (Aoki, 1983/2005, p. 120). Here, he created a new meaning in applying situational praxis to curriculum implementation.

To further escape the generalized, summative framework to "theorize" curriculum, Aoki et al. (1991) attuned to the significant inquiry of personhood. On this point, he said, "... narrative inquiry of lived experiences can disclose the existential texture of the beings" (p. xi) that we educators have come to be. That is, he encouraged educators to allow "theory" to unfold its existential essence—curriculum-as-live(d). Liu Baergen (2020), explains such inquiry Aoki invited educators to:

> probe the narratives of personhood as self-engaged with surrounding circumstances and questing and questioning for deeper meaning in the affairs of life, a situated, biographical understanding emerges through the composition of the enchanting discourse of culture, history, place, politics, class, gender, the way of knowing and the greater social welfare.
> (p. 30)

However, Aoki further conceded to a tension in curriculum scholarships between curriculum-as-lived and curriculum-as-plan and called on us to explore the tension between the two. He referred to curriculum-as-lived as the first-order curriculum world and he deemed curriculum-as-plan as the second-order curriculum world. He wrote:

> Curriculum-as-plan is an abstraction yearning to come alive in the presence of teachers and students. What it lacks is situatedness. A situated curriculum is a curriculum-as-lived. It is curriculum in the presence of people and their meanings. It is an experienced curriculum. I like to call it the first-order curriculum world.
> (Aoki, 1985/1991/2005, p. 231)

As a teacher educator and curriculum scholar, Aoki understood the tensionality between the first-order (the lived) and the second-order (the planed) curriculum worlds. Instead of surrendering to one or another curriculum world, Aoki (1985/1991/2005) suggested a "dialectic" mode of "between the first *and* second order curriculum worlds" (p. 231), curriculum-as-lived and curriculum-as-plan. To elaborate on this dialectic mode of *and*, Aoki spoke to his audience about the 1985 annual CACS conference symposium, divulged that he had hosted a focus theme, "Understanding Curriculum-as-Lived," where the first-order curriculum world was the hub. Aoki shared some remarks about the symposium, stating that "Canadian researchers from coast to coast," across various disciplines, displayed reasonable first-order curriculum scholarship (Aoki, 1985/1991/2005, p. 232) and also demonstrated their epistemological and ontological concerns. Aoki also noted that the science educators in Canada who had been softening to the second-order curriculum world had also undertaken a captivating "national study of school science-as-lived" (Aoki, 1985/1991/2005, p. 231). Even in the midst of this increasingly vibrant curriculum study, at the 1985 conference, Aoki was careful not to be carried away by this uplifting and lively research. He shared his insight: "I feel that we are now in a position to move towards a juxtaposition of curriculum-as-plan and curriculum-as-lived, which can be explored as twin moments of the same phenomenon, curriculum" (p. 232). Aoki called for the possibility of exploring the tension between the first *and* second curriculum worlds (p. 232).

Unplanned Curriculum

Following the heels of that conference, Aoki continued his relentless research into the tension between the first- and second-order curriculum worlds. In particular, he worked with principals and teachers in a local school district where he became inspired by Miss O, a Grade 5 teacher. Aoki placed a well-enunciated article in 1986, April/May issue of the *BC Teacher*, illustrating the teaching life of Miss O, her daily dwelling between the two worlds of curriculum-as-plan and curriculum-as-lived. He distinguished curriculum-as-plan as curriculum designed outside the classroom, far ahead of time, by the school district or the Ministry of Education. Such curriculum determines and stipulates what students and teachers should do in the language of aims, goals, and objectives. Here we find guidelines of evaluation pre-determined in a language of "ends means." In the eye of these instrumentalist curriculum planners, teachers are the installers of curriculum and implementing curriculum becomes strictly an instrumental activity. Aoki (1986/1991/2005) put it this way:

> We can see ... how truncated our understanding becomes when we see only a single curriculum-as-plan awaiting implementation. In this truncation, teachers are often technicized and transformed into mere technical implementers, and good teaching is reduced to mere technical effectiveness.
>
> (p. 163)

Aoki pointed out the danger under these circumstances: Teachers' "forgetfulness [of] what matters deeply in the situated world of the classroom," that is, "a forgetfulness that teaching is fundamentally a mode of being" (Aoki, 1986/1991/2005, p. 160). Aoki acknowledged that Miss O knew there exists another world in every classroom—the names of students, different cultures, lived experiences, surprises, and frustrations. This world holds the unplanned curriculum, a pedagogic environment alive with life stories. Here, both students and teachers are designing their learning plans in this curriculum-as-lived world. In this world, Miss O's students all have names, Johnny, Sandra, Nancy, and Susan, some with freckles, some with missing teeth, and all have personal hopes and dreams.

On the other side of the classroom, in the world of curriculum-as-plan, Miss O becomes accountable for teaching a legitimate, formalized curriculum, which of course, sustains her existence. However, this determined world persists at odds and is removed from the lived world of Grade 5 children. In the case of a caring teacher such as Miss O, Aoki said:

> She knows that whenever and wherever she can, between her markings and the lesson plannings, she must listen and be attuned to the care that calls from the very living with her own Grade 5 pupils ... She is asked to give a hearing to both simultaneously.
> (1986/1991/2005, p. 161)

A teacher such as Miss O understands that "the quality of life lived within the tensionality depends much on the quality of the pedagogic being that she is" (Aoki, 1986/1991/2005, p. 161). Teaching, Aoki articulated, is dwelling in the zone between where the tensionality resides as an inevitable act for a teacher. For him, teaching requires understanding, both epistemologically and ontologically, the tensioned zone between the two curriculum worlds. "Teaching as a mode of being" (Aoki, 1986/1991/2005, p. 163) means dwelling in that zone.

Aoki moved away from the instrumental understanding of curriculum-as-plan. He returned to the "isness" of curriculum to lead educators towards a world with uncertainties where the linguistic language is spoken and the grammatical rules may appear blurry. He took us to his world and shared his professional and private moments. He juxtaposed the lived moments that happen inside/outside the classroom, professional/personal traditions, and tensionality/openness. His critical-reflective style of theorizing spoke about curriculum in many ways.

Aoki continuously tried to refocus attention from the entrenched meaning of curriculum-as-plan and to distort the one-track view of understanding curriculum. He refocused educators towards the "being," the living experiences of teachers and students in the world, all with the understanding that the two curriculum worlds, plan and lived, can exist together, "a twin moment of two curriculum worlds" (Liu Baergen, 2020, p. 82). We wonder what Aoki might offer us today in an unprecedented situation concerning the two curriculum worlds as praxis becomes a living curriculum in the moment.

* * *

Mr. M, a Grade 4/5 teacher, accepted my[4] proposal to work with his students as a writer in residence of sorts. The project entailed students participating with me about various features of my children's novel in progress. I planned to visit their classroom once a week to work with them on background research, writing their own short scenes using the book's characters, and creating artwork around the story. I anticipated learning much from the students, the same age as my target audience.

A week before my first scheduled visit, schools closed in British Columbia due to the spread of a COVID-19 virus in Canada and globally (late March 2020). Teachers began adopting online platforms to continue teaching for the last months of the school year. Mr. M and I decided to start my project a few weeks later than planned, giving him time to rethink and reorganize his curriculum, as well as prepare students in their new virtual classroom.

I began the project differently than originally planned. I met with students in small groups online. I recorded myself reading my completed chapters and prepared the text for their reading. I corresponded with them by email. They sent me photos of their art and hand-written texts. Students sent me PowerPoint presentations of their background research related to the story. I heard about their favourite characters and why. By the end of June, I felt I had gotten to know them.

Mr. M made the project as fluid as possible for me while juggling a split-grade curriculum. He was dwelling between the two worlds of curriculum, profoundly attuned to the stressful situation. In such tensionality, he remembered what mattered—the personhood of each student and keeping them all motivated. For two months, I witnessed his focused praxis become a full and thoughtful lived-curriculum.

During that time, I thought about Ted Aoki's first world curriculum as lived and unplanned. Years ago, I had the great fortune of knowing Ted. I imagined a conversation with him about Mr. M. What would he say now? I revisited what he wrote about Miss O, the Grade 5 teacher who inspired him, who he wrote about. Taking the liberty of a writer, I fit Mr. M and his situation into the text Aoki wrote, featuring Miss O. I began to see the two worlds in double vision as one text (new words italicized).

Even before day 1 of *students online, Mr. M turns on his computer and his newly-created Grade 4/5 virtual classroom*. Because *Mr. M* is already a teacher, by *his* mere presence in the *online* classroom as teacher, *he* initiates a transformation of a sociocultural and physical environment into something different. *It is already late March. The schools across Canada closed abruptly due to the COVID-19, now a global pandemic*. Even before a pupil *joins the new online platform, Mr. M* silently asks: "Can I establish myself here as a teacher?" since the classroom's desks, walls, whiteboards, floor, books, and resources *go missing. All the things the students know as school.* And when the pupils join Mr. M *online, screens and faces* arrange themselves, as it were, around Mr. M's intention. They become *"confused," "uncertain," "unmotivated," "*hopeful," *"curious,"* and "teachable." The *virtual* environment ceases to be environment, and in its place comes the pedagogical situation, a lived situation *virtually* alive in the presence of people, *if not in the flesh.*

Within this situation, Mr. M soon finds that *his* pedagogic situation is living in tensionality—a tensionality that emerges, in part, from indwelling in a zone between two curriculum worlds: The worlds of curriculum-as-plan *that begun in September in a school*² and curriculum-as-lived experiences *in a new, necessary virtual space.*

A Contemplating Note

Discourse separating theory and practice, for Aoki, was not only philosophical, but indeed spoke to an ongoing, lived reality for classroom teachers. He pointed to philosophical roots of this dichotomy that position theory as fundamentally a mode of knowing, espousing rational, and utilitarian instrumentality. He argued further that the field of education has remained much aligned with Aristotle's preference of theoria over praxis—praxis as the first order of intellectual knowing and practice as the second order of applying the knowledge.

Aoki disrupted this centuries-long dualistic understanding by inviting us to a bridge as a pedagogical site. Rather than "seeing" theory and practice in division, he conjoined a "dialectic mode" of theory *and* practice as dwelling on that bridge to see with double vision. Here, he made a phenomenological move beyond a single way of seeing and knowing to a trans-epistemological process and contemplative mode of being.

To escape understanding theory as generalized abstraction, for the notion of curriculum in particular, Aoki returned to an ontological grounding of the [hu]man/world relationship that unfolds its existential essence. Thus, for him, curriculum-as-lived turned to explorations of "narrative inquiry of lived experiences that can disclose the existential texture of the beings that teachers and students have come to be" (Liu Baergen, 2020, p. 78). He knew well, however, that tensions and dilemmas will never seem to cease in classrooms. More so, Aoki (1987/2005) saw teachers' education caught up in the linearized form of theory *into* practice: "Curriculum and instruction courses as theorizing and the practicing of theories as practicum" (p. 358).

With such attunement to tensions and dilemmas "arising from the whatness of the generality and the isness of the particularity" (Liu Baergen, 2020, p. 78), Aoki advised us to dwell in sites of tensionality. He juxtaposed the lived moments that happen inside and outside the classroom, in professional and personal traditions and between tensionality and openness. His critical-reflective style of theorizing spoke to curriculum in multiple ways. He continuously refocused our attention from the entrenched meaning of curriculum-as-plan, distorting the one-track view of understanding curriculum.

He refocused us towards the "being," the living experiences of teachers and students in the world. He did so with the understanding that the two curriculum worlds, plan and lived, can exist together as "a twin moment of two curriculum worlds" (Liu Baergen, 2020, p. 82). This poetic thinking and dwelling of human in the world as openness to being-ness emanates what Aoki once described, every moment of practice is saturated in/with theory.

So now, decades later amid an existential human/world pandemic, we stand on the bridge/not bridge as a pedagogical site and contemplate how education unplanned will unfold. One eye to each side at once.

In a twin moment, two perspectives dance, like a pair of butterflies between flowers, in a space anew.

Notes

1 This narrative is the voice of Patricia Liu Baergen.
2 This passage came from Aoki's personal communication, April 29, 1999, to his colleague, Karen Meyer, at The University of British Columbia.
3 This passage originally came from Aoki's 1979 paper, titled "Reflection of a Japanese Canadian Teacher Experiencing Ethnicity," then later collected in his 2005 book, titled *Curriculum in a New Key*, edited by William F. Pinar & Rita L. Irwin. In 2020 Liu Baergen's book, titled *Tracing Ted Tetsuo Aoki's Intellectual Formation: Historical, Social and Phenomenological Influences*, Liu Baergen quoted this passage with her edited emphasis.
4 This narrative is the voice of Karen Meyer.
5 British Columbia elementary teachers were called back to the classrooms for June. Not all parents felt comfortable with this decision. Some parents kept their children at home. Teachers taught both online and face-to-face for to accommodate all students during the last four weeks of school.

References

Aoki, T. T. (1979/2005). Reflections of a Japanese Canadian teacher experiencing ethnicity. In W. F. Pinar & R. L. Irwin (Eds.), *Curriculum in a new key: The collected works of Ted T. Aoki* (pp. 333–348). Lawrence Erlbaum.

Aoki, T. T. (1981/2005). Toward understanding curriculum: Talk through reciprocity of perspectives. In W. F. Pinar & R. L. Irwin (Eds.), *Curriculum in a new key: The collected works of Ted T. Aoki* (pp. 219–228). Lawrence Erlbaum.

Aoki, T. T. (1983/2005). Curriculum implementation as instrumental action and as situational praxis. In W. F. Pinar & R. L. Irwin (Eds.), *Curriculum in a new key: The collected works of Ted T. Aoki* (pp. 111–123). Lawrence Erlbaum.

Aoki, T. T. (1984/2005). Competence in teaching as instrumental and practical action: A critical analysis. In W. F. Pinar & R. L. Irwin (Eds.), *Curriculum in a new key: The collected works of Ted T. Aoki* (pp. 125–135). Lawrence Erlbaum.

Aoki, T. T. (1985/1991/2005). Sings of vitality in curriculum scholarship. In W. F. Pinar & R. L. Irwin (Eds.), *Curriculum in a new key: The collected works of Ted T. Aoki* (pp. 230–233). Lawrence Erlbaum.

Aoki, T. T. (1986/1991/2005). Teaching as indwelling between two curriculum worlds. In W. F. Pinar & R. L. Irwin (Eds.), *Curriculum in a new key: The collected works of Ted T. Aoki* (pp. 159–165). Lawrence Erlbaum.

Aoki, T. T. (1987/1999/2005). Toward understanding computer application. In W. F. Pinar & R. L. Irwin (Eds.), *Curriculum in a new key: The collected works of Ted T. Aoki* (pp. 151–158). Lawrence Erlbaum.

Aoki, T. T. (1987/2005). Inspiriting the curriculum. In W. F. Pinar & R. L. Irwin (Eds.), *Curriculum in a new key: The collected works of Ted T. Aoki* (pp. 357–365). Lawrence Erlbaum.

Aoki, T. T., Berman, L. M., Hultgren, F. H., Lee, D., Rivkin, M., & Roderick, J. A. (1991). *Toward curriculum for being: Voices of educators.* State University of New York Press.

Liu Baergen, P. (2020). *Tracing Ted Tetsuo Aoki's intellectual formation: Historical, societal and phenomenological influences.* Routledge.

Nitobe, I. (2002). *Bushido: The soul of Japan.* Kodansha International.

Pinar, W. F., & Irwin, R. L. (Eds.). (2005). *Curriculum in a new key: The collected works of Ted T. Aoki.* Lawrence Erlbaum.

Figure 13.1 Nitobe Memorial Garden Lantern (Father Figure) | Photo: Simon Wong.

Index

a/r/tographer 41, 75; a/r/tography 10, 41, 59, 68, 70
abey 4, 10, 63, 80, 87
absence 30, 34–35, 39, 42–43, 54, 74, 129, 134, 146
access 19, 47, 55, 74, 116, 118, 139, 145, 149–150, 165; accessible 164; accessibility 170
accommodation 47, 67; accommodate 109, 136, 169
accountability 47, 67; accountable 53, 193
acknowledgment 22, 25, 165, 172
aesthetic 36, 51; aestheticism 144; aestheticist 145
agency 63, 67, 131–135, 137, 140, 160–161, 164, 167, 175
alive 8, 33, 97, 182, 191, 193, 195; aliveness 6, 8, 97, 160, 181
ambiguity 51, 56, 58, 67, 74, 88, 123, 146, 187
ambivalence 6, 56, 67
ancestral 2, 65, 116; ancestors 27, 82, 90; ancestry 24, 27
anecdotes 62, 109
Anthropocene 128, 139–140
anthropological 147, 159
anxiety 47, 49; anxious 49
art 67, 88, 151, 194; artist 56, 60, 70, 82, 91, 145–146, 151, 186; arts 12, 19, 58, 62–63, 144–147; liberal 165; making 146
art education 10, 46, 65–66, 68–70, art educator 46
artist/researcher/teacher 36–37, 41
arts-based research 3, 10, 62, 65, 70–71; education 10–11, 61
Asia 2, 117; Asian 26, 49–50, 74, 116; Asians 50; anti-Asian sentiments 49

assimilation 22, 25, 30, 38; assimilate 39; assimilated 132; assimilates 28
attunement 5–6, 8, 13, 48, 61, 71, 91, 148, 181–182, 195; attune 9, 17, 43, 161, 188; attuned 8, 97, 113, 148, 151, 181, 191, 193–194; attuning 4, 51, 56; re- 40
auditory 175
authentic 5, 51, 58, 168, 180, 186
auto-poetic 61, 68, 70–71
autobiography 3, 9–10, 17, 19, 26, 65, 68, 179; autobiographical 9, 17, 21, 24–26, 29–30, 40–41, 115, 180
autoethnographic 3, 9–10, 61, 94

beauty 37, 58, 89–90, 102, 157
becoming 3, 8, 9, 17, 23, 33, 36, 40, 42–43, 46–8, 51–52, 55, 70, 80–81, 90, 117, 131, 138, 148
beingness 12, 17, 53, 159, 161, 170, 176, 181–183
belonging 3, 9, 17–19, 21–26, 30, 38, 90, 119
bicycle writing 28
bifurcation 5, 67, 159, 177
bilingualism 38
binary 5–6, 12, 59, 117–118, 120, 123, 148, 161, 177, 188, 191; binaries 5, 9, 11, 113, 116–117, 120, 123–125, 150–151, 189
biography 41, 180; biographical 191
Black 74, 93
body 2, 8, 33–34, 38–39, 42, 86, 148, 151, 186; bodies 35, 145; bodily 41, 188
both/and 65, 67, 70, 72
boundary 81, 91; boundaries 47, 166, 186–187

breath 4, 34–35, 42, 58, 68, 80, 83, 90, 122, 148, 157; breathing 90, 122
bridge 2, 5, 9, 11, 19, 22–23, 26, 28–29, 34, 36, 43, 50–51, 53–54, 112–113, 123–125, 130–131, 135–18, 140, 177–179, 187–189
bridges 5, 11, 28–29, 68, 73, 116, 122–123, 125, 130, 187, 189

Canada 9, 17–19, 21–22, 24–25, 27–30, 38–39, 49, 53, 58, 72–73, 115, 117, 128, 132, 156, 190, 192, 194; Canadian 1–3, 5, 9, 17–19, 21–24, 26, 47, 49–51, 56, 66–67, 115–117, 156–157, 175, 178, 179, 186–187, 189, 192, 195–196; Canadianess 18
care 1, 52, 90, 97, 99, 110, 157, 168, 181, 193; caring 4, 88, 102, 193
Cartesian 87, 117, 156, 167, 169
categorizing 164,
categorise 85
centeredness 180; centered 164, 166; child 104; disciplined 171; human 147; learner 128; person 129–131; society 171; student 171, 178; teacher 171; technology 171
certainty 7, 49, 120–121
change 8, 46, 67, 87–88, 99, 129–130, 132–135, 138–140, 175; changed 47, 58; changes 128–129, 132, 167–168, 172
chaos 47, 81, 84
children 10–11, 24, 27, 48, 61, 63, 87, 91, 94, 96–97, 98–99, 100–105, 115, 122, 124, 146, 148–150, 193–194
China 49, 115, 117; Chinese 27
choice 11, 25, 46, 54, 109, 112, 144
circularity 130; circular 38, 118
citation 10, 59, 65, 68, 70, 176; citational 58, 62, 70
citizen 29; citizenship 22, 27
civic 3, 17, 19, 21–22, 26, 49, 166, 175
claim 22, 72, 119, 140, 178, 190; claiming 40
classroom 11, 22, 28, 52–53, 111, 116, 120, 122, 125, 130–131, 144, 166, 170, 176, 178, 180–182; classrooms 4, 6, 26, 65, 121, 163, 165, 168, 170 195; online 121; teacher 21, 28, 195; virtual 194; *see also* climate
climate (classroom) 50, 160, 165; climate (change) 87, 128–129, 132, 136, 139–140

Coast Salish 29
cognitive 131, 133, 137, 178; cognitively 178
collaborate 4, 116, 146, 165; collaboration 137; collaborative 102, 117, 125, 132, 146
colonization 21–22
commitment 4–5, 7, 46–47, 53, 56, 62, 67, 111, 176
commonality 25
communication 84, 118, 120, 125, 132, 137,
communications 29, 118, 120, 164, 169
community 3, 7, 9, 11, 12, 24, 26, 28, 35, 38–39, 47, 49, 50, 52, 69, 113, 118–119, 121, 132, 137–139, 145, 147–151, 181; communities 1, 3, 6, 22, 25, 49, 52, 80–81, 88, 131, 134, 137, 139, 146–147, 150
compassion 47, 82, 97; compassionate 81, 91, 172
competence 80, 121, 128–138; competency 133–134, 137, 160, 190
complexity 2, 5, 24, 68, 124, 169, 180
computer technology 121, 124–125, 147; *see also* technology
connect 2, 3, 5, 19, 24, 26, 50, 54, 65, 86, 94, 97–98, 103, 105, 113, 122–123, 125, 132, 129–133, 136–139, 180, 188; connection 24, 26, 39, 51, 54, 69, 102, 120–124, 129 136, 138–139, 148
consciousness 22, 25
contemplate 12, 33, 47, 53, 55, 81, 83, 115–116, 188–189, 196; contemplation 4, 48, 70, 84, 135, 167, 186, 189; contemplative 3, 4, 5, 17, 34, 36, 195
contemporary 1, 11, 13, 61, 66, 148, 150–151, 167, 190
context (educational) 7, 117, 119, 121, 133–133; Aokian 111, 163; contexts 3, 9, 11–12, 63, 80, 111–113, 115–117, 119, 124–125, 145, 147, 150, 159, 161, 172; contextual 125, 131, 137–138; curriculum 7, 132; of the time 48, 50, 55; teaching 164, 170
control 7, 28, 46, 48–49, 68, 85, 120–121, 160, 169
conversation 1, 3, 5, 8, 29–30, 46, 53, 61, 65–66, 68, 70, 84, 91, 94, 96, 98, 103–104, 107, 110, 115, 119, 129, 132, 137–138, 140, 144, 161,

Index 201

166–167, 168, 171, 182, 188, 194; complicated 175, 179; dialogue 18, 34, 129
correspondence 11, 21, 107, 109
cosmology 177; cosmos 36
courage 10, 46, 51, 53, 82, 88, 182
course (class) 1, 6, 26, 28, 54, 60, 65–66, 110, 176, 178–179, 182; evaluations 47, 50, 53–54
COVID-19 9, 11, 19, 47–49, 54, 69, 81, 116, 118, 121, 125–126, 194; virus 49, 74, 194; *see also* pandemic
crack 35, 68, 150, 186
creation 33, 35–36, 70–71, 81, 123, 135
creative 10, 81, 85, 91, 94, 96–97, 101, 104, 137, 146, 149, 170
crisis 19, 47–48, 50, 67, 109, 128, 139–140, 190
critical 4, 7, 11, 48, 53–55, 71, 99–100, 103–104, 109–110, 124, 130–135, 137, 139–140, 156, 163, 165, 169–170, 182, 193; critically 4–5, 50, 110–111, 121; reflection 54, 133, 135, 170; theory 52, 189–181; thinking 132, 140, 165
critique 5, 67–68, 180
cross-curricular 115; discipline 167
cultivation 46, 56, 135; cultivate 131, 135, 172; cultivated 116–117, 165; cultivating 52, 130–132, 137, 140, 175
culture 22, 29, 40, 49, 53, 74, 85, 88, 117, 119–120, 132, 134, 137, 165, 168, 170, 182, 190–191, 193
currere 12, 68, 71, 145, 179–180
curricula 6, 47, 52, 71, 82, 148, 164, 180; lived 73, 180
curriculum: -as-lived 68, 73, 110–111, 128, 130, 137, 149, 151, 159, 161, 175–179, 183, 188–189, 191–193, 195; -as-plan 29, 47, 99, 104, 130–131, 137, 146, 163, 166, 196; hidden 23; implementation 7, 113, 120, 135, 160, 190; inspirited 12, 157, 159, 176; planning 6, 178, 180; scholar 47, 163, 187, 189, 191; scholarship 159, 192; studies 1, 13, 22, 25, 30, 46, 58, 66, 107, 156–157; theory 24, 30, 66, 68, 70, 156, 176; theorizing 3, 9, 12, 22, 30, 144, 159, 176, 178; world 191–195
cyberbullying 115, 124–125

dance 33, 35–36, 42, 83, 88–89, 91, 196; dancing 35, 80, 82, 91, 187
data 67, 70–71, 168
de-intellectualization 160
decenter 9, 52
decolonization 25, 30, 74
dehumanization 53
dialectic 38, 53, 86, 119–120, 138, 161, 181, 188–189, 192, 195
dialogic 3, 146; dialogical 36
difference 8, 22–24, 29–30, 62, 67–68, 70, 72, 84, 88, 109, 117, 124, 129, 139, 144, 147, 149–150, 177; differences 3, 8, 28, 34, 53, 82, 88–89, 150, 187
digital 27, 71, 123–124; online 47, 51, 69, 115, 118, 120–121, 124–126, 194–195; virtual 69–70, 87, 194–195; virtually 122, 195
disabilities 150
discernment 7, 46, 50, 70, 111
discipline 68, 103; discipline (field) 3, 109, 111–112, 136, 145, 165–167, 192; disciplined 171; disciplinary 9, 12, 129, 136–137, 156, 161, 163–164, 166–167; disciplinarity 109
discrimination 21–22, 55
diversity 22, 24, 36, 39, 131, 137, 147, 149–150; diverse 3, 17, 80, 128, 144, 147, 149–150
double vision 86, 151, 161, 188–189, 194–195
dualism 187, 189; dualistic 187, 189, 195
dwell 1, 3, 5–7, 10, 12, 17, 19, 22–24, 36–38, 41–42, 51, 56, 58–60, 62, 65, 69, 112, 123, 125–126, 137, 139, 151, 172, 182, 186, 189, 195; dwelling 4–6, 8–10, 12, 17, 22–23, 29, 33–34, 36, 40, 50, 52–53, 59–60, 88, 90–91, 112, 123, 144–146, 151, 163, 172, 175, 188–189, 192–196

early childhood education 80
ecologic 52; ecological 3, 80; ecologically 1, 91
economy 48, 160; economic 52, 128, 131–132, 167–168, 175, 180
educational: journey 175, 182; research 9, 12, 26, 63, 156, 163, 168–169
ego 53, 117, 152
either/or 5, 67, 117, 167
elementary 21, 46, 111, 120, 190

emancipatory 133, 175; emancipated 81
embody 1, 62, 83, 125, 156; embodied 123; embodying 123
emotion 41, 48–49, 120, 133
empathy 96, 137
encounter 1, 9–10, 28, 38, 46, 61, 68, 100, 103, 144–146, 148–149, 175–180, 182–183
environmental 3, 131–132, 136, 139; environment 132, 137, 169–170, 193–195
epistemology 40; epistemologies 148; epistemological 54, 72, 147, 188–189, 192–193, 195
epistolary pedagogy 11, 109
equality 147
equity 2, 67, 131–132, 139–140, 147
ethics 19, 22, 48, 50, 65, 131–133, 177, 183
ethnic 38, 49, 51
etymology 68, 166; etymological 179; etymologically 164
Eurocentric 167
evaluating 4, 12, 163, 169
evaluation 7, 12, 35, 53, 72, 110, 122, 164, 168–170, 170–171, 192; course 47, 50, 53–54
everyday 9, 28, 61, 96, 157, 161, 187; everydayness 10, 94
evidence 131, 146, 168, 170
expectations 47, 54, 55, 111, 170, 181
experience 2–5, 9, 11–13, 17, 19, 21–23, 25–27, 30, 33–34, 36, 40–41, 47–48, 51, 54–55, 58, 60, 63, 65–66, 83–84, 88–89, 94, 96–97, 100, 102–104, 109, 116–118, 122–123, 125–126, 129, 133–134, 139–140, 144–145, 149–151, 159, 160, 164–165, 168–170, 172, 176, 178–180, 183, 190–191; experiential 7, 128–131, 139–140, 146; learning 63, 97, 99, 105, 120 150, 164, 189; lived 3, 11, 36, 38, 104, 116, 119, 125–126, 129–131, 134, 137–138, 146, 149, 163, 165, 168, 170–172, 176, 191, 193, 196; teaching 9, 19, 46–47, 51, 55
experimentation 84

facilitate 129, 138; facilitation 116, 129, 131, 134, 146–147
faculty 1, 18, 23, 58, 65, 67–68, 165–166, 168, 177

failure 85, 90, 135, 139
fair treatment 47
false binary 148
fear 24, 26, 42, 47, 50, 66
First Nations 24; *see also* Indigenous
freedom 42, 52, 149, 156; free 132, 135, 139, 156, 164; freely 102, 104
friendship 58, 68

gender 51–52, 55, 81, 191
genealogies 1, 159; genealogy 10, 58–60
generates 6, 8, 116; generated 118, 123, 133
generative 1, 6, 22, 33–34, 36, 42, 59, 82, 91, 112, 123, 140, 146, 149, 163, 170, 178; generating 150
gesture 4, 40, 61, 65, 70, 88–90, 168, 188
global 47, 49, 111, 128, 130–132, 137, 194; globally 12, 175, 194; globalization 30; globalized 149
grief 25, 28, 88
ground 5, 8, 34, 146, 171, 189; grounded 3, 28, 30, 37, 69, 91, 190; grounding 37, 65, 116, 195

habitual 4; habituate 125; habits 54–55, 168, 170
healing 4, 36, 85, 91; heal 46
health 47, 54
heart 5, 12, 35–38, 41–43, 61, 70, 80, 84–85, 89, 138–139, 157, 180, 186
hermeneutic 7, 8, 53, 121, 124–125 147, 169–170, 177; hermeneutical 19, 53
heterogeneity 24
hierarchy 5, 167; hierarchical 150–151
higher education 4, 9, 70, 134, 163, 165–166; *see also* post-secondary
history 2, 17–18, 22, 29, 47, 109, 116, 138, 145, 161, 164, 168, 170, 172, 176, 179–180, 191; historicity 179; histories 9, 17, 21–22, 24–26, 30, 112; historical 2, 22, 28–29, 81, 159, 165, 172, 177, 179, 182
holistic 131, 140, 180
home 2, 9, 21–28, 31, 38–39, 41, 47, 51, 66–67, 81, 86, 95, 110, 119, 122, 147
hope 10, 36, 39, 43, 47, 73, 81, 91, 98–99, 130–131, 134, 145, 180, 193; hopeful 90, 102, 195

Index 203

horizontal 8–9, 19, 33–34, 37, 39, 42–43, 84
human 7–10, 18–19, 23–24, 27, 29, 34, 36–38, 41–42, 46, 48, 50–54, 56, 67, 71–72, 91, 102, 117, 120, 122, 125, 132–134, 136–137, 139, 144, 146–147, 160–161, 164, 167–171, 190, 196; being-as-human 120–126, 131, 160, 181–182, 190; human-beingness 17; humanity 7, 19, 47, 53, 65, 164–165; humankind 29; humanly 1, 5, 29, 112; humans 7, 22, 123, 164, 167, 171; humanness 7, 51, 147, 190; more-than-human 9, 82; non-human 9, 134
humbly 108
humiliation 10, 23, 51–53, 147
humility 10, 37, 43, 51–53, 172, 180; humiliation 10, 23, 51–53, 147
hybrid 11, 111–112, 121, 123, 125–126; hybridity 6, 125; hybridization 123, 126

identity 6, 9, 21–22, 24, 30, 70, 72–73, 111, 115–117, 123, 125–126, 139–140, 150, 178–179
ideology 27, 48, 180
imagine 27, 37, 72, 87, 103, 123, 139, 188; imagined 90, 99, 188, 194
imaginaries 2, 72, 117, 123, 150, 167
immigrant 22, 25
immigration 30, 127
improvisation 34, 85, 94, 96, 104, 167; improvisational 104
in-between 2–3, 5–6, 17, 19, 33–34, 39–43, 58–60, 68, 125, 140, 151, 167, 172, 177–180, 183, 188
Indigenous 19, 22, 25, 27, 30, 74, 134
inhabit 10, 81, 160; inhabited 84; inhabiting 19, 140
inquiry 9, 22, 34; living 59, 66, 145, 163, 166, 168–171, 175, 191, 196; method 26; poetic 3, 33, 68, 71; writing 36–37
inspirited 9, 33, 36–41, 61, 65, 161, 186, 188; *see also* curriculum
institution 144, 147; institutional 2, 12, 67, 109, 144–145, 151, 164, 166, 170; institutions 25, 148, 151, 166
instrumentalization 12, 111, 117, 134, 160, 164; instrumentalism 7, 11–12, 116, 119–121, 123, 125, 135, 156, 189–190

intercultural 117, 187
interdisciplinary 12, 52, 115, 128, 131–132, 161, 163, 166–167, 172
intergenerational 1–2, 30, 146
interiority 9, 17, 36
intimate 25, 34, 41, 63, 89, 172, 177
intuition 34
invisibility 51, 53–55
Ismaili Muslim 9, 19, 33–34, 36, 43; Ismaili (Sufi traditions) 36
isness 3, 51, 89, 91, 159, 193, 195

Japan 17, 22–23, 58, 73, 115, 117, 119, 122, 186, 188; Japanese 2, 17–18, 21, 23–24, 30, 47, 51, 58, 60, 66, 72–74, 116–117, 123, 128, 186–189
Jazz 149
joy 94, 102, 105, 146, 157; joyful 46, 61, 82, 87, 96, 98, 105; joyous 12, 91, 157
justice 48, 71, 131–132, 147

knowledge system 83; knowledge systems 3, 25

land 2, 3, 19, 21–22, 25, 27–30, 74, 123
landscape 4, 9, 25, 33, 61–63, 67–68, 71, 82, 110, 112, 117–118, 176–177
language 3, 8, 9, 11, 17–19, 23–24, 30, 33–36, 38–41, 48–50, 52, 59, 61, 68, 70, 72, 74, 81, 87, 89, 109, 119, 146–147, 149–150, 171, 177–181, 192–193; languaging 4
leadership 3, 6, 11, 51, 67, 71, 82, 113, 128–132, 135, 138–140, 163
light 9, 19, 33, 35–37, 40–43, 156–157, 166
liminal 3, 68
linger 5, 8–9, 12, 34, 36, 43, 50–51, 53–54, 58, 60, 70, 90, 109, 112, 116, 125, 136, 151, 175–176, 182
listen 8, 11, 28, 33, 36, 41, 58, 61, 71, 83, 97–98, 100–102, 104, 113, 148, 151, 168, 193
living inquiry 9, 59; *see also* curriculum
loss 19, 43, 54, 67, 74, 120
love 1, 34, 36–37, 42, 74, 82, 89, 95–98, 100, 104, 144, 157; loved 47, 60, 87; self 54

margin 24, 51; 109, 168
material 9, 12, 33–34, 36, 43, 66, 71, 145, 157, 167; materiality 68, 179

meditative 186; meditation 2, 34, 186
memory 2, 21, 38, 41, 117, 119, 122–123, 151, 156, 186
mentorship 11, 129, 145
metaphor 2, 8, 11, 19, 22, 29–30, 34, 50, 55, 68, 86, 90, 113, 122–123, 130–131, 136, 180, 188; metaphoric 24, 29, 33–34, 44
method 3, 26, 41, 65, 68, 70–71, 103, 121, 171; methods 46, 67, 124, 128, 169; methodology 4, 11, 25, 41, 112, 115, 125
Métis 28
metonymy 8, 34, 90, 107; metonymically 8, 86
metrics 164, 169–170
microaggression 51
mindful 42, 46, 61, 101, 151
minority 26, 38, 49, 89
moral 47, 49; morality 177
mother tongue 19, 38–39, 119; mother language 38, 72, 119
multi-disciplinary 129, 161, 166–167
multiplicity 1, 3–5, 11, 17, 33, 47, 51–52, 56, 90, 112, 116–118, 122, 160, 176, 178, 180–181
music 3, 10–12, 35, 63, 84, 94–105, 111–113, 144–145, 147–151, 186–187
Musqueam 2, 21, 65, 116

narrative 9–10, 17–18, 21–23, 26, 61–63, 66, 68, 70, 81, 94, 112, 144, 187, 191, 195
narrative inquiry 66, 191, 195
nation 81, 156
natural 82, 87, 96, 103, 117, 132, 186; naturally 121
neoliberalism 9, 48–49, 54
Nitobe Memorial Garden 2, 5, 10–11, 58–60, 66, 115–116, 119, 122–123, 125, 160, 186–187
normative 54, 134, 144–145, 147, 149–150
nothingness 35, 87

objective 6, 120, 124, 146, 170
objectives 99, 130–131, 135, 146, 169, 192
objects 119, 164, 179
ontology 40, 49; ontological 3, 19, 34, 53–54, 68, 159, 170, 177, 179–180, 188, 192, 195; ontologically 72, 193
orality 84

orientation 7, 46, 53–62, 144–145, 160, 164, 169–172
other (the) 8, 19, 38, 46, 50, 55–56, 119, 139, 172; otherness 17, 81, 147–148; alterity 51
outcomes 46, 119, 131, 134–135, 160, 165–169
output 146, 149
outside 12, 21, 47, 58, 70, 91, 109, 145, 148–149, 167–168, 172, 192–193, 195
outsider 11, 18, 21–23, 27, 49, 72, 170
outward 37, 84

Pacific 2, 22, 24, 28–29, 123, 187, 189
pandemic 47, 49, 65, 126, 128, 136, 194, 196
paradigm 7, 12, 48, 53, 129–130, 144–145, 160, 164; paradigmatic 159
paradox 56–57, 80; paradoxically 166
patience 82, 89; patiently 101
pause 1, 4–5, 10, 34, 54, 65, 121, 136–138, 160, 175, 186
pedagogy 1, 9, 11–12, 33–34, 36, 52, 66, 72, 81, 104–105, 107, 109, 111, 128, 132, 134, 140, 156–157, 159, 165, 168, 175, 180, 182; pedagogic 4, 7, 13, 48, 50, 52–53, 56, 102, 161, 168, 181–182, 193, 195; pedagogical 7, 9, 11–13, 33, 36, 40–41, 49, 67, 91, 96–97, 101, 103, 105, 107, 111–112, 129, 135, 159–161, 163–165, 167, 169–170, 172, 176, 178, 180–183; pedagogue 7, 9, 19, 51, 55, 63
perceptiveness 164–165, 172
performance 33, 145–146, 149, 153, 160, 169, 187
performative 85, 145; performativity 170
phenomenology 54–55, 57; phenomenological 19, 34, 40, 42, 156, 180, 188–189, 191, 195
philosophy 1, 84, 176; philosophical 159, 167, 171, 195; philosophies 3, 166–168; philosophizing 4
physical 5, 10, 22, 29, 43, 120, 123, 132, 137, 194; physicality 55, 120; physically 118, 122, 126
piano 4, 10–11, 39, 41–42, 61, 63, 94–105
place 1, 2, 3, 9–10, 17–19, 21–30, 33, 37–38, 42–43, 50, 52–53, 61, 66,

71, 80–81, 85, 87, 90, 102, 116, 123, 125, 146–148, 151, 161, 166, 170, 172, 180–181, 186, 188, 190–191, 195; *see also* dwelling
plan 29, 47, 99, 104, 130–131, 137, 146, 163, 166, 196
plants 10, 61, 63, 80–82, 84, 86, 88–90
play 3, 9, 39, 52, 61, 63, 65, 80, 82, 84, 88, 90–91, 117, 148, 170, 186–187; piano 94–105
plural 90; plurality 36; pluralism 38
poet 34–35, 37, 42, 50
poet*h*ics 10, 63, 83
poetic 3, 9, 21–22, 26, 33–34, 36–37, 41–42, 61, 66, 68, 70, 71, 84–86, 90, 168, 186, 189, 196; poetics 9, 19, 30, 71, 82
poetry 3, 9, 22, 28, 33–34, 36–41, 61, 68, 71–72, 90, 146
policy 18, 23, 150, 156
polyphonic 85; polyphonically 52, 84
positive 5, 83, 86, 88, 90, 132, 150, 168
positivist 145–145, 147, 188
post-secondary 11, 129, 138; *see also* higher education
post-structural 156
potentiality 47, 51, 85, 146, 148–149, 180, 188, 190
power 2, 5, 34, 48, 52, 56, 58, 67, 70, 81, 86; powerful 90, 156, 180
practical 24, 53, 113, 131–132, 134–137, 148, 166, 170, 190
practice 4, 9, 11–13, 21, 30, 33, 36, 48, 54–55, 58, 62–63, 66, 68, 70–71, 85, 87, 90, 99–100, 102–104, 110, 112, 117–118, 128, 132, 134, 138–140, 145–146, 148, 150–151, 159, 161, 163–168, 172, 175–177, 180–181, 186–191, 195–196
practitioners 30, 111, 149, 163
pragmatic 164, 169, 177–178
pragmatics 177–178
pragmatism 144
praxis 7, 11, 36, 65, 81, 113, 116, 119–123, 125, 128–131, 133–140, 159, 161, 182, 189–191, 194–195
precarity 47
predictable 52; predictability 49
presence 4, 6, 19, 23, 30, 34–35, 39–43, 51, 53–56, 58, 66, 69, 71, 74, 97, 104, 171, 183, 186, 191, 195; absence 34; subjective 66

present 9, 33–34, 39, 55–56, 94, 97, 99, 102, 104, 118, 123, 125, 151, 165, 172
privilege 5, 50, 66, 157
professional development 165, 177
public 49–50, 58, 146, 163

qualitative 67, 70
quantitative 67, 146
quarantine 47
queer 66, 74

racial 49–51, 55; racializing 54–55
racism 9, 48, 49, 54; racist 23, 38
radical 8, 11, 66, 85, 144, 147, 149
re-conceptualist 156; reconceptualizing 165; reconceptualize 137
reciprocity 27, 91; reciprocal 33–34; reciprocate 39
reflect 2–3, 11, 17, 23, 28, 33, 42, 65, 69, 105, 112, 116, 119, 121, 136–140, 165–166, 188
reflection 9, 12, 54, 66, 121, 129, 131, 133, 135–140, 164–165, 167, 170, 176, 180–182, 190–191
refuge 27, 47
refugees 82
relation 1, 3–4, 6, 8–10, 12–13, 17, 19, 22, 25, 30, 51, 53–56, 63, 65, 67, 72, 81, 89–91, 116, 144, 167, 171–172, 188; relationality 22, 68, 70; relationship 6, 9, 12–13, 18, 22, 25–27, 29–30, 91, 102, 111, 115–116, 119, 125, 135, 138–139, 151, 163–164, 178, 195
religious 177
render 163, 170; renderings 10
representation 2, 34, 62, 66–67, 70, 109, 171
research creation 70–71
resolve 67
resound 8, 33, 41, 65, 89, 91, 151, 189
respect 7, 25, 27, 38, 82, 94, 96, 100, 119, 137; respectfully 27
responsibility 9, 26–27, 30, 49–50, 52, 55, 67, 87–89, 103, 122, 132, 175
responsive 7, 148, 150; responsiveness 175
restorative 176
return 1, 5, 10, 21, 28, 30, 46, 56, 65, 72
reveal 6–7, 17–18, 25, 86, 113, 121, 147–148, 151, 160, 181; revelation 34, 36; revelations 37, 69

rhetoric 11, 84; rhetorical 39, 58
rhizomatic 110; rhizomean 33–34, 37
rhythm 8, 10, 28, 35, 37, 42, 81, 89, 101, 148, 186–187; rhythmic 23, 41, 52, 90
ritualistic 4

sacred 36, 81, 89, 157
scarcity 47
scholarship 1–2, 4, 9, 10, 12, 17, 40–42, 46, 58, 60, 62–63, 65, 70, 107, 109, 144–145, 159, 163, 165, 168, 171, 192
Scholarship of Curriculum Practice (SoCP) 163
Scholarship of Teaching and Learning (SoTL) 3, 9, 12, 159, 161
school 7, 18, 21–23, 25, 28, 38, 58, 60, 71–72, 81, 95, 99, 111, 120, 122, 124, 137, 144, 177, 181, 186, 190, 192, 194–196
seeing 4, 24, 30–31, 48, 60, 82, 86, 151, 159, 188–189, 191, 195
self 4, 10, 17–19, 22, 24, 26, 38, 46, 49–52, 54, 56, 67, 71–73, 81–82, 85–86, 112, 117, 119, 129–130, 133–134, 148, 157, 161, 167, 172, 177, 181–182, 191
sensory 8, 41, 188
service 4, 49, 149, 165–167, 189
səl'ilwəta?ɬ (Tsleil-Waututh) Nations 21, 27, 29, 65
silence 10, 40, 42–43, 66, 80, 88, 116, 148, 168; silenced 26; silences 10, 34, 81
similarities 82
singular 90, 102, 124
situated 2, 6, 12, 22, 56, 116, 120, 129, 146, 159, 167, 179, 182, 188–189, 191, 193
slow 4, 40, 62, 85, 90, 98, 148; scholarship 4
social 17, 23, 26, 28, 30, 34, 48–49, 51, 54–55, 71–72, 80, 109, 118–122, 124–125, 129, 131–140, 145, 150, 166–167, 169, 181–182, 191
society 3, 24, 29, 48, 81, 135, 156, 168, 171, 180, 182; societal 80–81, 134–135, 137
sonare 41, 176
sound 8, 33, 41, 55, 66, 89, 90, 96, 148, 168, 186, 189; re- 109; re/sound 148; re/sounding 149; sounding 33, 83, 90, 149; sounds 12, 33, 42, 80, 90, 148, 161, 175, 183

space 3–6, 8–10, 12, 17, 19, 21–23, 29–30, 33–34, 36–37, 40, 42, 49–50, 52–53, 56, 58–60, 62, 65, 68, 70, 80, 83, 91, 96, 109–110, 112, 116–118, 123, 125, 136–140, 144, 146–151, 163, 167, 172, 175, 177–180, 187–188, 195–196; between 147; time 17
species 80, 83, 90
spirit 1, 33, 36, 43, 53, 90, 148
spiritual 9, 17, 19, 33–34, 36, 38, 43, 80, 157, 175
spirituality 12, 36, 157
standard 147,
standards 132, 147, 170
stories 3, 9–12, 17, 22, 25–28, 39–41; 52, 61–63, 81, 84–86, 94–96, 99–100, 102, 105, 115, 122, 145, 151, 176, 183, 193
storytellers 27; storytelling 3, 4, 85, 146
storywork (Archibald) 27
strange 22, 73, 82, 84, 88,
stranger 17, 22, 165; strangers 49–50
stress: pandemic 47; stressed 166, 170; stressful 146, 194
students 1, 3, 6–7, 10–12, 21–23, 25–28, 30, 47, 52–54, 58–59, 65–66, 72–73, 94–97, 99–105, 112, 115–122, 129–135, 137–140, 156–157, 161, 165–168, 170–171, 175, 177, 180–183, 190–196
studio 62, 65–66, 68, 71, 94–95, 97–98, 103, 149
study 1, 3, 9, 11–12, 58, 60, 62, 66, 71, 107, 116, 131, 144–145, 157, 163, 165–167, 170, 177–180, 192; studying 12, 66, 84, 124, 171
subject 8, 23, 52, 54, 74, 85, 119, 125, 177–178, 182, 190
subjectivity 7, 175–176, 178, 190; subjectivities 147, 178
subjects 72, 74
success 85, 90, 135, 146; successful 189
suffering 46, 49, 85, 88, 90
Sufi 9, 33, 36
sustainability 3, 11, 111, 113, 128–138, 140, 170
syllabus 6, 182; syllabi 110
symbolic 29, 39
synergy 27; synergistic 34
synthesize 25
system 3, 9, 25, 47–49, 83, 87, 134, 144, 149, 151, 161, 166, 189
systemic 9, 129

teach 11, 22, 52, 54, 70, 90–98, 103–105, 121, 125, 156, 160–161, 167, 179–182
technical 7, 104, 150, 178, 189–190, 192
technology 3, 11, 29, 30, 111–112, 115–118, 120–122, 124–126, 147, 164, 167, 171, 176, 179, 190
temporal 3, 5, 10, 65, 72, 180; temporality 180
tensionality 2–5, 8, 13, 17, 23, 47–48, 50, 104, 140, 146, 181, 187, 191, 193–195
theology 177, 179
theoria 71, 190, 195
theory 9, 12–13, 23–25, 30, 52, 66, 68, 70–71, 128, 138, 140, 145, 150–151, 156, 159, 161, 163–165, 167–168, 172, 176–178, 182, 187–191, 195–196
third space 6, 9, 33–34, 112, 123, 125, 137, 179; third spaces 11, 19, 112
time 3–4, 10, 23, 28, 38, 40, 46–48, 50, 52–55, 55, 70–71, 80–81, 83–84, 87–90, 98, 100–103, 107, 110, 115–116, 119, 122, 125–126, 128, 138–139, 144, 146–147, 151, 156, 165–166, 170, 192, 194
tradition 12, 36, 61, 69, 84, 112, 149, 153, 156, 177, 180, 193, 195; traditional 2, 9, 21, 27, 30, 65, 113, 116, 124, 129, 139, 148, 150–151, 166, 186–187, 190; ;
traditionally 27, 147, 86
transcendence 34, 41, 72
transform 18, 24, 51, 133, 170, 182, 190
transformation 67, 111–112, 125, 133–140, 170, 175, 194; transformational 133–135, 138
trauma 19, 30, 74; traumatic 9, 46

universe 35, 37, 107
university 22, 24, 46, 107, 111, 119, 129, 145, 156, 176–177; The University of British Columbia 1–2, 10, 18, 21, 58, 65, 116, 186
unknowable 146, 148
unknown 26, 39, 46, 156

value 10, 26, 30, 38, 48, 56, 67, 71, 94, 100–104, 120, 122, 129–140, 151, 159–161, 164, 166–168, 170, 175, 177, 188
Vancouver 9, 19, 21, 28, 38, 67, 81, 95, 116, 126

vertical 9, 33–34, 37, 39, 42–43, 90; verticality 41, 84; vertically 37, 91
visual 28, 53, 69, 71, 118, 145–146, 176; visualize 130–131, 139–140; visualizing 37, 113, 128
voice 1–3, 10, 13, 25–26, 28, 42, 55, 71, 81–82, 84–85, 107, 175, 181–183, 187–188
vulnerability 10, 19, 46, 51, 53

Wales 10, 80–81, 84; Welsh 80–81, 83–85, 89
walk 10, 17, 19, 34, 50, 55, 58, 60, 81, 85, 87–88, 97, 116, 119, 122, 144; walking 11, 21, 25, 54, 58, 88, 99, 112, 115–116, 122–123, 125, 157, 183; walks 3, 10, 17, 63, 86–87
wander 81, 85, 91; wanders 10; wandered 90, 186; wandering 88, 187
ways of being 1, 3, 7, 25, 34, 56, 60, 80, 97, 99–103, 111, 118, 125, 148
well-being 1, 38, 96
Western 2, 28, 117, 168, 187–188, 190
whatness 3, 159, 195
whirling 4, 9, 19, 33, 35–37
white(ness) 54, 66
wisdom 4, 62, 84
wit*h*ness 91; wit*h*nessed 81
wonder 25, 29, 81, 84, 87, 94, 96, 99, 102, 179, 181, 193
world 1, 3, 7–8, 9–10, 12, 17–18, 24–25, 34, 36, 38–41, 50–51, 53, 55–56, 60, 63, 66, 68, 71–72, 80–82, 87–91, 104–105, 107, 111, 128, 132, 138–140, 144, 147–149, 151, 157, 171, 187–188; being-in-the-world 1–4, 7, 10, 54–55
World War II 2, 17, 21, 23, 51
write 1–2, 4, 10, 21–24, 27, 29–30, 33–38, 40–41, 43, 48, 51, 54, 60, 71, 81–82, 123; writer 2, 9, 12, 49, 159, 194; writers-in-residence 146, 194

Xenophobia 9, 48–49, 54
xʷməθkʷəy̓əm (Musqueam) 2, 21, 65, 116

young: children 11, 96, 99, 101–105; people 27, 113, 149
youth 17, 23, 40, 115, 128, 135, 146

Zen 186–187
zone (of) between 6, 8, 50, 146, 152, 193, 195

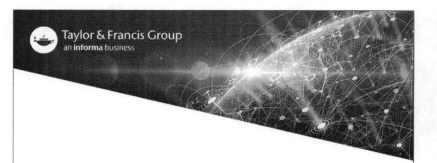

Printed in the United States
by Baker & Taylor Publisher Services